The Corps of Discovery

Staff Ride Handbook for the Lewis and Clark Expedition

Charles D. Collins, Jr.
and the Staff Ride Team
Combat Studies Institute

Combat Studies Institute
US Army Command and General Staff College
Fort Leavenworth, Kansas 66027-1352

CONTENTS

	page
Illustrations	iii
Foreword	v
Introduction	vii

I. The US Army and the Lewis and Clark Expedition 1

    President Jefferson's Vision 1
    Raising the Corps of Discovery 1
    The Journey of Exploration (14 May 1804 to September 1806) 5

II. The Corps of Discovery 19

    The US Army in 1803-1804 19
    Organization of the Corps of Discovery 21
    Weapons 24
    Transportation 28
    Logistics Planning and Support 33
    Medical Support 34

III. Suggested Route and Vignettes 37

    Introduction 37
    Day 1, Marias River to the Upper Portage Camp 39
    Day 2, Gates of the Mountains to the Three Forks 75
    Day 3, The Jefferson River to Camp Fortunate 95
    Day 4, Salmon River Reconnaissance to Travelers' Rest 133
    Day 5, The Challenge of the Rocky Mountains 163

IV. Integration Phase for the Lewis and Clark Staff Ride 195

V. Support for the Lewis and Clark Staff Ride 203

Appendix A. Members of the Expedition 207

Appendix B. Detachment Orders 221

Appendix C. Uniforms of the Lewis and Clark Expedition 241

Appendix D. Visuals 265

Bibliography 293

ILLUSTRATIONS

Figures

page

1. The Corps of Discovery (1 April to 25 May 1804) 22
2. The Corps of Discovery (14 May 1804 to 6 April 1805) 22
3. The Corps of Discovery (7 April 1805 to 29 June 1806) 23
4. The Corps of Discovery (30 June to 12 August 1806) 23
5. Transportation: Waterborne – Pittsburgh to Camp Fortunate 29
6. Transportation: Waterborne – Canoe Camp to the Pacific and Back 30
7. Transportation: Waterborne – Camp Fortunate to St. Louis 31

Tables

Tailored Staff Rides 38

Map

Map of the Lewis and Clark Expedition 11

Stand Maps

Day One

Map 1-1, Marias River to the Upper Portage Camp 39
Map 1-2, Stands 1 and 2 41
Map 1-3, Stand 3 50
Map 1-4, Stand 4 53
Map 1-5, Stand 5 56
Map 1-6, Stands 6 and 7 60
Map 1-7, Stand 8 67

Day Two

Map 2-1, Gates of the Mountains to the Three Forks 75
Map 2-2, Stand 1 76
Map 2-3, Stand 2 79
Map 2-4, Stand 3 82
Map 2-5, Stand 4 86
Map 2-6, Stand 5 90

Day Three

Map 3-1, The Jefferson River to the Shoshone Indians 95
Map 3-2, Stand 1 97
Map 3-3, Stand 2 100
Map 3-4, Stand 3 104

	page
Map 3-5, Stand 4	107
Map 3-6, Stand 5	110
Map 3-7, Stand 6	115
Map 3-8, Stands 7A, B, and C	119
Map 3-9, Stand 8	123

Day Four

Map 4-1, Salmon River Reconnaissance to Travelers' Rest	133
Map 4-2, Stands 1 and 2A	135
Map 4-3, Stands 2B and C	139
Map 4-4, Stands 3A, B, and C	146
Map 4-5, Stand 4	152
Map 4-6, Stands 5A and B	156

Day Five

Map 5-1, The Challenge of the Rocky Mountains	163
Map 5-2, Stand 1	165
Map 5-3, Stands 2 and 3	168
Map 5-4, Stands 4 and 5	172
Map 5-5, Stands 6, 7, 8, 9, and 10	177
Map 5-6, Stand 10	186
Map 5-7, Stand 11	191

FOREWORD

Since the early 20th century, officers of the US Army have honed their professional knowledge and skills by conducting staff rides to historical battlefields. In most cases, these educational exercises have focused on the tactical and operational levels of war, through a detailed examination of a major battle or campaign. The Lewis and Clark staff ride presented in this booklet, by contrast, focuses on a US Army mission to explore the unknown during a time of peace.

By studying the Lewis and Clark Expedition of 1804-1806, traveling the route, and visiting the places where key decisions were made, the military professional can gain a greater appreciation of what it means to be a leader in today's Army and gain an enhanced understanding of the time-honored leadership principle of Be, Know, Do. The captains had commendable character, the "Be" of Be, Know, Do. They had the courage to do what was right regardless of the circumstances or the consequences. In short, they lived the Army values of honor, loyalty, and selfless service. The captains also repeatedly demonstrated well-honed interpersonal, conceptual, technical, and tactical skills, the "Know" of Be, Know, Do. They mastered their tasks and constantly strove to add to their knowledge and skills. Most important, the captains' actions demonstrated the Army values of duty, respect, integrity, and personal courage, the "Do" of Be, Know, Do. Their mastery of agile and adaptive leadership was the single most important factor in the success of their mission.

In many ways, Captains Lewis and Clark faced a more daunting leadership challenge in their journey into the unknown than that faced by the crews of the Apollo missions to the moon. In their epic journey to the Pacific and back, they had no communication with "Houston Control" and had to rely completely on their own skills, judgment, and resources. Fortunately, they were equal to the challenge, and they had their commander's clear intent from the president. They serve today as outstanding examples of what an Army leader must Be, Know, Do. They understood what a leader must be, a person of character; they demonstrated what a leader must know, mastery of the profession; and they exercised what a leader must do, take charge and motivate others to accomplish the mission, however daunting the obstacle.

May 2004   Lawyn C. Edwards
                                 Colonel, Aviation
                                 Director, Combat Studies Institute

INTRODUCTION

Ad bellum Pace Parati: prepared in peace for war. This sentiment was much on the mind of Captain Arthur L. Wagner as he contemplated the quality of military education at the Infantry and Cavalry School at Fort Leavenworth, Kansas, during the 1890s. Wagner believed that the school's curricula during the long years of peace had become too far removed from the reality of war, and he cast about for ways to make the study of conflict more real to officers who had no experience in combat. Eventually, he arrived at a concept called the staff ride, which consisted of detailed classroom study of an actual campaign followed by a visit to the sites associated with that campaign. Although Wagner never lived to see the staff ride added to the Leavenworth curricula, an associate of his, Major Eben Swift, implemented the staff ride at the General Service and Staff School in 1906. In July of that year, Swift led a contingent of 12 students to Chattanooga, Tennessee, to begin a two-week study of the Atlanta Campaign of 1864.

The staff ride concept pioneered at Leavenworth in the early years of the 20th century remains a vital part of officer professional development today. At the US Army Command and General Staff College, the Army War College, ROTC detachments, and units throughout the world, US Army officers arestudying war vicariously in peacetime through the staff ride methodology. That methodology (in-depth preliminary study, rigorous field study, and integration of the two) need not be tied to a formal schoolhouse environment. Units stationed near historic sites can experience the intellectual and emotional stimulation provided by standing on the hallowed ground where soldiers once contended for their respective causes. Yet units may find themselves without many of the sources of information on a particular campaign that are readily available in an academic environment. For that reason, the Combat Studies Institute has begun a series of handbooks that will provide practical information on conducting staff rides to specific campaigns and battles. These handbooks are not intended to be used as a substitute for serious study by staff ride leaders or participants. Instead, they represent an effort to assist officers in locating sources, identifying teaching points, and designing meaningful field study phases. As such, they represent a starting point from which a more rigorous professional development experience may be crafted.

The Lewis and Clark Expedition 1804-06 is an effective vehicle for a staff ride. It raises a variety of teaching points that are relevant to today's officer. In addition, the expedition exemplifies the values that have guided the American soldier to the present day.

The *Staff Ride Handbook for the Lewis and Clark Expedition* provides a systematic approach to the analysis of this key operation. Part I consists of an expedition overview that establishes the context for the individual actions to be studied in the field. Part II surveys the Army during the early 19th century, detailing the organization, weapons, transportation, logistic support and medical support for the Corps of Discovery. Part III consists of a suggested itinerary of sites to visit to obtain a concrete view of the expedition in its several phases. For each site, or "stand," there is a set of travel directions, a discussion of the action that occurred there, and vignettes by participants in the expedition that further explain the action and which also allow the student to sense the human drama of the journey into the unknown. Parts IV and V provide information on conducting a staff ride along the Lewis and Clark route, the integration phase, and logistics considerations. Appendix A provides biographical sketches of key expedition members. Appendix B provides a copy of the 'Detachment Orders' written by the officers and NCOs of the corps. Appendix C overviews the uniforms worn by the expedition members, and Appendix D provides copies of the visuals used at the instructional stands. An annotated bibliography suggests sources for further study.

I. THE US ARMY AND THE LEWIS AND CLARK EXPEDITION*

President Jefferson's Vision

Thomas Jefferson, author of the Declaration of Independence and third president of the United States, did much to help create the new nation. Perhaps his greatest contribution was his vision. Even before he became president, Jefferson dreamed of a republic that spread liberty and representative government from the Atlantic Ocean to the Pacific Ocean. As one of the leading scientific thinkers of his day, he was curious about the terrain, plant and animal life, and Indian tribes of the vast, unknown lands west of the Mississippi River. As a national leader, he was interested in the possibilities of agriculture and trade in those regions and suspicious of British, French, Spanish, and Russian designs on them.

On 18 January 1803, months before President Jefferson had acquired the region from France through the famous Louisiana Purchase, he sent a confidential letter to Congress, requesting money for an overland expedition to the Pacific Ocean. Hoping to find the Northwest Passage, Jefferson informed Congress that the explorers would establish friendly relations with the Indians of the Missouri River Valley, help the American fur trade expand into the area, and gather data on the region's geography, inhabitants, flora, and fauna.

To conduct the expedition, Jefferson turned to the U.S. Army. Only the military possessed the organization and logistics, the toughness and training, and the discipline and teamwork necessary to handle the combination of rugged terrain, harsh climate, and potential hostility of the endeavor. The Army also embodied the American government's authority in a way that civilians could not. Indeed, the Army provided Jefferson with a readily available, nationwide organization that could support the expedition—no small consideration in an era when few national institutions existed. Although the expedition lay outside the Army's usual role of fighting wars, Jefferson firmly believed that in time of peace the Army's mission went beyond defense to include building the nation.

Raising the Corps of Discovery

The man that Jefferson wanted to lead the expedition was an Army officer: his personal secretary, Capt. Meriwether Lewis. A friend and

---

* Section I of the handbook is a reprint of the U.S. Army Center of Military History's brochure (CMH Pub 70-75-1) written by David W. Hogan, Jr. and Charles E. White.

neighbor of Jefferson's, the 28-year-old Lewis had joined the Virginia militia to help quell the Whiskey Rebellion of 1794 and then had served for eight years as an infantry officer and paymaster in the Regular Army. In Lewis, Jefferson believed he had an individual who combined the necessary leadership ability and woodland skills with the potential to be an observer of natural phenomena.

Before Congress approved funds for the expedition, Lewis had already begun his preparations. From Jefferson he learned how to use the sextant and other measuring instruments. Together they studied Alexander MacKenzie's account of his 1793 Canadian expedition to the Pacific coast and the maps in Jefferson's collection. The president even had a special map made for Lewis that detailed North America from the Pacific coast to the Mississippi River Valley, with emphasis on the Missouri River. While the president drafted his instructions for the expedition, the captain worked on his planning and logistical preparations. In the evenings they discussed their concepts of the operation.

Leaving Washington in March, Lewis traveled to the Army's arsenal at Harpers Ferry (at that time in Virginia), where he obtained arms, ammunition, and other basic supplies while supervising the construction of an experimental iron boat frame he had designed. Next, Captain Lewis went to Lancaster and Philadelphia, Pennsylvania, where Jefferson had arranged for some of the nation's leading scientific minds to instruct Lewis in botany and natural history, medicine and anatomy, geology and fossils, and navigation by the stars. While in Philadelphia, Lewis purchased additional supplies, including a new condensed food, "portable soup." He also arranged for the Army to provide transportation for his nearly four tons of supplies and equipment from Philadelphia to Pittsburgh. Lewis then set off for Washington for a final coordination meeting with President Jefferson.

When Lewis returned to Washington in mid-June, he was nearly two months behind his original schedule. He had hoped to be in St. Louis by 1 August; but after three intensive months of preparation, Lewis realized that the successful accomplishment of his mission would require more men and another officer. Now the president handed the captain his formal instructions. Foremost among Jefferson's expectations was an all-water route to the Pacific. Lewis was told to explore and map the rivers carefully, to learn all he could about trade routes and traders of the region, and to study every Indian tribe along the way. Jefferson ordered Lewis to treat the Indians with dignity and respect and to invite their chiefs to come to Washington for a visit. Lastly, Captain Lewis was to describe the geography of the region and to bring back samples of plant and animal life. As they discussed the expedition, Jefferson acknowledged that it would require more men and another leader.

With Jefferson's consent, Lewis wrote to his friend and former comrade, William Clark, offering him the assignment as co-commander. Both Lewis and Clark had served in the Legion of the United States under General Anthony Wayne a decade earlier. Clark had been an infantry company commander but had resigned his lieutenancy in 1796 to attend the business affairs of his older brother, General George Rogers Clark. In addition to approving the choice of William Clark, Jefferson ordered the War Department to give Lewis unlimited purchasing power for the expedition. Moreover, the president authorized the captain to recruit noncommissioned officers and men from any of the western army posts. On 4 July 1803, news arrived of the Louisiana Purchase, which resolved any international problems affecting the expedition. The next day Lewis set off for Pittsburgh.

Pittsburgh, as a riverboat-building center in 1803, provided a logical starting point for the expedition chartered to discover an all-water route to the west coast. While in Philadelphia in May, Lewis had placed an order for a keelboat for the mission. Arriving in Pittsburgh, Lewis found the builder had only just begun construction, which would take another six weeks. Lewis worried about his ability to get down the Ohio River, with its diminishing flows, and up the Mississippi River before winter set in.

Other frustrating news followed. The shipment of supplies had not yet arrived from Philadelphia. The driver had decided that the weapons were too heavy for his team and had left them at Harpers Ferry, so Lewis had to hire another teamster to bring the arms to Pittsburgh. Good news came from Clark, who had accepted Lewis' invitation to join the expedition. Clark told Lewis he would be ready to go when the keelboat reached Louisville, Kentucky. In the meantime, he would recruit only quality men: the word was out, and Clark already had many young frontiersmen eager to join the expedition. Lewis was delighted with this news, knowing Clark was an excellent judge of men.

Lewis finally left Pittsburgh on 31 August. With him were seven soldiers from the Army barracks at Carlisle, Pennsylvania, three prospective recruits, the pilot of the boat Lewis had hired in Pittsburgh, and one or two additional hands. It took them six weeks to travel down the shallow Ohio River to Louisville. Along the way Lewis had stopped for a week in Cincinnati to rest his men and take on provisions. Arriving in Louisville on 14 October, he hired a local pilot to guide the boat safely through a daunting set of rapids known as the Falls of the Ohio, then on a short way to Clarksville, Indiana Territory. Once there, Lewis set off to meet his cocaptain. Over the next two weeks, Lewis and Clark selected the first enlisted members of the expedition. They included: Sgts. Charles

Floyd and Nathaniel Pryor and Pvts. William Bratton, John Colter, Joseph and Reuben Field, George Gibson, George Shannon, and John Shields. (Colter and Shannon may have joined Lewis before he had reached Cincinnati.) These men became known as the Nine Young Men from Kentucky. Clark also decided to bring along his servant, York, a black man of exceptional size and strength.

The keelboat and two smaller, flat-bottom boats (called by their French name, pirogue) departed Clarksville on 26 October and arrived two weeks later at Fort Massac in southern Illinois Territory, about thirty-five miles upstream from the junction of the Ohio and Mississippi Rivers. Here, Lewis hired the respected Shawnee/French hunter, guide, and interpreter George Drouillard, and accepted from the post two privates: John Newman and Joseph Whitehouse. The seven soldiers from Carlisle Barracks who had been temporarily assigned to bring the keelboat down the Ohio River remained behind at Fort Massac. The party left Fort Massac on 13 November and reached the confluence of the Ohio and Mississippi Rivers the next evening. The men camped there for a week, while Lewis and Clark measured both the Ohio and Mississippi Rivers and Lewis taught Clark how to make celestial observations. The expedition then set out for St. Louis.

As they turned upstream into the powerful Mississippi River, Lewis and Clark immediately realized they needed more men. All three boats were badly undermanned, and the expedition seldom progressed more than a mile an hour moving upstream. On 28 November the men reached Fort Kaskaskia, some fifty miles south of St. Louis. The next day Lewis remained behind to confer on personnel matters and to requisition supplies, while Clark took the boats to Cahokia, a few miles below St. Louis. Lewis left Fort Kaskaskia on 5 December and arrived at Cahokia the next day. Following two days of talks with Spanish authorities, the party left Cahokia and reached St. Louis early on the morning of 11 December.

Upon arriving at St. Louis, Lewis left the party to handle logistical arrangements and to gather intelligence on Upper Louisiana. Clark took the party upriver about eighteen miles to the mouth of the Wood River, a small stream that flowed into the Mississippi River directly across from the mouth of the Missouri River. Here, Clark constructed Camp River Dubois, which was finished by Christmas Eve 1803.

Once the camp was established, Clark set about preparing for the arduous journey ahead. Throughout the winter months he selected and trained personnel, modified and armed the keelboat and pirogues, and assembled and packed supplies. For all his efforts, William Clark never received the captaincy Lewis had promised him. Instead, the War

Department commissioned Clark a Lieutenant of Artillery. Nevertheless, Lewis called Clark Captain and recognized him as co-commander, and the men of the expedition never knew differently.

On 31 March 1804, Lewis and Clark held a ceremony to enlist the men they had selected as members of "the Detachment destined for the Expedition through the interior of the Continent of North America." In addition to the eleven men previously selected, Lewis and Clark chose: Sgt. John Ordway, Cpl. Richard Warfington, and Pvts. Patrick Gass, John Boley, John Collins, John Dame, Robert Frazer, Silas Goodrich, Hugh Hall, Thomas Howard, Hugh McNeal, John Potts, Moses Reed, John Robertson, John Thompson, Ebenezer Tuttle, Peter Weiser, William Werner, Issac White, Alexander Willard, and Richard Windsor. In their Detachment Order of 1 April 1804, Captains Lewis and Clark divided the men into three squads led by Sergeants Pryor, Floyd, and Ordway. Another group of five soldiers led by Corporal Warfington would accompany the expedition to its winter quarters and then return to St. Louis in 1805 with communiqués and specimens collected thus far.

With their military organization established, Lewis and Clark began final preparations at Camp River Dubois and in St. Louis for their trek up the Missouri River. Clark molded the men into a team through a regimen of drill and marksmanship training, while Lewis was busy in St. Louis arranging logistical support for the camp and obtaining intelligence on the expedition's route and conditions along the way. Discipline was tough, and Clark made sure that the men were constantly alert, that they knew their tasks on both river and land, that their camps were neat and orderly, and that they cared for their weapons and equipment. He dealt firmly with any form of insubordination or misbehavior. At the same time he rewarded the winners of marksmanship contests and those who distinguished themselves on their work details. Clark's fine leadership proved effective, as the expedition recorded only five infractions during its two-and-a-half-year trek, a record unmatched by any other Army unit of the time.

The Journey of Exploration (14 May 1804 to 23 September 1806)

On the afternoon of Monday, 14 May 1804, Clark and his party left Camp River Dubois, crossed the Mississippi River, and headed up the Missouri. The Expedition proceeded slowly toward St. Charles, because Clark wanted to ensure the boats were loaded properly for the journey. Two days later they reached St. Charles, made adjustments to the loading plan, and awaited Lewis. At St. Charles, Clark also enlisted two additional boatmen: Pvts. Pierre Cruzatte and Francois Labiche. Both knew the tribes of the Missouri River Valley and would serve as interpreters. On 20 May, Lewis arrived from St. Louis with a group of prominent St. Louis citizens who wanted to see the expedition launched. The next afternoon, a crowd lining the riverbank bade farewell to Captains Lewis and Clark and their expedition.

"The Commanding Officers" jointly issued their Detachment Orders for the Expedition on 26 May. This decree established a routine while making it clear to the men that this was a military expedition into potentially hostile territory. Lewis and Clark refined the organization previously agreed upon at Camp River Dubois. The three original squads were redesignated "messes" and manned the keelboat, while Corporal Warfington's detachment formed a fourth mess and rode in the "white" pirogue. The civilian boatmen formed the fifth mess and rode in the "red" pirogue. Because he was the better boatman, Clark usually stayed on the keelboat while Lewis walked on shore and made his scientific observations. Occasionally, they would rotate and Lewis would catalog specimens on the keelboat.

Captains Lewis and Clark now commanded through the three sergeants, who rotated duties on the keelboat. One always manned the helm, another supervised the crew at amidships, and the third kept lookout at the bow. The senior sergeant was Ordway, who acted as the expedition's first sergeant. He issued daily provisions after camp was set up in the evening. Rations were cooked and a portion kept for consumption the next day. (No cooking was permitted during the day.) Sergeant Ordway also appointed guard and other details. The guard detail consisted of one sergeant, six privates, and one or more civilians—fully one third of the entire party. The guard detail established security upon landing and maintained readiness throughout the encampment. All three sergeants maintained duty rosters for the assignment of chores to the five messes. The cooks and a few others with special skills were exempted from guard duty, pitching tents, collecting firewood, and making fires. Drouillard was the principal hunter and usually set out in the morning with one or more privates and rejoined the expedition in the evening with meat.

The expedition generally made good time up the Missouri River. Thanks largely to the total commitment of the crews, the keelboat and pirogues averaged a bit more than one mile per hour against the strong Missouri current. With a wind astern, the crews usually doubled their speed. Along the way, the expedition conquered every navigational hazard the Missouri River offered. In addition, the men also overcame a variety of physical ills: boils, blisters, bunions, sunstroke, dysentery, fatigue, injuries, colds, fevers, snakebites, ticks, gnats, toothaches, headaches, sore throats, and mosquitoes. As the expedition traveled north, its members became the first Euro-Americans to see some remarkable species of animal life: mule deer, prairie dog, and antelope. Wildlife became more abundant as the expedition moved upriver. The likelihood of meeting traders and Indians also increased.

As the men traveled north, they encountered more than a dozen parties of traders, sometimes accompanied by Indians, coming downriver on rafts or in canoes loaded with pelts. On 26 June the expedition reached the mouth of the Kansas River. On 21 July, some six hundred miles and sixty-nine days upstream from Camp River Dubois, the expedition reached the mouth of the Platte River. On 28 July Drouillard returned from hunting with a Missouria Indian. The next day Lewis and Clark sent boatman "La Liberte" (Jo Barter) with the Indian to the Oto camp with an invitation for their chiefs to come to the river for a council.

At Council Bluff on Friday morning, 3 August 1804, the expedition held its first meeting with six chiefs of the Oto and Missouria tribes. This amicable council set the pattern for later meetings between the expedition and Native Americans. The outstanding characteristic of these councils was the mutual respect between the expedition and its native hosts. At midmorning, under an awning formed by the keelboat's main sail and flanked by the American flag and troops of the expedition, Captains Lewis and Clark awaited the Indian chiefs. The two captains wore their regimental dress uniform, as did Sergeants Ordway, Floyd, and Pryor, Corporal Warfington, and the twenty-nine privates. As the Oto and Missouria delegation approached, the soldiers came to attention, shouldered their arms, dressed right, and passed in review. Captain Lewis then stepped forward to deliver his long speech announcing American sovereignty over the Louisiana Territory, declaring that the soldiers were on the river "to clear the road, remove every obstruction, and make it a road of peace," and urging the Oto and Missouria tribes to accept the new order. According to Private Gass, the chiefs were "well pleased" with what Lewis said and promised to abide by his words. The chiefs and officers then smoked the peace pipe and Lewis distributed peace medals and other gifts to the chiefs. The council closed with a demonstration of the expedition's air gun, designed to awe the Indians. Like a BB gun, the air gun operated by air pressure, was nearly silent, and was capable of firing a .31-caliber round forty times before recharging. Upon conclusion of the council, the expedition continued upriver.

Tragedy struck the expedition on 20 August when Sgt. Charles Floyd died of what modern medical authorities believe was peritonitis from a perforated or ruptured appendix. Floyd had been ill for some weeks, but nothing Lewis or Clark did seemed to help. On 19 August he became violently ill and was unable to retain anything in his stomach or bowels. Lewis stayed up most of the night ministering to him, but Floyd passed away just before noon the next day. That afternoon the expedition buried Floyd with full military honors near Sioux City, Iowa, on the highest hill overlooking a river the men named in tribute to their stricken comrade. Sgt. Charles Floyd was the only member of the Lewis and Clark Expedition to lose his life. Two days later the captains ordered the men to choose Floyd's replacement. Pvt. Patrick Gass received nineteen votes, while Pvts. William Barton and George Gibson each received five. In their orders of 26 August, Lewis and Clark appointed Patrick Gass to the rank of sergeant in "the corps of volunteers for North Western Discovery." This was the first time the captains used this term to describe the expedition.

The Corps of Discovery entered Sioux country on 27 August near Yankton, South Dakota. As the boats passed the mouth of the James River, a young Indian boy swam out to meet one of the pirogues. When the expedition pulled to shore, two more Indian youths greeted them. The boys informed Lewis and Clark that a large Sioux village lay not far up the James River. Anxious to meet the Yankton Sioux, the captains sent Sergeant Pryor and two Frenchmen with the Indians to the Sioux village. They received a warm welcome and arranged for the chiefs to meet Captains Lewis and Clark. On the morning of 29 August, the Corps of Discovery met the Yankton Sioux, with both parties dressed in full regalia. As the Sioux approached the council, the soldiers came to attention, raised the American flag, and fired the keelboat's bow swivel gun. The Yanktons also had a sense of drama. Musicians playing and singing preceded their chiefs as they made their way to the American camp. After greeting one another, Lewis gave his basic Indian speech. When he finished, the chiefs said they would need to confer with the tribal elders. Lewis was learning Indian protocol, which required of him patience and understanding. The captains then presented the chiefs with medals, an officer's coat and hat, and the American flag. After the formalities were over, young Sioux warriors demonstrated their skill with bows and arrows. The soldiers handed out prizes of beads. In the evening the men built fires, around which the Indians danced and told of their great feats in battle. The Corps of Discovery was truly impressed with the peaceful Yankton Sioux. Later, the same could not be said about the Teton Sioux.

From the time they had left St. Louis, Captains Lewis and Clark knew they would eventually have to face the aggressive Teton Sioux. Careful diplomacy would be required. On one hand, the Teton Sioux had a bad reputation for harassing and intimidating traders and demanding toll. On the other hand, of all the tribes known to Jefferson, it was the powerful Teton Sioux whom he had singled out in his instructions for special attention. Jefferson urged Lewis and Clark "to make a friendly impression" upon the Sioux. Acutely aware of the often-violent tactics the Teton Sioux used to control the Upper Missouri, the expedition, in Clark's words, "prepared all things for action in case of necessity."

On the evening of 23 September, just below the mouth of the Bad River (opposite present-day Pierre, South Dakota), three Sioux boys swam across the Missouri River to greet the Corps of Discovery. Anxious to begin talks, the captains told the boys that their chiefs were invited to a parley the following day. But the next afternoon, as the Corps of Discovery was preparing for the council, Pvt. John Colter (who had gone ashore to hunt) reported that some Teton warriors had stolen one of the expedition's horses. Suddenly, five Indians appeared on shore. As the captains tried to speak with the Indians, they realized that neither group understood the other. Later that evening, Lewis met with some of the Sioux leaders, who promised to return the horse. In his journal, Lewis reported "all well" with the Sioux.

Early on Tuesday morning, 25 September, on a sandbar in the mouth of the Bad River, the Corps of Discovery met the leaders of the Teton Sioux: Black Buffalo, the Grand Chief; the Partisan, second chief; Buffalo Medicine, third chief; and two lesser leaders. The council opened on a generous note, with soldiers and Indians offering food to eat. By ten o'clock both banks of the river were lined with Indians. At noon the formalities began. Lacking a skilled interpreter, Lewis made a much shorter speech, but one that upheld the essential elements established in his earlier talks. After the Corps of Discovery marched by the chiefs, Lewis and Clark presented them with gifts suited to their stature. Evidently unaware of factional Sioux politics, the captains inadvertently slighted the Partisan and Buffalo Medicine. The chiefs complained that their gifts were inadequate. Indeed, they demanded that the Americans either stop their upriver progress or at least leave with them one of the pirogues loaded with gifts as tribute. Hoping to divert their attention, Lewis and Clark took the three chiefs in one of the pirogues to the keelboat, where Lewis demonstrated his air gun. Unimpressed, the chiefs repeated their demands. After some whiskey, the Partisan pretended to be drunk. Fearing a bloody melee, Clark and three men struggled to get the Indians ashore. When the pirogue landed, three young warriors seized the bow cable. The Partisan then moved toward Clark, speaking roughly and staggering into him. Determined not to be bullied, Clark drew his sword and alerted Lewis and the keelboat crew to prepare for action. Suddenly, soldiers and Indians faced each other, arms at the ready. A careless action by an individual on either side might have touched off a fight that might have destroyed the expedition. Fortunately, the members of the corps held their fire, and Lewis, Clark, and Black Buffalo calmed the situation.

Over the next two days both sides tried to ease tensions. The Sioux held an impressive ceremony at their village on the evening of 26 September. After Black Buffalo spoke, he said a prayer, lit the peace pipe, and offered it to Lewis and Clark. After the solemnities were over, the Corps of Discovery was treated to all of the Sioux delicacies, and hospitality reigned in the camp. At nightfall, a huge fire was made in the center of the village to light the way for musicians and dancers. Sergeant Ordway found the music "delightful." Shortly after midnight the chiefs ended the festivities and returned with Lewis and Clark to the keelboat, where they spent the night. The next day Lewis and Clark made separate trips to the Sioux villages and presented more gifts. On 28 September, as the Corps of Discovery made final preparations for departure, Black Buffalo and the Partisan made their now-familiar demand that the expedition remain with them. Both Lewis and Clark were weary of the constant demand for gifts and sensed trouble from the well-armed Sioux warriors lining the banks of the river. After an angry exchange of words, Lewis tossed some tobacco to the Indians. Realizing that he could not keep the expedition from leaving, Black Buffalo ended the confrontation and allowed the boats to pass.

News of the Expedition's confrontation with the Teton Sioux spread rapidly up and down river. Captains Lewis and Clark had demonstrated sound leadership and bold determination, while the training, discipline, and teamwork of the men had gained them much prestige. While the success of the expedition at Bad River was due in large part to Chief Black Buffalo, who sought to avoid bloodshed, the fact that the Sioux had permitted the Americans to pass gave hope to the tribes of the upper Missouri. Between 8 and 12 October, the Corps of Discovery visited the Arikara villages in north central South Dakota. The councils went smoothly: The Arikara chiefs were pleased with their gifts and amazed with the air gun, while the captains learned much about the surrounding country and its tribes. On 26 October, five days after the first snow fell, the expedition arrived near the junction of the Knife and Missouri Rivers, roughly sixty miles upstream from present-day Bismarck, North Dakota, and 1,600 miles from Camp River Dubois. This was the home of the Mandan and Hidatsa tribes.

Described as "the central marketplace of the Northern Plains," the five Mandan and Hidatsa villages attracted many Europeans and Indians alike. With a population of nearly 4,400, this was the largest concentration of Indians on the Missouri River. After visiting all five villages, Lewis and Clark prepared for their important council scheduled for 28 October.

This would be the largest council yet, bringing together leaders from the Mandan, Hidatsa, and Arikara tribes. That Sunday weather prevented Lewis and Clark from holding their meeting, so the captains spent the day entertaining the chiefs who had arrived and reconnoitering the Missouri River for a good location for their winter quarters. On 29 October, just three days after arriving, Captains Lewis and Clark held their most impressive council to date. After the usual display of American military prowess, Lewis gave a speech that not only stressed American sovereignty, but also sought harmonious relations among the tribes themselves. Next came the distribution of gifts to the chiefs. Then Lewis ended the proceedings with a display of his air gun, "which appeared to astonish the natives very much."

With the onset of winter, the Corps of Discovery had to find a suitable place for their camp. On 2 November, Captain Clark selected a site directly opposite the lowest of the five Indian villages and two miles away from it. The next day the Corps of Discovery set to work building a triangular-shaped structure that consisted of two converging rows of huts (or rooms), with storage rooms at the apex (the top of which provided a sentry post) and a palisade with gate at the base or front. The walls were about eighteen feet high, and the rooms measured fourteen feet square. The men finished the fort on Christmas Day 1804 and named it Fort Mandan in honor of their neighbors. For security, the captains mounted the swivel cannon

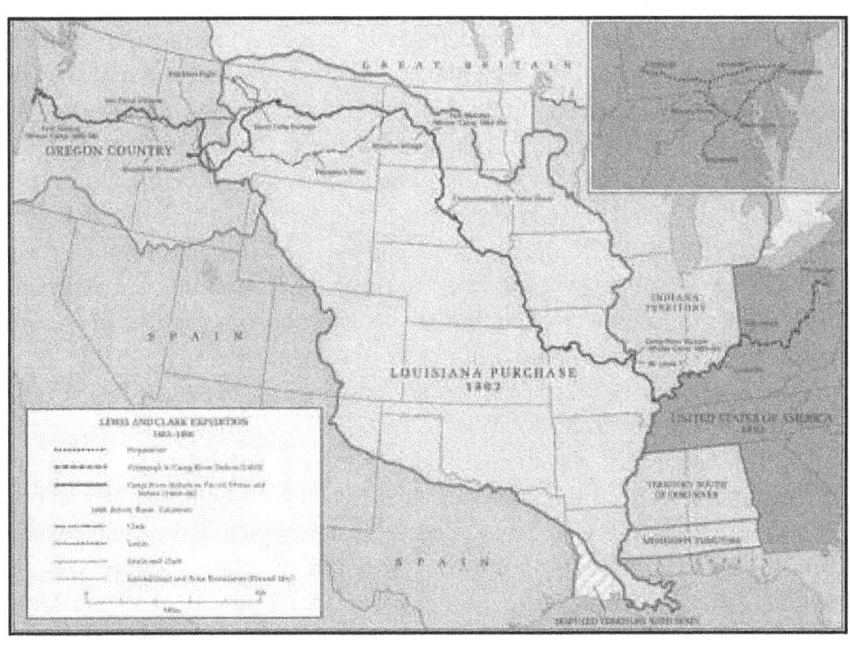

Map of the Lewis and Clark Expedition

from the bow of the keelboat on the fort, kept a sentry on duty at all times, refused Indians admittance after dark, and kept the gate locked at night.

While at Fort Mandan, the Corps of Discovery continued its association with the Indians. The soldiers took part in Indian hunting parties and social events and built goodwill by providing rudimentary medical care and the services of their blacksmith, John Shields, to the tribes. They took time to speak with British and French-Canadian traders who were well established with the Indians, and gained valuable intelligence. On 27 October, they hired Rene Jessaume as an interpreter with the Mandan. A week later they recruited French-Canadian fur trader Baptiste Lepage into the permanent party to replace Private Newman, who had been "discarded" from the expedition for "repeated expressions of a highly criminal and mutinous nature." Then they hired another French-Canadian fur trader, Toussaint Charbonneau, as an interpreter. The 44-year-old Charbonneau had been living and trading among the Hidatsa for the past five years and had been active on the Upper Missouri since at least 1793. Later, in March 1805, Lewis and Clark hired Charbonneau to accompany the expedition west and agreed that he could bring along his young Shoshone wife, Sacagawea, who had given birth a month earlier to a boy they named Jean Baptiste.

On 6 April 1805, Lewis and Clark sent the keelboat back to St. Louis. In the keelboat were Corporal Warfington; six privates (including Newman and Reed, who had been discharged from the expedition for desertion); Gravelines, the pilot and interpreter; two French-Canadian traders; and an Arikara chief returning to his village. The next day the remainder of the Corps of Discovery departed the Mandan villages in two pirogues and six dugout canoes heading north. Along the way west, the Expedition continued to note abundant plant and wildlife. The scenery was stunning, and spirits were high. On 14 April Clark saw his first grizzly bear. Eleven days later the corps reached the mouth of the Yellowstone River and camped there. On 10 May the men saw their first moose. A week later Clark noted in his journal that the men were beginning to be use deerskins to make moccasins and leggings, as the original uniform trousers were wearing out.

Lewis and Clark faced their first major navigational test on 2 June 1805. Arriving at the junction of two large rivers, the captains needed to decide correctly which fork was the Missouri. Between 4 and 8 June, Lewis and a party reconnoitered the northwest branch, which Lewis later named the Marias River, while Clark and another group explored the southwestern branch. After comparing their notes, reevaluating their intelligence, and studying the maps they had brought from St. Louis, Lewis and Clark determined that the southwestern branch was the Missouri River, even though all their men thought otherwise. Nevertheless, in a great tribute to their leaders, the men followed Lewis and Clark, although they believed the captains were wrong. Then, on 13 June, Lewis saw a majestic sight: the Great Falls of the Missouri River. The captains had been right. Here, the Corps of Discovery made camp and prepared for the great portage.

Lewis and Clark were proud of their men. The Corps of Discovery was "zealously attached to the enterprise, and anxious to proceed." Indeed, as Lewis wrote, there was not "a whisper of discontent or murmur" among the men, who acted in unison and "with the most perfect harmoney [sic]." That the Corps of Discovery was a tough, resourceful, and tightly knit group was due to the great leadership of the two captains, who complemented each other so well and had molded their troops into a confident and cohesive force. They would need that confidence and cohesiveness during the arduous eighteen-mile portage around the Great Falls. Over the next three weeks, the Corps of Discovery struggled up steep slopes, over prickly pear cactus thorns and jagged ridges, around gullies and ravines, in the scorching summer heat to complete their passage of the falls. The expedition rested for two days and continued the journey on 14 July.

On 12 August, the Corps of Discovery reached the source of the Missouri River. The next day an advance party of Lewis, Drouillard, and two privates encountered the Shoshones. Using friendly hand signals and gifts, the soldiers managed to win the trust of the Indians. Four days later Clark and the rest of the Corps of Discovery joined Lewis and established Camp Fortunate. At the council that evening, Sacagawea was there to interpret. But before the meeting began, she recognized the Shoshone chief Cameahwait as her brother. She immediately embraced him. Lewis wrote that the reunion was "really affecting." More gifts, promises of future trading, and the good fortune that the chief of the Shoshones was the brother of Sacagawea enabled the party to secure horses and guides for the journey along the Continental Divide and over the rugged Bitterroots to the country of the Nez Perce Indians. The hard, forced march across the Rockies along the Lolo Trail, where the freezing cold and lack of food pushed the Corps of Discovery to the limits of its endurance, ended in late September, when the advance party under Clark met the Nez Perce.

On 23 September, Lewis and Clark held a council with Twisted Hair and some lesser chiefs of the Nez Perce. Anxious to get to the Pacific (and of the fact that they were no longer in U.S. territory), the captains dispensed with the usual displays of American military might and instead passed out medals and gifts, explained their mission to Twisted Hair, and requested his assistance in building canoes for the expedition. Indeed, the soldiers were so weak from crossing the Rockies that they could hardly move and spent nearly a week recovering. The Nez Perce could have easily destroyed the expedition, but thanks largely to their generosity and kindness, the canoes were finished by 6 October, and the Corps of Discovery was ready for its final leg to the Pacific.

On 7 October, the Expedition began its journey down the Clearwater, Snake, and Columbia Rivers to the ocean. In dealing with the tribes they encountered along the way, Lewis and Clark followed their usual practice of expressing joy at meeting the Indians, urging them to make peace with their neighbors, handing out gifts, and promising more trade goods from future American traders. To impress the tribes, the Corps of Discovery occasionally paraded in formation or showed off a magnifying glass, the air gun, or another device. Friendly talk and displays of the expedition's military prowess usually impressed the Indians and guaranteed safe passage, although the soldiers were less successful in halting the intertribal warfare.

In the distance lay the Pacific Ocean. On 7 November, the soldiers spotted an inlet from the Pacific near the mouth of the Columbia River. "Great joy in camp," Clark wrote in his journal, "we are in view of the Ocian [sic] . . . this great Pacific Octean [sic] which we been so long anxious to See [sic]." As soon as they arrived at the ocean, Lewis and Clark began reconnoitering for a site to make their winter camp. After exploring the region along the northern shore of the Columbia near the ocean, the Corps of Discovery crossed the Columbia to its southern side, where it was more sheltered from the heavy winds and rough seas. There, the soldiers built Fort Clatsop close to the present location of Astoria, Oregon.

The men of the Corps of Discovery named their winter quarters after the local tribe, as they had the previous winter. Fort Clatsop was about fifty feet square, with two structures that faced each other. One structure was divided into three rooms that housed the three enlisted messes. The other structure was divided into four rooms, one of which served as quarters for the captains and another the Charbonneau family. The third was the orderly room, the fourth a smokehouse. Palisade walls joined these two structures. At one end was the main gate; at the other a smaller, "water gate" (fresh spring water was about thirty yards away). In the middle of the fort was a parade ground. On 30 December the Expedition completed Fort Clatsop as its winter quarters, establishing tight security to safeguard its equipment and to avoid any trouble. Clark wrote that "the Sight [sic] of our Sentinal [sic]" brought a sense of peace and security to the Corps of Discovery.

Life at Fort Clatsop was depressing. Of the 112 (some say 102) days the expedition was there, it rained every day except twelve, and only half of those were clear days. Most of the men suffered from being constantly wet and cold, and their clothing was rotting off their backs. Making salt was a vital diversion, but boiling ocean water was a slow and tedious process.

After two months the operation produced only one bushel of salt. Without salt, preserving food in the wet and humid weather was a serious problem. To make matters worse, hunting parties had a difficult time finding enough palatable food for the expedition. Despite these challenges, Lewis and Clark kept everyone busy, including themselves. Lewis spent much of his time writing in his journal on botanical, ethnological, meteorological, and zoological topics, while Clark completed the first map ever made of the land between North Dakota and the Pacific coast. Together they discussed what they had seen and learned from the Indians.

After three months of constant rain, dietary problems, fleas, and boredom, the Corps of Discovery left Fort Clatsop on 23 March 1806. Concerned with the security of the expedition, the two captains wanted "to lose as little time as possible" getting to the Nez Perce. They decided to return along the same path they had come, satisfied that it was the best possible route. Even though security was rigid, at various points on the way up the Columbia, Lewis and Clark had to use the threat of violence to preclude trouble with the Indians. In early May they finally reached their old friends, the Nez Perce. Once again, the Nez Perce demonstrated their hospitality by feeding and taking care of the Corps of Discovery. During a two-month stay with the Nez Perce, Lewis and Clark held councils with the tribal elders, while their men participated in horse races and other games with young Indian warriors. Clark also used his limited medical skills to created more goodwill. These activities built great relations with the Indians. Indeed, Lewis wrote the Nez Perce considered Clark their "favorite physician."

On 10 June, the Corps of Discovery set out toward the Lolo Trail, over the objections of the Nez Perce. The Indians had warned Lewis and Clark that the snow was still too deep to attempt a recrossing of the Rockies. Eager to get home, the captains ignored this sound advice and proceeded on without Indian guides. In a week the expedition found itself enveloped in snow twelve to fifteen feet deep. Admitting that the going was "difficult and dangerous," Lewis and Clark decided to turn back. "This was the first time since we have been on this long tour," Lewis wrote, "that we have ever been compelled to retreat or make a retrograde march." Sergeant Gass agreed, and noted that most of the men were "melancholy and disappointed." Two weeks later, the Corps of Discovery set out once again, this time with Indian guides. Averaging nearly twenty-six miles a day, the expedition took just six days to reach the eastern side of the Rockies. On 30 June, Lewis and Clark set up camp at Travelers Rest. There, the Corps of Discovery rested for three days before implementing the final portion of its exploration.

According to the plan Lewis and Clark had formulated at Fort Clatsop, they split their command into four groups. Captain Lewis, Sergeant Gass, Drouillard, and seven privates would head northeast to explore the Marias River and hopefully meet with the Blackfeet to establish good relations with them. At the portage camp near the Great Falls, Lewis would leave Gass and three men to recover the cache left there. Captain Clark would take the remainder of the expedition southeast across the Continental Divide to the Three Forks of the Missouri. There, he would send Sergeant Ordway, nine privates, and the cache recovered from Camp Fortunate down the Missouri to link up with Lewis and Gass at the mouth of the Marias River. Clark, four privates, the Charbonneau family, and York would then descend the Yellowstone River to its juncture with the Missouri River. Meanwhile, Sergeant Pryor and three privates would take the horses overland to the Mandan villages and deliver a letter to the British North West Company, seeking to bring it into an American trading system Lewis sought to establish. Lewis and Clark would unite at the juncture of the Missouri and Yellowstone Rivers in August.

The willingness of Lewis and Clark to divide their command in such rugged, uncertain, and potentially dangerous country shows the high degree of confidence they had in themselves, their noncommissioned officers, and their troops. In addition to the physical challenges the expedition would certainly meet, war parties of Crow, Blackfeet, Hidatsa, and other tribes regularly roamed the countryside and threatened to destroy the expedition piecemeal. By dividing their command in the face of uncertainty, Lewis and Clark took a bold but acceptable risk to accomplish their mission.

Separated for forty days, the Corps of Discovery proceeded to accomplish nearly all its objectives. Lewis and his team successfully explored the Marias but narrowly escaped a deadly confrontation with the Blackfeet in which two Indians died. What had begun as a friendly meeting turned into a tragedy. On the afternoon of 26 July, Lewis came upon several Blackfeet, greeted them, handed out a medal, a flag, and a handkerchief, and invited them to camp with his party. They agreed. Lewis was thrilled, but at the same time somewhat apprehensive: the Nez Perce, the Shoshoni, and other plains tribes had warned Lewis to avoid their traditional enemy. At council that evening, Lewis discussed the purpose of his mission, asked the Blackfeet about their tribe and its trading habits, and urged them to join an American-led trade alliance. During the discussion, Lewis noticed that the Indians possessed only two guns; the rest were armed with bows, arrows, and tomahawks. The meeting concluded with smoking the pipe. Nevertheless, after standing first watch, Lewis woke Reubin Field and ordered him to observe the movements of the Blackfeet and awaken him and the others if any Indian left the camp.

At daybreak Joseph Field was standing watch without his rifle. As the Blackfeet crowded around the fire to warm themselves, Field realized he had carelessly left his rifle unattended beside his sleeping brother Reubin. Suddenly, Drouillard's shouts awakened Lewis, who noticed Drouillard scuffling with an Indian over a rifle. Lewis reached for his rifle, but it was gone. He drew his pistol, looked up, and saw an Indian running away with his rifle. At the same time, another Indian had stealthily slipped behind Joseph Field and grabbed both his and Reubin's rifles. The men chased the Indians, and Lewis and Drouillard managed to recover their rifles without incident. But when the Field brothers caught the Indian with their rifles, a fight ensued and the Blackfoot died of a knife wound to his heart. After recovering the weapons, the soldiers saw the Blackfeet attempting to take their horses. Lewis ordered the men to shoot if necessary. Running after two Blackfeet, Lewis warned them to release the horses or he would fire. One jumped behind a rock while the other raised his British musket toward Lewis. Instinctively, Lewis fired, hitting the Indian in the abdomen. The Blackfoot fell to his knees but returned fire. "Being bearheaded [sic]," Lewis wrote, "I felt the wind of his bullet very distinctly." Fearing for their lives, Lewis, Drouillard, and the Field brothers began a frantic ride southeastward to reunite with Sergeants Gass and Ordway at the mouth of the Marias. This they accomplished on 28 July, after riding nearly 120 miles in slightly more than twenty-four hours.

As Lewis and his party made their way from the site where they had encountered the Blackfeet, Sergeant Ordway's group had recovered the cache at Camp Fortunate, proceeded down the Missouri River, and linked up with Sergeant Gass without incident. Gass' team had already recovered the cache at the portage camp at the Great Falls and was awaiting Lewis and Ordway. Meanwhile, while Clark and his party were exploring the Yellowstone River, Pryor could not complete his mission. On the second night out, a Crow raiding party stole all the soldiers' horses. Demonstrating their ingenuity, Pryor and his men kept their cool, walked to Pompey's Pillar (named in honor of Sacagawea's infant son, whom Clark nicknamed "Pomp"), killed a buffalo for food and its hide, made two circular Mandan-type bullboats, and floated downriver to link up with Clark on the morning of 8 August. Four days later, Lewis and his group found Clark along the banks of the Missouri River.

Clark was astonished to see Lewis lying in the white pirogue recovering from a gunshot wound in the posterior, but he was relieved to learn it was not serious. While hunting on 11 August, Private Cruzatte apparently had mistaken Lewis for an elk. On 14 August, the Expedition reached the Mandan villages. After a three-day visit with the Mandans, the Corps of Discovery bit farewell to the Charbonneau family and Private Colter (who had requested an early release so he could accompany two trappers up the Yellowstone River) and proceeded down the Missouri River. On 1 September, Lewis and Clark held a council with some friendly Yankton Sioux. Three days later the Corps of Discovery stopped to visit the grave of Sergeant Floyd.

On the morning of 23 September 1806, the Corps of Discovery arrived at St. Louis to the cheers of crowds lining the riverfront. Over the past two hundred years, the Lewis and Clark Expedition has become famous as an epic of human achievement, covering nearly eight thousand miles in two years, four months, and ten days. Although the Corps of Discovery did not locate an uninterrupted, direct route to the Pacific Ocean as Jefferson had hoped, the expedition strengthened the nation's claim to the Pacific Northwest and paved the way for future Army expeditions, which helped to open the American West to commerce and settlement. The two captains and some of their men kept detailed journals and brought back invaluable geographic and scientific data, including 178 new plants and 122 previously unknown species and subspecies of animals. They also made friends with several Indian tribes and gave the nation a foothold in the region's fur trade.

The U.S. Army had made a singular contribution to the success of the Lewis and Clark Expedition. The Army furnished the organization and much of the manpower, equipment, and supplies. Military discipline and training proved crucial, both to winning over potentially hostile tribes and to overcoming the huge natural obstacles to crossing the continent. The journey of the Corps of Discovery demonstrated, as today's force continues to, that the U.S. Army has many roles and helps the nation in many ways.

II. THE CORPS OF DISCOVERY

The US Army in 1803-1804

The Regular Army of the United States of America was in a period of transition in 1803. The old Continental Army that fought in the War for Independence had been disbanded, and the new Army that would fight the War of 1812 would not begin its buildup until 1810. Much of this transition and change reflected the American people's mistrust of a large standing army. They believed that the oceans served as a protective shield from other countries and that the militia could be raised in time to meet any foreign threat. As a result, the Army went through five major reorganizations between 1784 and 1803 as it struggled to find its place in the new nation.

Congress discharged all but 80 men of the Continental Army in 1784. Then, less than a year later, Congress authorized 700 men for the 1st US Infantry to guard the northwest frontier. In 1792 the legislators increased strength allocations and reorganized the Army into the Legion of United States. The Legion, specifically designed to fight Indians on the northwest frontier, consisted of four sub-legions, each with two battalions of infantry and single companies of rifles, artillery, and cavalry. Both Meriwether Lewis and William Clark served as junior officers in the Legion. In 1794 the Legion played a major role in putting down the Whiskey Rebellion in western Pennsylvania.

The decisive defeat of the Indian alliance at the Battle of Fallen Timbers in 1794 resulted in increased responsibilities for the Army. These new responsibilities exceeded the capabilities of the legionary organization and required an increase in size of the Army. The Army was now required to garrison numerous forts along the northwest frontier, negotiate treaties with Indian tribes, administer frontier law, and manage affairs between the Indian tribes and white settlers. Then, in 1799, the fear of war with France caused an additional buildup of the regular army. Most of the new units were disbanded, though, when tensions between the two countries decreased. However, several enlisted soldiers who initially joined the Army during the buildup of 1799 would later be members of the Corps of Discovery.

The new century brought with it major changes for the Army. The War Department designated Brigadier James Wilkinson as the commanding general in 1800, and the nation elected Thomas Jefferson as the third president of the United States. Wilkinson gave the Army a new look when he revised uniform regulations in 1801 and, in 1802, began downsizing the force in accordance with instructions from the president. Wilkinson's new look included short haircuts and uniforms similar to European standards.

One who aided in downsizing the Army was the president's personal secretary, Captain Meriwether Lewis. Under the direction of the president and the secretary of war, Lewis compiled an order of merit list for the 269 officers serving in the Army. The criteria for the list not only included military proficiency but also rated whether they supported or opposed the current administration's Republican policies. Most of the 76 officers released from active duty were Federalists.

In 1803, the Army had only 3,220 officers and men. It consisted of two regiments of infantry and one regiment of artillery. Each infantry regiment was authorized 800 officers and men divided into 10 companies. Each regiment was commanded by a colonel and also had one lieutenant colonel, a major, an adjutant, and a sergeant major. The 10 companies rarely served together and were usually spread between distant frontier posts. The artillery regiment had 1,600 officers and men divided into 20 companies. As with the infantry, a colonel commanded the artillery regiment. However, the artillery colonel had a lieutenant colonel, four majors, and an adjutant to assist in the administration of the regiment. The artillery companies were widely separated, serving in coastal forts and along the frontier. Both infantry regiments and Captain Amos Stoddard's company of artillery provided volunteers for the Corps of Discovery.

The individual soldiers of the early 19th-century Army were a hardy lot. The nation was predominantly rural, with four out of every five citizens living on farms. The average household in 1800 had 6 to 10 people who lived in a small house with only one or two rooms. From childhood, they were accustomed to hard work, long days, and crowded living conditions. The average soldier was a volunteer and a native-born American. It was not until years after the Louisiana Purchase that the Army contained more diverse cultural backgrounds. In some ways, the Corps of Discovery led the way in this respect, having two half-French, half-Omaha Indian soldiers, Pierre Cruzatte and François Labiche, and one German-born soldier, John Potts.

The average age for an American soldier in 1803 was 26. However, many were as young as 17 or as old as 44. The Corps of Discovery was very close to the Army average with the average age for the 23 privates in the permanent party being 27. The youngest was Private George Shannon at 18 and the oldest was Private John Shields at 34. The soldiers of the corps also mirrored the Army as a whole, coming from numerous professions. These included: carpenters, blacksmiths, gunsmiths, tailors, musicians, interpreters, navigators, and hunters. The character and nature of the Army, from which Lewis and Clark solicited volunteers for the Corps of Discovery, was molded by the changes and transitions leading up to 1804.

The Army, because of its remote frontier assignments, had the proven ability to organize, equip, train, and lead a small unit into the unknown West. The captains, Lewis and Clark, had the logistics skills needed for planning and executing a major operation. The captains and their sergeants had the leadership skills needed to build and maintain a functioning team. Most important, the individual soldiers and the team as a whole had the tenacity, training, and determination needed to journey into the unknown.

Organization of the Corps of Discovery

The Army in 1803 had no existing table of organization for a corps of discovery. However, both Lewis and Clark were well acquainted with the organization and capabilities of an infantry company. The infantry company of their time was authorized one captain, one 1st lieutenant, one 2nd lieutenant, four sergeants, four corporals, four musicians, and 64 privates. In reality, the harsh and remote frontier duty meant that most units were drastically understrength. Frontier forts normally had a garrison of one or two companies. The average garrison strength of 39 officers and men for a fort on the frontier in 1804 was comparable to the size of the Corps of Discovery.

The captains organized the noncommissioned officers and men in a manner similar to that of an infantry company by dividing them into squads and messes. The 1804 squad was authorized 12 men, divided into two messes. The mess was an administrative unit that prepared and ate food together. In practice, squads of reduced-strength units normally had only one mess.

While wintering at Fort Dubois, the captains organized the volunteers into three squads led by Sergeants Floyd, Ordway, and Pryor. They also directed the sergeants to form two messes in each squad. The same detachment orders, dated 1 April 1804, also identified which soldiers would constitute what they called "the Permanent Party," those men who would go all the way to the Pacific (see Figure 1).

The captains created an additional mess under Corporal Warfington on 4 May 1804. They later simplified their organization by reducing the number of messes in each squad to one in the detachment orders dated 26 May 1804. They reorganized the corps into five squads or messes. Three squads headed by the sergeants constituted the permanent party. A fourth squad led by Corporal Warfington was designated as the return party, which would return to the east after the first winter. Baptiste Deschamps headed a fifth squad of civilian contract boatmen (see Figure 2).

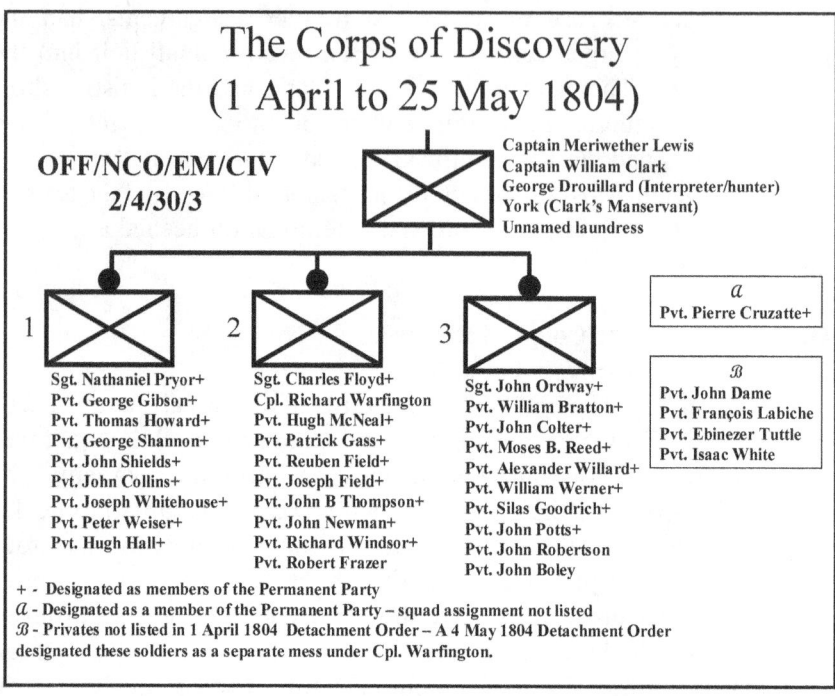

Figure 1

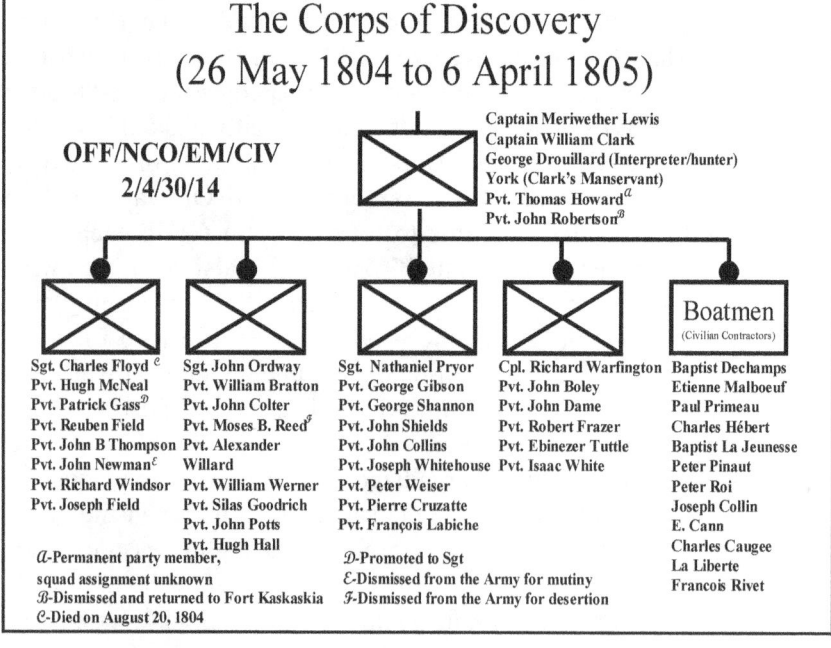

Figure 2

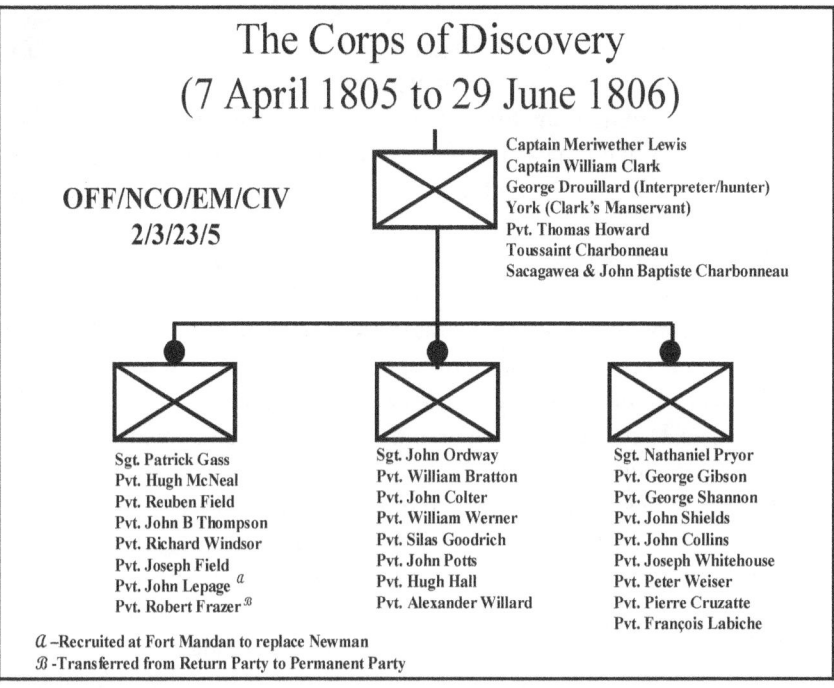

Figure 3

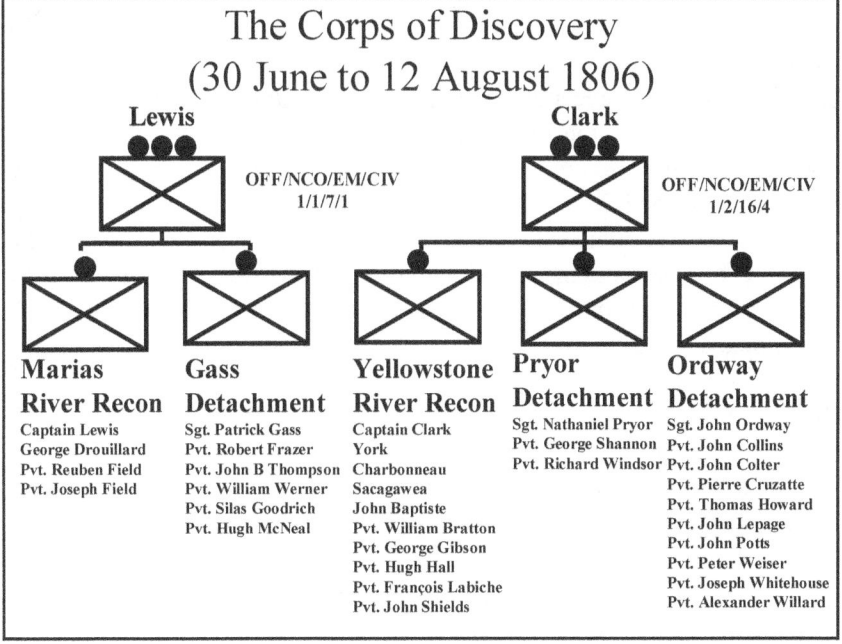

Figure 4

Corporal Warfington's squad and the remaining contract boatmen (some of the boatmen were discharged at Fort Mandan), returned to the east in the keelboat after wintering at Fort Mandan. The captains continued west with the remaining three squads on 7 April 1805. The Corps of Discovery continued to use the three-squad organization for the remainder of the journey to the west and most of the eastward return trip (see Figure 3).

Although the Corps of Discovery kept the three-squad organization during the first part of its 1806 return to the east, the captains decided to divide the corps so that more ground could be explored east of the Rocky Mountains. This required a significant task reorganization of the Corps of Discovery. During the period between 30 June and 12 August 1806, the Corps of Discovery operated as five separate detachments, each with different missions (see Figure 4).

Captain Lewis' group explored the Marias River. Sergeant Gass' detachment prepared the Upper Portage Camp cache for the portage around the Great Falls. Captain Clark's group explored the Yellowstone River. Sergeant Pryor's detachment had the mission to move the horse herd from the head of the Yellowstone to the Mandan village. Finally, Sergeant Ordway's three-fold mission was to move the canoes from Camp Fortunate down the Missouri River to the Great Falls, take charge of the portage, and then link up with Captain Lewis at the junction of the Missouri and Marias Rivers (see Section I for more details and the activities of the separate groups).

The captains' decision to organize as a modified infantry company allowed them and the volunteers to operate in a familiar and proven organizational structure. The multiple squad organization provided the flexibility needed when moving through uncharted and possibly hostile environments. Equally important, it allowed the sergeants to concentrate on NCO business and the captains to accomplish officer business. Together the captains and their sergeants established a command climate that promoted successful mission accomplishment.

Weapons

The Army of 1803 had a varied array of weapons. Some were best suited for the brutal linear combat of the day; others were more suited for skirmishing and hunting. Although no exact list of weapons exists for the Corps of Discovery, a fairly accurate list can be compiled by studying the journals.

Model 1792 Contract Rifles. One of the most significant issues concerning the weapons of the Lewis and Clark Expedition is the question of which rifle they carried. We know that Lewis procured 15 rifles from the Harpers Ferry Arsenal. Gary E. Moulton's edition of the journals and Stephen Ambrose's *Undaunted Courage* identified the rifles as Harpers Ferry 1803 Rifles. However, many scholars today believe the 15 rifles were Model 1792 contract rifles.

The War Department did not authorize the development of the Harpers Ferry 1803 Rifle until two months after Lewis visited the arsenal. The arsenal developed the first prototype in December 1803 and began production in the 2nd quarter of 1804. These dates are long after Lewis departed the Harpers Ferry Arsenal with his 15 rifles.

The rifles that Lewis procured were most likely Model 1792 contract rifles. The Army had contracted almost 3,500 of these .45- to .47-calibers rifles in two procurements, the first in 1792 and the second in 1794. The Army reorganized after the Battle of Fallen Timbers and disbanded the Legion of the United States. As a result, the force structure no longer contained rifle-armed units, and the Army placed hundreds of Model 1792 contract rifles into storage.

The most probable theory is that Lewis selected 15 of the best rifles and directed the Harpers Ferry Armory to modify and refurbish them. The modifications completed by the arsenal included replacing trigger locks and attaching sling swivels. The armory stamped the locks with "Harpers Ferry 1803." This 1803 stamp is probably the main reason for the belief that the rifles were Harpers Ferry 1803 Rifles. Lewis also directed the gunsmiths to manufacture spare locks for each of the rifles and to shorten the barrels from 42 inches down to about 36 inches. The shorter barrels made the rifles handier for travel in boats and moving through rough terrain.

Pennsylvania or Kentucky Long Rifles. Some of the men on the expedition may have carried their own Pennsylvania or Kentucky long rifles. The average Pennsylvania or Kentucky long rifle was .45 caliber, weighed 9 pounds, and had a barrel length of 40 inches. Like the Model 1792 contract rifles, these long rifles were extremely accurate to 200 yards.

Model 1795 Musket and Bayonet. Most of the volunteers recruited from the frontier forts would have been armed with the Model 1795 Musket and Bayonet. This was the standard infantry arm for the period. The musket was approximately five feet long and weighed almost 9 pounds. The musket had a relatively high rate of fire for the day. A well-trained soldier could fire three shots a minute (four if he began with a loaded weapon). It fired a heavy .69-caliber ball but was only accurate to about 100 yards. The musket-armed soldier could also attach a bayonet to the weapon. The bayonet allowed the musket to be used as a thrusting spear for close combat. The Model 1795 Musket Bayonet varied in length from 13 to 16 inches. Although intended for melee combat, the bayonet was most commonly used as a utility tool.

Fusils. Several journal entries mentioned the use of fusils by various members of the Corps of Discovery. The journals specifically indicated that both Clark and Toussaint Charbonneau owned fusils. A fusil was a lighter, shorter, and smaller-caliber version of the smoothbore musket. A military fusil was sometimes issued to officers and NCOs. It was also a civilian term that applied to any well-made and elegantly crafted smoothbore musket.

Air Gun. The air gun, mentioned often by Lewis in the journals, was much more than the modern day BB gun. The air gun was a .31 caliber rifle that looked like a Kentucky long rifle. The air reservoir was in the butt of the weapon and could be pumped up to 900 pounds per square inch. The fully charged weapon could fire up to 20 shots. The maximum range is not known, but journal entries indicate that it could be fired with accuracy to 50 yards. The air gun had an unusually loud discharge and often was used as a signal to guide hunters into the night camp. The primary purpose of the air gun was to impress the Indians during shooting demonstrations. Air gun demonstrations are mentioned 26 times in the journals.

Pistols. The pair of horseman's pistols Lewis obtained from the Philadelphia Arsenal were most likely Model 1799 flintlock pistols. Hundreds of these pistols would have been placed in storage after Jefferson disbanded all regular cavalry in the Army. Lewis also purchased a pair of pocket pistols with secret triggers for a sum of $10. Lewis frequently mentioned his pistols in journal entries. Most notably, he recorded the use of one of his horseman pistols in the skirmish with the Blackfeet Indians. It is highly probable that Clark also carried pistols. His most notable entry about pistols was that he traded a pistol for a horse on 29 August 1805.

Blunderbusses and Cannons. The journals also mentioned two blunderbusses and a small, 1-pounder cannon. The blunderbusses were short shoulder arms with a bell mouth. They were basically heavy shotguns used in an antipersonnel role. The small cannon had a bore of about 2 inches and could either fire 16 musket balls or a 1-pound solid shot. The blunderbusses and the cannon were mounted on swivel mounts on the keelboat. The corps probably mounted the weapons on the walls of Fort Mandan during the second winter encampment. They cached all three weapons during the portage around the Great Falls. The corps recovered them on the return trip, and Lewis presented the small cannon to a Hidatsa chief as a gift.

Edged Weapons. The members of the Corps of Discovery also carried a variety of swords, spontoons, knives, and tomahawks. Both Lewis and Clark carried swords on the expedition. They mentioned the use of swords during the encounter with the Lakota Sioux and in other formal parades for the Indians. Typically, sergeants during this period also carried short swords. However, the journals made no reference of the NCOs carrying swords.

Officers during this time period also carried spontoons to signify their rank. The spontoon was a 6 1/2-foot wooden pole with an iron spearhead. We know from journal entries that both the captains sometimes carried spontoons. Although the spontoon was intended primarily as a ceremonial mark of rank, the two captains tended to use them for more practical purposes. Lewis frequently used his as a walking stick, and other references referred to them being used as rifle rests. The most spectacular events regarding their use were the accounts of Lewis using his spontoon against a grizzly bear and Clark using his to kill a wolf.

In addition to the weapons already mentioned, it is probable that all the corps members carried knives and tomahawks. During the planning phase of the expedition, Lewis ordered 15 knives and 18 tomahawks from the government stores. Because the rifle had no bayonet, the riflemen usually carried a tomahawk to use in close combat. The knife could also be used for close combat, but both weapons were most commonly used as utility tools.

Weapons Summary. The number and variety of weapons in the Corps of Discovery gave the unit the flexibility needed for its journey into the unknown. The corps had the firepower to defend itself and the ability to hunt and sustain itself during the long journey. The musket's higher rate of fire provided the necessary firepower for the unit to face an enemy force in a firefight. The attachment of the bayonet to the muskets gave the Corps of Discovery the ability to defend itself against an enemy in close combat. The major deficiencies of the musket were its short range and lack of accuracy. The corps supplemented the firepower of the muskets with pistols, edged weapons, blunderbusses and the cannon. Although they were some of the best weapons available for early 19th-century warfare, muskets were not good weapons for hunting. The rifles supplemented musket fire with accurate and long-range skirmish fire. More important, they provided the corps with excellent weapons for hunting. The major shortcoming of the rifle was its slow rate of fire. A trained rifleman could fire one or two shots per minute compared to the trained soldier with a musket who could fire three or four shots a minute. The mixture of weapons provided the Corps of Discovery with the flexibility needed for almost any frontier situation.

Transportation

The Corps of Discovery traveled nearly 8,000 miles in two years, four months, and 10 days. It initially moved upstream along the Missouri and Jefferson Rivers. For the first 16 months, the members of the corps dragged, pulled, pushed, and rowed their boats against the prevailing current. Next, they walked or rode horses over the Rocky Mountains. Then, for the first time in 18 months, they canoed downriver on the final westward leg of the trip toward the Pacific. The corps waited out the winter on the west coast and then reversed the route back to St. Louis. In the last six months of the journey, the men struggled upriver toward the west face of the Rockies, then over the mountains, and finally downriver all the way to St. Louis. The Corps of Discovery thus used several different modes of transportation to accomplish its epic journey. These included: a keelboat, pirogues, canoes, horses, and bullboats.

The Keelboat. A keelboat was a large flat-bottom boat with a heavy timber (the keel) running down the of the entire center length of the boat. The purpose of the keel was to absorb the shock of striking underwater obstructions. Lewis had his keelboat built in Pittsburgh during the summer of 1803. The boat measured 55 feet long, 8 feet wide, and had a 3- to 4-foot draft. It used a 32-foot sailing mast and had 22 oars for propulsion. However, poling was the most common method for moving upstream, whereby the men planted long poles along the bottom of the river and pushed the boat upstream. The captains mounted a small swivel cannon on the bow and a blunderbuss on each side for protection against hostile forces. The boat included a cabin and lockers for storage. The locker tops also served as walkways for poling. It had a total carrying capacity of 12 to 14 tons. The corps used the keelboat on the first phase of its journey from St. Louis to Fort Mandan. After the first winter, the keelboat withdrew to St. Louis with the return party (see Figure 5).

The Pirogues. In 1803, the term *pirogue* (pronounced per-rogue) was a common name used on the Ohio River for any long, narrow, flat-bottom,

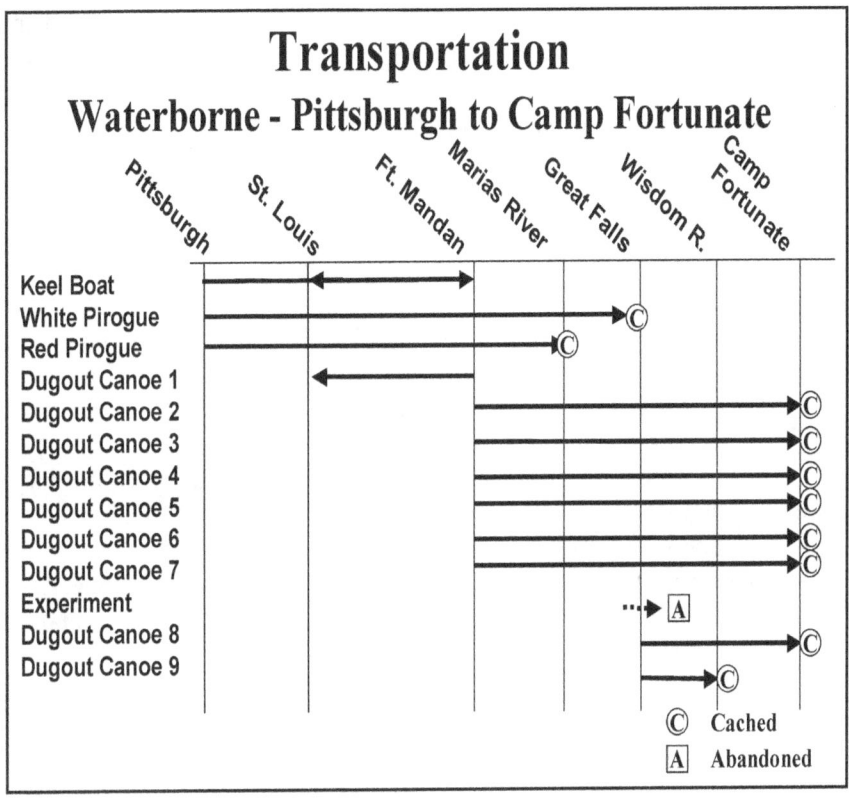

Figure 5

plank-sided boat. Lewis purchased two pirogues on the upper Ohio River. The first, called the "red pirogue," a flat-bottom plank craft with a square stern, was about 41 feet long and 9 feet wide. It was capable of carrying about 9 tons of cargo. The red pirogue was equipped with seven oars, a rudder, and a mast. The second was called the "white pirogue." This boat was slightly smaller and more stable than the red pirogue. The white pirogue was also equipped with a mast and sail. The corps cached the red pirogue with other excess baggage at the junction with the Marias River. The second pirogue was cached at the Great Falls. On the return trip, the captains found that the recovered red pirogue had rotted. They removed all useable material from it, including its iron nails, and then abandoned it. The corps found the white pirogue in good condition and floated it back to St. Louis (see Figures 5 and 7).

Canoes. The corps' primary means of transportation after making the portage around the Great Falls was canoes. The corps built 16 canoes during the journey: 11 made from cottonwood trees on the east side of the Rockies and five made from ponderosa pines on the west side of the Rockies. They also obtained several additional canoes from the Indians.

At Fort Mandan, they built seven dugout canoes. The men built these by hollowing out large cottonwood logs with axes. After the first winter, they took six of the dugouts, along with the two pirogues, up the Missouri River. The seventh canoe returned to St. Louis with the keelboat. Next, they portaged the canoes around the Great Falls on homemade carts. After portaging the Great Falls, they constructed two more canoes from cottonwood logs to make up for the failure of Lewis' iron boat, the *Experiment* (discussed later in this section). From the falls, they then continued to struggle upstream to the source of the Missouri. The corps cached one canoe at the junction of the Wisdom River and the other seven at Camp Fortunate (see Figure 5).

After traversing the Rockies on horseback, the members of the corps built five dugouts from ponderosa pines. These were built using the Nez Perce method of burning and chipping out the hollow of the log. On the Clearwater River, they traded one of the dugouts for an Indian canoe. After wintering at Fort Clatsop, they abandoned one of the dugouts and obtained

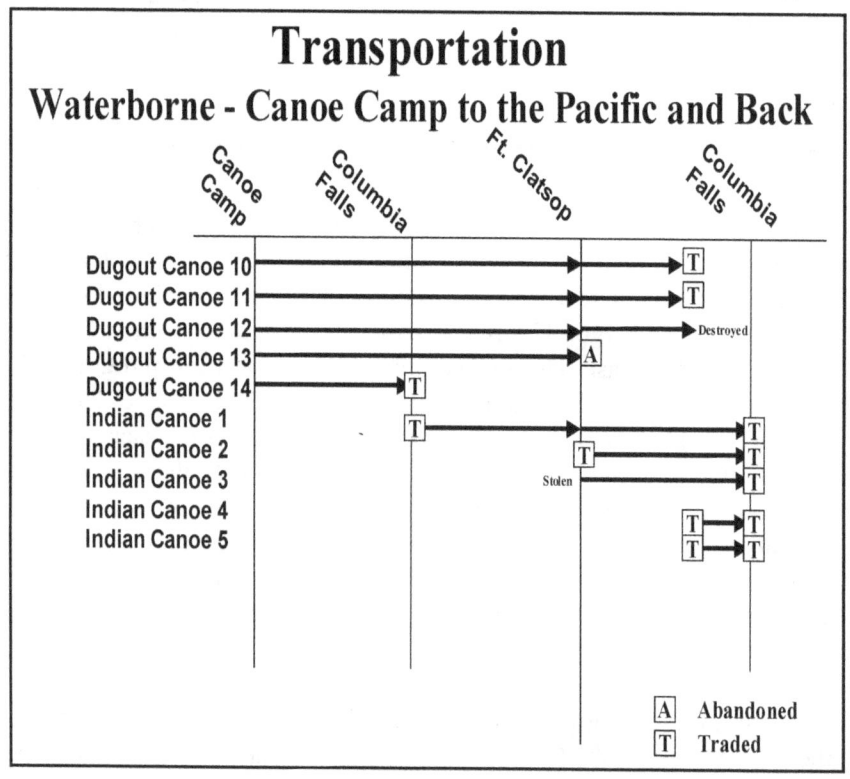

Figure 6

two additional canoes from the Indians for the eastward return trip. They purchased one with trade goods and stole another from the Clatsop Indians. The Indian canoes were lighter and better designed than the dugouts. With their higher, curved sides, they were less susceptible to being swamped in rough waters than the dugouts were. They lost one of the dugouts in an accident while struggling upriver and bartered away the remaining two for Indian canoes. Eventually, they traded all their remaining canoes for horses and continued eastward over the mountains (see Figure 6).

Clark's party recovered the seven dugout canoes cached at Camp Fortunate during its eastward journey in 1806. The men dismantled one of the canoes to get materials to repair the other six. Then Sergeant Ordway's detachment sailed the repaired canoes back to Great Falls, where they abandoned one of the canoes and portaged the remaining five around the falls. The reunited corps later used all five of these canoes on the journey back to St. Louis.

Clark had the men build two cottonwood dugout canoes during his exploration of the Yellowstone River. He increased their stability by lashing them together to form a crude catamaran. The members of the

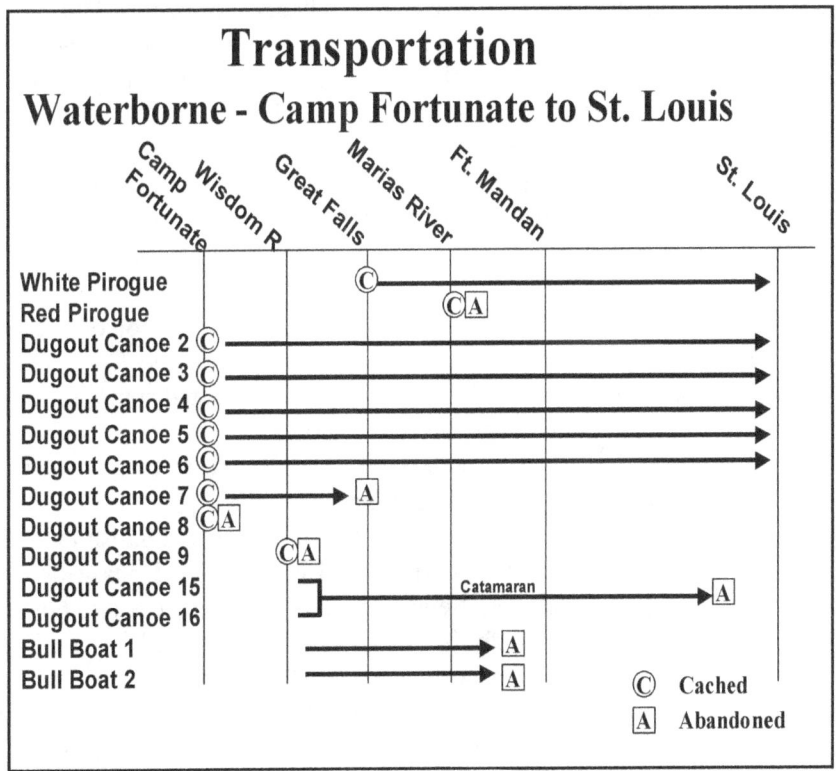

Figure 7

corps floated the catamaran most of the way to St. Louis but abandoned it just short of the city (see Figure 7).

***The* Experiment.** The *Experiment* was a collapsible iron-frame boat that Lewis designed and had built by ironworkers at Harpers Ferry. The corps carried the frame all the way to the Great Falls. The plan was that the *Experiment* would replace the pirogues after the portage around the falls. The *Experiment* was basically a large canoe frame. It was 36 feet long, 4 feet wide, and 26 inches deep. It was capable of hauling almost 2 tons of cargo. Unfortunately, the *Experiment* failed because there was no pine pitch available on the treeless prairie to waterproof the hull made of skins.

Lewis had the iron frame disassembled and put in the cache near the Upper Portage Camp. When Lewis returned to the area in 1806, he had it dug up and found the iron frame rusted but still serviceable. It is unknown whether the corps abandoned the frame at the Great Falls or perhaps later used its iron as trading material with the Mandan Indians.

Bullboats. Another form of transportation that played an important role throughout the expedition was the use of skin boats or bullboats. The corps learned to make these boats during their stay with the Mandan Indians. The bullboat was a crude saucer-shaped frame of sticks with a large animal hide stretched around it. The members of the corps used this type of boat (or sometimes even more crude log rafts) to make river crossings. The most notable use of bullboats was when Sergeant Pryor's Detachment lost its horses to a Crow Indian raiding party and built bullboats to float several hundred miles down the Yellowstone to catch up with Clark's group.

Horses. Adding the increased transport strength of horses was a critical part of Lewis' plan to cross the mountains of the Continental Divide. As early as July 1805, his journal entries indicated some sense of desperation to find the Shoshone Indians and obtain horses. He recognized that, without the horses, the corps would not be able to cross over the mountains and reach the Pacific Ocean before winter.

The corps used horses obtained from the Shoshone and Salish Indians to cross the Rocky Mountains during the 1805 westward phase of the expedition. At Camp Fortunate Lewis estimated that he needed 25 horses and successfully bartered with the Shoshone Indians for 29 horses. The horses were important for transporting personnel but were most critical for carrying supplies, which had previously been transported in seven dugout canoes. Lewis updated his transportation estimate after the corps' first week in the mountains. The rough and mountainous terrain quickly eroded the physical condition of the horses. To replace seven of his worn-out horses, Lewis coordinated a trade with the Salish Indians. In addition to the seven replacements, he was able to acquire 11 more horses in the trade.

It is doubtful that the corps could have survived the 1805 crossing without the horses. Available game was too sparse to sustain the corps through hunting. Without the supplies carried by the packhorses and the eating of three colts, the corps' crossing of the Bitterroot Mountains would probably have failed.

The packhorses also carried critical trade goods needed to establish good relations with the Nez Perce Indians on the west side of the mountains. The Nez Perce welcomed the exhausted corps in 1805 and readily agreed to care for the corps' horses when the expedition continued to the west in canoes. In the 1806 eastward phase of their journey, the Nez Perce provided critical support to the corps. Through a combination of bartering and receiving gifts, the corps departed the Nez Perce homeland and began the eastward crossing of the mountains with more than 66 horses. Each of the 33 members of the corps had at least two horses, one for riding and another for baggage.

The corps' horses also played a vital role in the 1806 eastward portage of the Great Falls. In 1805 it took the 32 men and one woman of the corps 14 days to conduct the westward portage of the Great Falls. In 1806, Sergeants Ordway and Gass, 14 men, and four horses executed the portage in only eight days. This marked difference, for the most part, can be attributed to the prudent acquisition and use of horses. During the first portage the soldiers of the corps served as beasts of burden by harnessing themselves to the portage wagons and dragging the canoes around the falls. In 1806 the men used horses to accomplish the same task in significantly less time.

Logistics Planning and Support

Logistics planning played a major role in the success of the expedition. Equally important was the captains' demonstrated ability to solve logistics issues in innovative ways and obtain host nation support from the Indians.

Lewis accumulated many of the supplies that the expedition was going to need while still on the East Coast. He collected almost 2 tons of goods, using the $2,500 Congress had allocated for the expedition. These included: scientific and mathematical instruments, camp supplies, presents and trade goods for the Indians, clothing, arms and ammunition, medicine and medical supplies, a traveling library, and boats to haul the supplies.

The captains showed significant innovation in both logistics planning and execution. Lewis directed the armory to attach sling swivels to the rifles. This allowed the men to sling the weapons on their backs and free their hands for other work. Also, Lewis' foresight to bring spare weapon parts gave the corps the ability to repair damaged and worn-out weapons. His idea to store gunpowder in sealed, lead containers protected the unit's gunpowder from numerous canoe overturns in the river. The lead containers also provided a resource for the manufacture of more bullets. The captains also numbered and marked all storage bags stowed on the boats. This made it easy to inventory supplies and provided ready identification of needed items without digging through numerous storage bags.

Lewis' decision to include a significant number of trade items in the original packing list probably saved the expedition from failure. Without the host nation support from the Indian nations, the corps could not have survived its two years in the wilderness. The horses provided by the Shoshone and Salish Indians allowed the corps to cross the Rocky Mountains before the onset of winter in 1805. Host nation support provided by the Nez Perce Indians was equally important. They saved the Corps of Discovery from exhaustion in 1805 and provided the horses needed to cross the mountains again in 1806.

Medical Support

The Corps of Discovery had no designated medical personnel during its journey into the unknown. The Army rarely assigned doctors below brigade or regimental level. In small units, such as the corps, the officers were responsible for the health of their men. Despite the lack of specialized medical support and its struggles to overcome food shortages, a harsh environment, exhaustion, illness, and injury, the corps had only one fatality. Sergeant Charles Floyd died on 20 August 1804, near present-day Sioux City, Iowa, from what modern medical experts believe was a ruptured appendix. Ironically, he probably would have died even if hospital care had been available because contemporary medical science had no cure available for this ailment.

Both Lewis and Clark had the common military training required for treating military injuries such as broken bones, cuts, gunshot wounds, and boils. Lewis, as a young boy, had also learned much about herbal medicine from his mother, a renowned country doctor. President Jefferson supplemented Lewis' skills by arranging for him to receive training in medical science from the country's leading medical expert, Dr. Benjamin Rush.

The state of medical science in 1803 was not advanced much beyond what was known in medieval times. Scientific medicine was based upon the Depletive Theory. This theory taught that, if a person was sick, there was a bad substance inside the body that had to be removed. Doctors conducted the removal by sweating, increased urination, vomiting, purging, or bloodletting. Most of the available scientific medicines of the day were developed to cause one of those actions.

The list of medicines that Lewis purchased in Philadelphia for the expedition shows that he stocked both herbal remedies and scientific medicines. The list included: cinnamon, cloves, dried rhubarb leaves, nutmeg, tarter emetic, jalap root, Peruvian bark, glauber salts, nitre, laudanum, vitriol, benzoin, mercury chloride ointment, and Rush's Pills. Most of these were meant to purge the body, with Dr. Rush's "Thunderclapper" pills being the most infamous. These pills were extremely strong laxatives frequently prescribed by the captains for almost any ailment. However, many of the other items on the list were legitimate medicines. Peruvian bark contained quinine, making it a valid medicine, and benzoin was an effective disinfectant (although they had no concept of germs). Clark regularly used vitriol as an eyewash, which medical science did not fully replace until after World War II. Laudanum was a very effective pain reliever since its main ingredient is opium. The training Lewis received from Dr. Rush concentrated on how to administer these medicines, what dosages to give, and which medicines to use for which symptoms.

The corps experienced a variety of medical problems during the journey: Sacagawea almost died at the Great Falls of the Missouri, and twice the expedition had to stop because one of the captains was too sick to travel. Moreover, a significant number of the men contracted venereal disease; Lewis was shot in the thigh; and there were constant reports of men with tumors and boils. Sacagawea recovered after they ceased using scientific medicine and used the herbal medicine technique of administering mineral water. It was probably rest, definitely not the frequent administrations of Rush's pills, which cured Clark from what today is suspected to have been Colorado Tick Fever.

The captains treated each case with tremendous care and concern. However, with the exception of their treatment of boils, tumors, and blisters with bandages and time, most of their applications of the scientific method probably caused more harm than good. The primary reason the members of the corps survived their many trials and tribulations, along with the damaging effects of 1803 medical science, was that they were young, in good health, and in excellent physical condition.

III. SUGGESTED ROUTE AND VIGNETTES

Introduction

During the two-year course of the Lewis and Clark Expedition (14 May 1804 to 23 September 1806), the Corps of Discovery explored thousands of miles of uncharted territory. Because of the wide chronological and geographical span of the expedition, it is necessary to exercise selectivity in packaging a staff ride that can be executed within a reasonable amount of time.

The resulting itinerary involves considerable driving time. The full itinerary, with discussions at each stand, takes approximately five days. The package focuses on the events between 2 June and 7 October 1805. During this period, the Corps of Discovery faced its first major navigational dilemma, reached the source of the Missouri River, crossed the Rocky Mountains, and resumed waterborne movement on rivers that flowed into the Pacific. The primary theme of the study is the discussion of today's Army values and other leadership issues. Individual groups can tailor travel schedules and discussion themes to accommodate the time available and the particular interests of the group. Table One (Tailored Staff Rides) shows recommendations for tailored itineraries.

Be aware that not all of the stands cited in the itinerary are designated by signs or monuments. For this reason, directions are as specific as possible in terms of mileages, road names, and landmarks. Even so, roads and landmarks may change over time, and mileage numbers are no more accurate than the odometer of the vehicle. A set of detailed road maps will help prevent unintended detours.

Journal entries are from *The Journals of the Lewis & Clark Expedition (August 30, 1803 – September 26, 1806),* published as a project of the Center for Great Plains Studies by the University of Nebraska Press, 1986. Gary E. Moulton served as the editor for this outstanding and valuable project. Moulton's editorial goal, as stated in the introduction to his works, was to: "provide the users with a reliable text that is largely uncluttered with editorial interference. By using the text from the full edition, I have retained the enigmatic writing of the journalists that has so captivated, bedeviled and delighted readers for nearly two hundred years." (quoted in *The Lewis and Clark Journals, An American Epic of Discovery*, by Gary Moulton, lvii).

To maintain the spirit of Moulton's work, CSI only added editorial comments to help clarify or complete unclear passages. [Editorial comments appear in square brackets.]

Tailored Staff Rides					
5-Day Staff Ride	4-Day Staff Ride	3-Day Staff Ride	2-Day Staff Ride	1-Day Staff Ride	
Day 1, Marias River to the Upper Portage Camp Recommended End of Day Lodging in Great Falls, MT	Day 1, Marias River to the Upper Portage Camp				
Day 2, Gates of the Mountains to the Three Forks Recommended End of Day Lodging in Three Forks, MT	Day 2, Gates of the Mountains to the Three Forks	Start at Three Forks	Start at Three Forks		
Day 3, Jefferson River to the Shoshone Indians Recommended End of Day Lodging in Salmon, ID	Day 3, Jefferson River to the Shoshone Indians	Day 3, Jefferson River to the Shoshone Indians	Day 3, Jefferson River to the Shoshone Indians	Day 3, Jefferson River to the Shoshone Indians	
Day 4, Salmon River Recon to Travelers' Rest Recommended End of Day Lodging in Lolo, MT	Day 4, Salmon River Recon to Travelers' Rest	Day 4, Salmon River Recon to Travelers' Rest	Day 4, Salmon River Recon to Travelers' Rest		
Day 5, The Challenge of the Rocky Mountains		Day 5, The Challenge of the Rocky Mountains			

Day 1
Marias River to the Upper Portage Camp
(2 June to 15 July 1805)

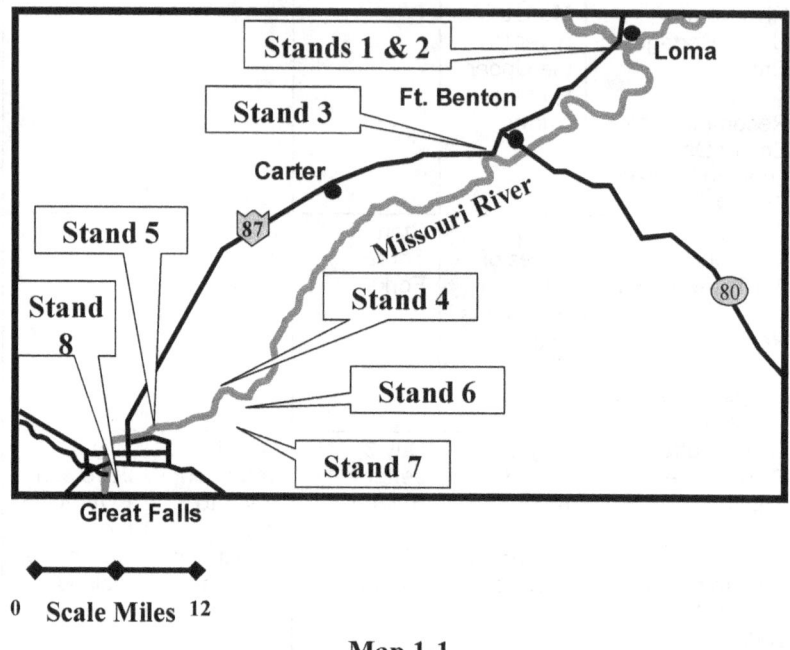

Map 1-1

Stand 1, The Corps of Discovery (interpretive display at Decision Point, Loma, MT)

Stand 2, Decision at the Marias (Decision Point, Loma, MT)

Stand 3, Leader's Recon (SW of Fort Benton, MT)

Stand 4, The Great Falls (Ryan Dam Park, Great Falls, MT)

Stand 5, Crooked Falls and Beautiful Falls (east of Lewis and Clark Interpretive Center, Great Falls, MT)

Stand 6, Portage Creek (Salem Bridge Turnaround, east of Great Falls, MT)

Stand 7, Willow Run Camp and the Great Portage (Salem Road Overlook, east of Great Falls, MT)

Stand 8, Upper Portage Camp (Great Falls, MT)

End the Day at Great Falls, MT

Day 1
Stand 1 (The Corps of Discovery) and Stand 2 (Decision at the Marias)

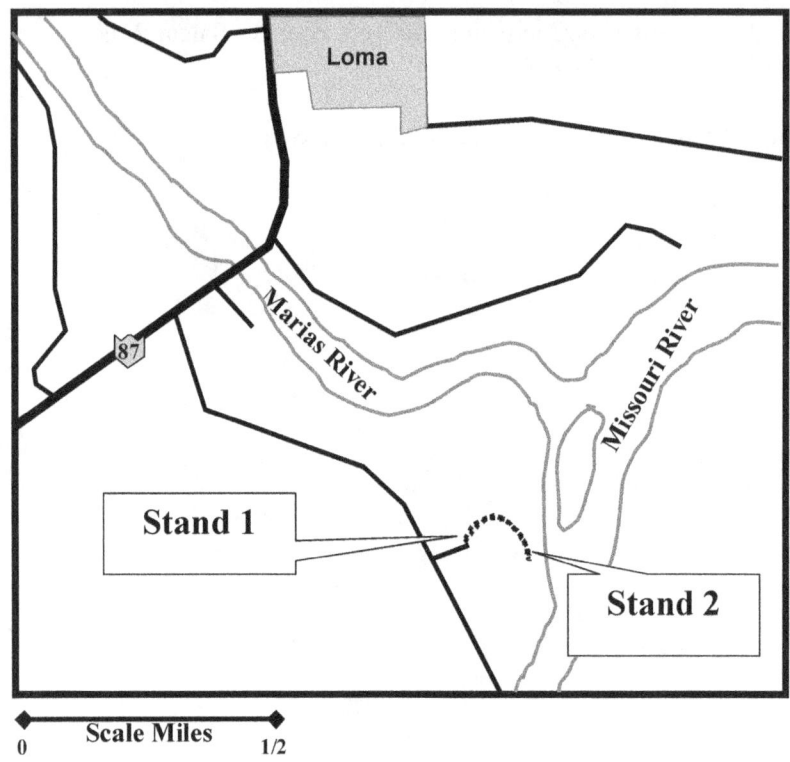

Map 1-2

Stand 1
The Corps of Discovery
(January 1803 – May 1805)

Directions: Go 11 miles northeast of Fort Benton on US 87, then turn right and go 0.5 miles on a gravel road just to the west of Loma Bridge (follow the signs to Decision Point Overlook). Park and orient the group on the interpretive display for the first stand.

Orientation (See Visual 1-1, Appendix D): This stand is near the location where the Corps of Discovery camped in early June 1805. The purpose of the stand is to provide an overview of corps activities from January 1803 to May 1805. St. Louis, Missouri, where the corps officially started the expedition, is just under 2,000 miles to the east; and Fort Mandan, were they spent the previous winter, is about 500 miles to the east.

Situation: Thomas Jefferson assumed the office of President of the United States in 1801. At the time, the western boundary of the United States was the Mississippi River, and the vast majority of the population lived within 50 miles of the Atlantic Ocean. Jefferson, always fascinated by the West, had previously tried to organize expeditions across the continent. Now that he was the president, he decided to try once more. In early 1803, he sent a secret communication to Congress seeking authorization and $2,500 for the expedition. Upon obtaining the approval of Congress, Jefferson selected his personal secretary, Captain Meriwether Lewis, to command the expedition.

In the spring of 1803, Captain Lewis started the logistics planning process and began purchasing supplies for the expedition. These included: portable shelters, clothing, Indian trading goods, weapons, medicines, emergency food, navigational and cartographic instruments and construction tools. He then traveled to Philadelphia, where the nation's leading experts instructed him in botany, navigation, medicine, and zoology. Lewis also decided that the expedition required a second officer and selected a former Army comrade, William Clark, to share command of the expedition. The importance of the expedition increased with the advent of the Louisiana Purchase. President Jefferson purchased a vast chunk of the western part of the continent for only 3 cents an acre. His investment of $15 million dollars doubled the size of the United States.

Lewis changed his base of operations to Pittsburgh in the summer of 1803. Before the year ended he oversaw the construction of a keelboat and purchased two smaller boats. He floated the boats and supplies down the

Ohio River toward the Mississippi River and St. Louis. Along the way, he picked up Clark and several volunteers. The expedition arrived in St. Louis late in December of 1803 and established Camp River Dubois on the east side of the river. Lewis spent most of the winter in St. Louis purchasing supplies and gathering intelligence, while Clark and the rest of the group remained at the camp. Clark used the time to drill the men and mold them into a disciplined military unit. He also used his time to observe the men and select from the group the best individuals for the expedition.

On 14 May 1804, the Corps of Discovery began its journey up the Missouri River in the keelboat and two smaller boats. They proceeded on, using sails, oars, poles, and many times ropes for dragging the boats up the Missouri River. The Corps of Discovery's progress was slow and laborious, a good day being 10 to 15 miles progress. They celebrated the nation's first Fourth of July west of the Mississippi by firing their small cannon, issuing an extra ration of whiskey, and naming a creek, Independence Creek (less than 30 miles northwest of present-day Fort Leavenworth, KS).

As the captains continued westward, they met with several different Indian nations. They promised each of the tribes a future of prosperity if the tribes would maintain peace and trade only with the United States. Near what is now Sioux City, Iowa, Sergeant Charles Floyd became the expedition's first and only fatality. He died from what was probably a burst appendix. In late September, near what is now Pierre, South Dakota, the expedition encountered the Teton Sioux (the Lakota). The Sioux demanded one of the boats as a toll for moving farther upriver. The expedition and the Indians came very close to fighting, but the refusal of the captains to accede to the demands and the diplomacy of a chief named Black Buffalo calmed the situation.

The Corps of Discovery reached the villages of the Mandans and Hidatsas on 24 October 1804 (north of what is now Bismarck, North Dakota). The villages contained over 4,000 inhabitants, more than lived in St. Louis or even Washington, D.C. at the time. The captains decided to stay the winter there and built Fort Mandan across the river from the main village. While wintering at Fort Mandan, the captains hired Toussaint Charbonneau and his young Shoshone wife, Sacagawea, as interpreters.

On 7 April 1805, the captains dispatched the keelboat with the return party downriver. The boat carried reports for the president along with maps and scientific specimens. That same day, the permanent party headed west. In late April they entered what is now Montana. By late May they had reached the vicinity of central Montana.

Vignette 1: "The object of your mission is to explore the Missouri River, and such principal streams of it, as, by its course and communication with the waters of the Pacific Ocean, whether the Columbia, Oregon, Colorado, or any other river, may offer the most direct and practical water-communication across the continent, for the purposes of commerce..." (Thomas Jefferson, Letter to Lewis, quoted in Donald Jackson, ed. *Letters of the Lewis and Clark Expedition*, vol. 1, 61.)

Vignette 2: (Note: Lewis penned these words just 75 miles east of the junction of the Missouri and Marias Rivers). "...from this point, I beheld the Rocky Mountains for the first time, I could only discover a few of the most elevated points above the horizon... these points of the Rocky Mountains were covered with snow, and the sun shone on it in such a manner as to give me a most plain and satisfactory view. While I viewed those mountains I felt a secret pleasure in finding myself so near the head of the heretofore conceived - boundless Missouri; but when I reflected on the difficulties which this snowy barrier would most probably throw in my way to the Pacific Ocean, and the sufferings and hardships of myself and party in them, it in some measure counterbalanced the joy I had felt in the first moments in which I gazed on them; but, as I have always held it a crime to anticipate evils, I will believe it a good, comfortable road untill I am compelled to believe otherwise." (Captain Lewis, 26 May 1805, quoted in Gary Moulton, ed., *The Journals of the Lewis & Clark Expedition*, vol. 4, 201.)*

Teaching Points:

Leadership. How much did the captains' *leadership* contribute to the success of the mission during this phase of the journey?

Logistics Planning. The captains recognized the need to plan, manage, synchronize, and integrate key combat service support functions. How important was the *logistics planning* to the success of the expedition?

Duty and Personal Courage. The captains' sound leadership and bold determination exemplified the Army values of *duty* and *personal courage* during their negotiations with the Teton Sioux. Could today's combat leaders find themselves in similar circumstances?

Training, Discipline, and Teamwork. The corps' training, discipline, and teamwork allowed them to successfully navigate the lower and middle

---

* All vignettes retain the enigmatic writing of the journalists. See the introduction to Section III for an explanation of the editorial principles used with the journal entries.

Missouri and to survive their first winter in the wilderness. What lessons can we learn from the captains on building a successful unit?

Stand 2
Decision at the Marias
(2 – 9 June 1805)

Directions: From the interpretive display, take the trail to the top of the hill that overlooks the junction of the Missouri and Marias Rivers.

Orientation (See Visuals 1-1 and 1-2, Appendix D): At this location, the captains faced their first major navigational decision on which route to take. Modern-day channeling of the Missouri has significantly changed the appearance of the forks. In 1805 the two rivers were relatively equal in width. The Missouri was not as wide and controlled as it appears today. In 1805 it flowed much more rapidly and the channel had numerous bends and turns along the present-day river bottom. Additionally, the channel divided around numerous small islands. Modern day channeling and erosion control have also changed the appearance of the west fork, today's Marias. In 1805, the captains described it as big and muddy.

Situation: On 2 June 1805, the Corps of Discovery reached two apparently equal rivers converging to form the Missouri. All the men believed the north fork was the true Missouri; Lewis and Clark believed the south fork to be the Missouri. The captains had to make a critical decision on which fork they should take. A wrong decision would have had significant consequences. It was already late in the year; they needed to reach and cross the mountains before winter. A wrong decision might also have compromised their leadership with the men.

Private Pierre Cruzatte, the experienced Missouri River pilot, firmly believed the north fork to be the Missouri. All the men respected Cruzatte's experience and were inclined to agree with him. The north fork (today's Marias) did come from the westward direction of the mountains, and it flowed wide and muddy, just as the Missouri had done all the way back to St. Louis. Lewis believed that, because it flowed muddy, the source of the north fork must lie in the plains and not in the mountains. Further, the clear flowing water and smooth tumbled stones on the bottom of the south fork indicated to Lewis that the south fork must flow out of the mountains making it the true Missouri. His own visual sighting of the mountains a few days before indicated to him that, as near as the mountains appeared, the waters should logically flow clear rather than muddy. His analysis of the two forks in relation to the close proximity of the mountains; along with the use of his Jefferson map and information received from the Mandans, convinced Lewis they needed to take the south fork.

Despite their belief that the south fork was the Missouri, the captains wanted to be certain; they wanted more information before making such a critical decision. They decided to allow the main body of the corps to rest and reorganize while they led reconnaissance teams up both forks to gather additional information. They knew, based on information gleaned from the Mandan Indians, that the true Missouri would have a great waterfall. Between 4 and 8 June, Lewis explored the north fork, traveling an estimated 77 miles. He reasoned that the north fork veered too far to the north to be the route to the Pacific and concluded that his earlier estimation was correct; the slow-moving current and muddy waters must surely flow from the plains.

Clark explored the south fork between 4 and 6 June. He was concerned that he did not find the Great Falls and that the river led him to the southwest, but he felt confident that the river would eventually turn westward toward the mountains. He reasoned that the width and depth of the river indicated the south fork was the main channel. The captains were so certain that the south fork was the Missouri that they named the north fork the Marias (after a cousin of Lewis back in Virginia).

On the 9th of June, the captains briefed the men on their decision to take the south fork. The men continued to put their trust in Cruzatte and were not convinced that the south fork was the true Missouri. However, they understood that the authority and burden of command rested with the officers. They told the captains "they were ready to follow us anywhere we thought proper to direct."

Vignette 1: "This morning early we passed over and formed a camp on the point formed by the junction of two large rivers... An interesting question was now to be determined; which of these rivers was the Missouri... to mistake the stream at this period of the season, two months of the traveling season having now elapsed, and to ascend such stream to the rocky Mountain or perhaps much farther before we could inform ourselves whether it did approach the Columbia or not, and then be obliged to return and take the other stream would not only loose us the whole of this season but would probably so dishearten the party that it might defeat the expedition altogether..." (Captain Lewis, 3 June 1805, quoted in Gary Moulton, ed., *The Journals of the Lewis & Clark Expedition*, vol. 4, 246.)

Vignette 2: "...the bed of the N. fork composed of some gravel but principally mud; in short, the air and character of this river is so precisely that of the missouri below that the party with very few exceptions have already pronounced the N. fork to be the Missouri; myself and Cap. C.

not quite so precipitate have not yet decided but if we were to give our opinions I believe we should be in the minority...what astonishes us a little is that the Indians who appeared to be so well acquainted with the geography of this country should not have mentioned this river on wright hand if it be not the Missouri; *the river that scolds at all others*, as they call it if there is in reality such a one, ought agreeably to their account, to have fallen in a considerable distance below, and on the other hand if this right-hand or N. fork be the Missouri I am equally astonished at their not mentioning the S. fork which they must have passed in order to get to those large falls which they mention on the Missouri..." (Captain Lewis, 3 June 1805, quoted in Gary Moulton, ed., *The Journals of the Lewis & Clark Expedition*, vol. 4, 248.)

Vignette 3: "Captain C. and myself concluded to set out early the next morning with a small party each, and ascend these rivers untill we could perfectly satisfy ourselves of the one, which it would be most expedient for us to take on our main journey to the Pacific. accordingly it was agreed that I should ascend the right-hand fork and he the left. I gave orders to Sergt Pryor, Drewyer, Shields, Windsor, Cruzatte, and La Page to hold themselves in readiness to accompany me in the morning. [Note: Lewis repeated refers to George Drouillard as "Drewyer."] Capt. Clark also selected Reubin and Joseph Fields, Sergt. Gass, Shannon, and his black man, York, to accompany him. we agreed to go up those rivers one day and a halfs march or further if it should appear necessary to satisfy us more fully of the point in question..." (Captain Lewis, 3 June 1805, quoted in Gary Moulton, ed., *The Journals of the Lewis & Clark Expedition*, vol. 4, 250.)

Vignette 4: "I determined to give it a name and in honour of Miss Maria W-d. called it Maria's River. it is true that the hue of the waters of this turbulent and troubled stream but illy comport with the pure celestial virtues and amiable qualifications of that lovely fair one; but on the other hand it is a noble river; one destined to become in my opinion an object of contention between the two great powers of America and Great Britain with rispect to the adjustment of the North westwardly boundary of the former..." (Captain Lewis, 8 June 1805, quoted in Gary Moulton, ed., *The Journals of the Lewis & Clark Expedition*, vol. 4, 266.).

Vignette 5: "...today we examined our maps, and compared the information derived as well from them as from the Indians and fully settled in our minds the propryety of addopting the South fork for the Missour*i*, as that which it would be most expedient for us to take... I endeavored to impress on the minds of the party, all of whom, except Capt. C. being still firm in the belief that the N. fork was the Missouri and that which we ought to take; they said very cheerfully that they were ready to follow us any wher we thought proper to direct but that they still thought that the other was the river and that they were affraid that the South fork would soon termineate in the mountains and leave us at a great distance from the Columbia…" (Captain Lewis, 9 June 1805, quoted in Gary Moulton, ed., *The Journals of the Lewis & Clark Expedition*, vol. 4, 269-271.)

Teaching Point: **Personal Courage.** The captains demonstrated the physical aspect of *personal courage* in their negotiations with the Teton Sioux. How does Lewis' decision to name the north fork the Marias River exemplify another part of the Army value of personal courage?

Day 1
Stand 3
(Leader's Recon)

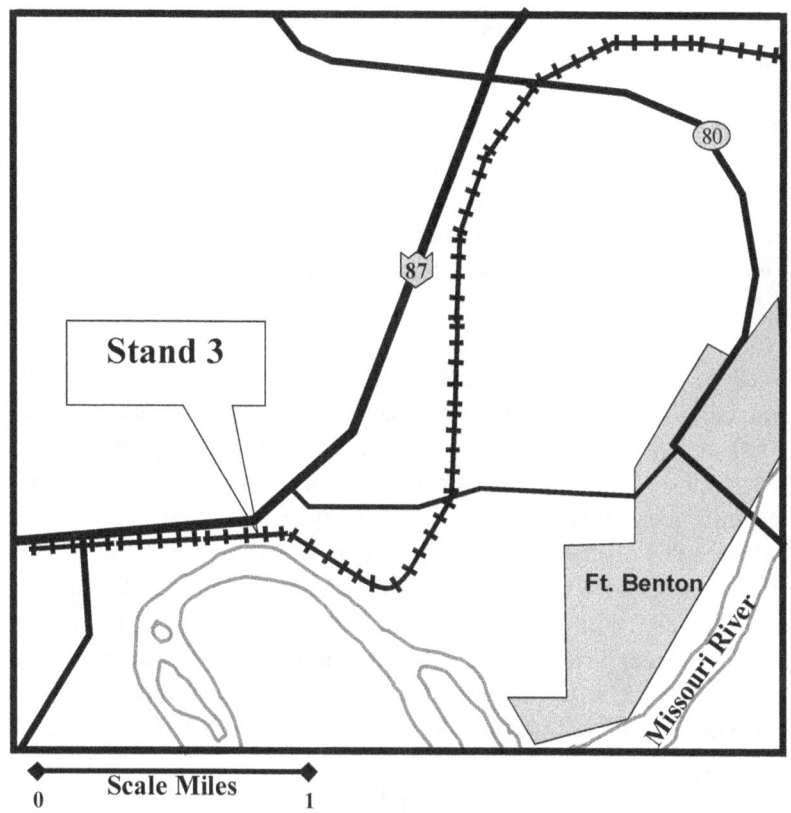

Map 1-3

Stand 3
Leader's Recon
(9 - 12 June 1805)

Directions: Proceed south on US 87 past Fort Benton. After passing the junction for Highway 386, pull into the interpretive display turnout on the south side of the road.

Orientation (See Visual 1-3, Appendix D): Orient the group on the great bend in the Missouri River. The junction of the Missouri and Marias Rivers is 13 miles to the northeast. Clark passed through this area on 5 June during his initial reconnaissance of the south fork. Lewis also passed through here on 12 June in his effort to confirm that the south fork was the Missouri.

Situation: The captains, still concerned because Clark had not found the Great Falls on his initial reconnaissance, decided on 9 June to mitigate the risk of a wrong decision by sending an advance party led by Captain Lewis up the south fork to confirm that it was, indeed, the Missouri River. The main body of the Corps of Discovery would follow one day later. Lewis delayed his departure for one day due to a severe stomach ailment. Sacagawea was also very ill, and Clark employed the accepted practice of bleeding as a method of treatment. The rest of the men spent the day drying out equipment and repairing the canoes. Additionally, Private Shields took advantage of the extra time to repair Lewis' air rifle and some of their other weapons using some of the spare weapon parts that Lewis had had the foresight to bring.

Lewis departed on 11 June with the small advance party consisting of Drouillard and three other men. They camped that evening just northeast of present-day Fort Benton, and Private Goodrich, the expedition's best fisherman, caught a sauger and a goldeye for the group's dinner. Both species were new to science, so Lewis, despite his fatigue and continuing stomach ailments, meticulously recorded in his journal detailed descriptions of the fish. Lewis also experimented with concoctions made from chokecherries and twigs to ease his violent stomach cramps. Amazingly, his choice of chokecherries did actually help to ease the discomfort of his stomach problems.

The next day, Lewis and his group continued up the Missouri. Clark followed with the main body and traversed the great bend of the Missouri on 12 June 1805. He had used the one-day delay to reorganize the corps for movement and to cache excess supplies at the forks. He also left the red pirogue behind at the forks because its carrying capacity was no longer needed.

Vignette 1: "Cruzatte who had been an old Missouri navigator and who from his integrity knowledge and skill as a waterman had acquired the confidence of every individual of the party declared it as his opinion that the N. fork was the true genuine Missouri and could be no other. finding them so determined in this belief, and wishing that if we were in an error to be able to detect it and rectify it as soon as possible it was agreed between Capt. C. and myself that one of us should set out with a small party by land up the South fork and continue our rout up it untill we found the falls or reached the snowy Mountains, by which means we should be enabled to determine this question prety accurately…" (Captain Lewis, 9 June 1805, quoted in Gary Moulton, ed., *The Journals of the Lewis & Clark Expedition*, vol. 4, 271.)

Vignette 2: "Shields renewed the main Spring of my air gun we have been much indebted to the ingenuity of this man on many occasions; without having served any regular apprenticeship to any trade, he makes his own tools principally and works extremely well in either wood or metal, and in this way has been extremely serviceable to us, as well as being a good hunter and an excellent waterman…" (Captain Lewis, 10 June 1805, quoted in Gary Moulton, ed., *The Journals of the Lewis & Clark Expedition*, vol. 4, 275.)

Vignette 3: "we Set out at 8 oClock & proceeded on verry well… the bluff are a blackish Clay & Coal for about 80 feet. the earth above that for 30 or 40 feet is brownish yellow…" (Captain Clark, 12 June 1805, quoted in Gary Moulton, ed., *The Journals of the Lewis & Clark Expedition*, vol. 4, 281.) [Note: There is no coal in the bluffs. The black band of rock is actually Marias River Shale.]

Teaching Point: **Respect.** How does the captains' decision to mitigate risk exemplify the Army value of *respect*? In what ways does Lewis' comment about Private Shields demonstrate respect? Why was it important for them to demonstrate respect?

Day 1
Stand 4
(The Great Falls)

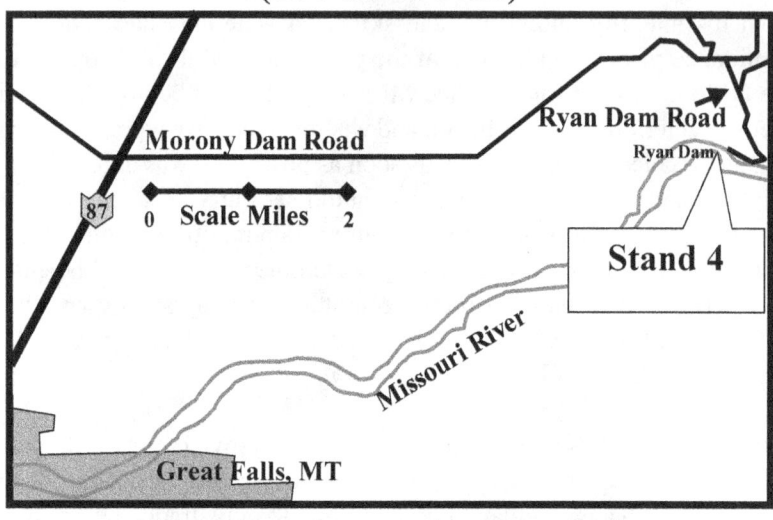

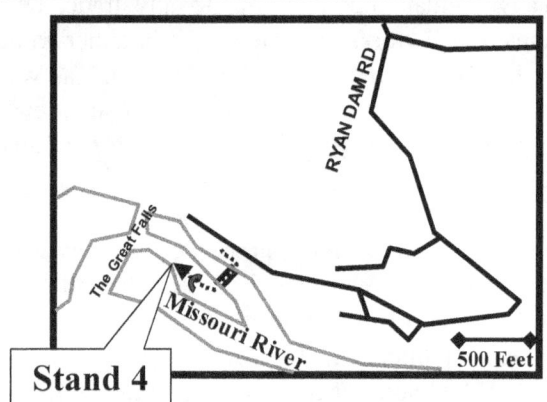

Map 1-4

**Stand 4
The Great Falls
(12 – 14 June 1805)**

Directions: Continue south on US 87 toward Great Falls. Approximately 3 miles north of Great Falls, turn left (east) on Morony Dam Road. Then go approximately 8 miles and turn south on Ryan Dam Road. Follow signs to Ryan Dam Park. After parking, cross the footbridge and move through the picnic pavilion to the high point overlooking Ryan Dam.

Orientation (See Visual 1-3, Appendix D): Lewis reached this area on 13 June 1805. From here the Missouri River flows to the northeast. It is 50 miles northeast to the junction with the Marias River and approximately 8 miles upriver to the present-day city of Great Falls. Ryan Dam has significantly changed the hydrology of the Great Falls.

Situation: Lewis had not made significant progress on the 11th because he was still dealing with a troubling stomach aliment. He felt much better on the 12th, and his group was able to forge ahead 27 miles. That day they killed two bears and left the meat hanging beside the river for Clark's group. They also saw, from a high point, the distant Rocky Mountains with their peaks covered in snow. Game was very plentiful, and that evening they dined on the best parts of a buffalo, an antelope, three mule deer, and about a dozen fish: a hearty banquet for only four men.

Lewis moved the group out at sunrise on the 13th. He was anxious to find the falls and unwilling to be delayed by the need for the men to hunt. He instructed them to obtain the day's lunch and meet him at the river. As he scouted ahead, he soon heard the roaring of falls. He had found "the grandest sight I ever beheld," the Great Falls of the Missouri, proof that he and Clark had been correct.

Vignette 1: "…from this hight we had a most beatifull and picturesk view of the Rocky mountains which wer perfectly covered with Snow and reaching from S.E. to the N. of N.W.- they appear to be formed of several ranges each succeeding range rising higher than the preceding one untill the most distant appear to loose their snowey tops in the clouds…" (Captain Lewis, 12 June 1805, quoted in Gary Moulton, ed., *The Journals of the Lewis & Clark Expedition*, vol. 4, 280.)

Vignette 2: "I had proceeded on this course about two miles with Goodrich at some distance behind me whin my ears were saluted with the agreeable sound of a fall of water, and advancing a little further I saw the spray arrise above the plain like a collumn of smoke which would frequently dispear again in an instant caused I presume by the wind which blew pretty hard from the S.W. I did not however loose my direction to this point which soon began to make a roaring too tremendious to be mistaken for any cause short of the great falls of the Missouri. here I arrived about 12 OClock having traveled by estimate, about 15 miles. I hurried down the hill which was about 200 feet high and difficult of access, to gaze on this sublimely grand spectacle..." (Captain Lewis, 13 June 1805, quoted in Gary Moulton, ed., *The Journals of the Lewis & Clark Expedition*, vol. 4, 283-284.)

Teaching Point: **Trust and Loyalty.** Lewis' decision to send an advance party on the south fork showed respect for the men's belief that the north fork was the Missouri. How did the consequences of that decision help to build *trust and loyalty* within the corps?

Day 1
Stand 5
(Crooked Falls and Beautiful Falls)

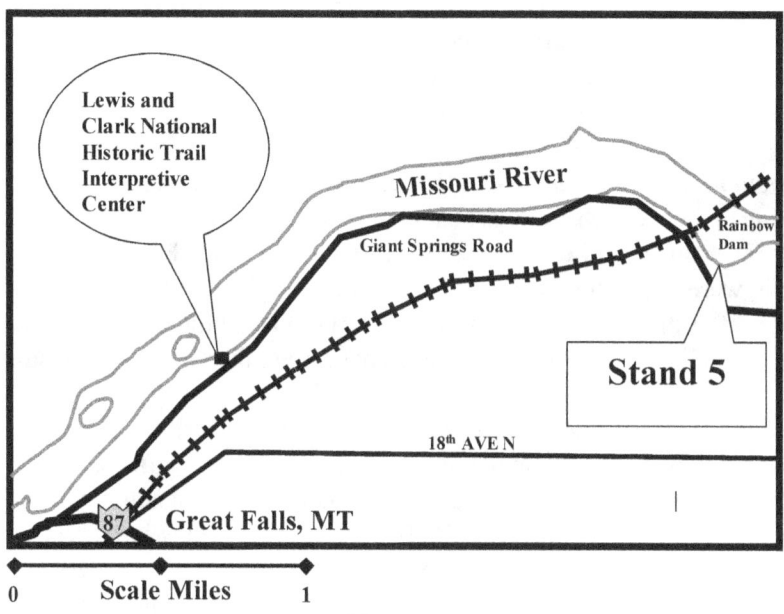

Map 1-5

Stand 5
Crooked Falls and Beautiful Falls
(14 June 1805)

Directions: Return to US 87 along Ryan Dam Road and Morony Dam Road. At US 87 proceed south toward Great Falls. Continue on US 87 into Great Falls. Immediately after crossing the Missouri River turn left on River Drive. After approximately 1.6 miles, turn left onto Giant Springs Road. Then, approximately 1.4 miles past the Lewis and Clark Interpretive Center, turn left into Rainbow Dam Overlook.

Orientation (See Visual 1-4, Appendix D): The dams have significantly changed the scene that Lewis beheld in June 1805. The view below is Rainbow Dam and what Lewis called Beautiful or Handsome Falls. The Crooked Falls were a quarter of a mile downriver and the Great Falls another 9 miles after that. Colter Falls (now submerged) is ½ mile upstream. Finally, the Upper Falls (now Black Eagle Dam) are another 2 ½ miles upstream.

Situation: On 14 June, Lewis dispatched a note to Clark verifying that the south fork was indeed the Missouri. He decided that, while he waited for Clark and the main body of the Corps of Discovery to catch up, he would recon a route around the falls. He believed, based on his interpretation of the information provided to him by the Hidatsa Indians, that there was only one fall and that the portage would take one day. The Hidatsa Indians had been there many times and certainly understood that there was a series of falls. The message of a series of falls must have been lost in the translation. Besides, the Hidatsas had come to the falls by horse and would not actually have had to portage around them. They instead would have taken one day to pass around the falls on horseback.

Lewis was amazed by the beauty of what he saw that day, but he also must have been very concerned by what it all meant to his projected portage timetable. He discovered that the first 5 miles beyond the Great Falls was a stretch of continuous rapids. He then discovered three more falls in quick succession and a fourth farther upriver. In all, he found more than 12 miles of rapids and five falls. His journal entries for this day read much like an excited tourist enjoying the sites. However, the entries also showed that Lewis was updating his commander's estimate of where and how to make the portage. He noted that numerous ravines cut the north bank and would make a portage on that side difficult. More important, he reasoned that, because the river turned to the south, the shorter portage route would be on the south bank.

During his reconnaissance, Lewis came close to losing his life or, at a minimum, being severely injured. He had shot a buffalo about 6 miles west of Beautiful Fall near where the river makes the bend to the south. In a moment of inattention, he failed to reload his rifle and allowed a grizzly bear to approach unnoticed. He was forced to defend himself against the charging bear with his spontoon. The encounter ended with the bear beating a hasty retreat and Lewis vowing never to leave his rifle unloaded again.

Vignette 1: "…about ten OClock this morning while the men were engaged with the meat I took my gun and espontoon and thought I would walk a few miles and see where the rapids termineated above, and return to dinner. accordingly I set out and proceeded up the river about S.W. after passing one continued rappid and three small cascades of abut for or five feet each at the distance of about five miles I arrived at a fall of about 19 feet… just above this rappid the river makes a suddon bend to the right or Northwardly. I should have returned from hence but hearing a tremendous roaring above me I continued my rout across the point of a hill a few hundred yards further and was again presented by one of the most beautiful objects in nature, a cascade of about fifty feet perpendicular… here the river pitches over a shelving rock, with an edge as regular and as streight as if formed by art, without a nich or brake in it; the water descends in one even and uninterrupted sheet to the bottom, wher, dashing against the rocky bottom rises into foaming billows of great hight and rappidly glides away, hising flashing, and sparkling as it departs… I now thought that if a skillful painter had been asked to make a beautifull cascade, he would most probably have pesented the precise immage of this one; nor could I for some time determine on which of those two great cataracts to bestoe the palm, on this, or that which I had discovered yesterday; at length I determined between these two great rivals for glory, that this was *pleasingly beautiful*, while the other was *sublimely grand…*" (Captain Lewis, 14 June 1805, quoted in Gary Moulton, ed., *The Journals of the Lewis & Clark Expedition*, vol. 4, 289-290.)

Vignette 2: "I scelected a fat buffaloe and shot him very well, through the lungs; while I was gazeing attentively on the poor animal discharging blood in streams from his mouth and nostrils, expecting him to fall every instant, and having entirely forgotten to reload my rifle, a large white, or reather, brown bear, had perceived and crept on me within 20 steps before I discovered him; in the first moment I drew up my gun to shoot, but at the same instant recolected that she was not loaded, and that he was too near for me to hope to perform this opperation before he reached me, as he was then briskly advancing on me; it was an open level plain, not a bush within miles nor a tree within less than three hundred yards of me; the riverbank was sloping and not more than three feet above the level of the water; in short, there was no place by means of which I could conceal myself from this monster untill I could charge my rifle; in this situation I thought of retreating in a brisk walk as fast as he was advancing untill I could reach a tree about 300 yards below me, but I had no sooner terned myself about but he pitched at me, open mouthed and full speed, I ran about 80 yards and found he gained on me fast, I then run into the water the idea struck me to get into the water to such debth that I could stand and he would be obliged to swim, and that I could in that situation defend myself with my espontoon. Accordingly, I ran hastily into the water about waist deep and faced about and presented the point of my espontoon, at this instant he arrived at the edge of the water within about twenty feet of me; the moment I put myself in this attitude of defense he suddenly wheeled about as if frightened, declined the combat on such unequal grounds, and retreated with quite as great precipitation as he had just before pursued me as soon as I saw him run of[f] in that manner I returned to the shore and charged my gun, which I had still retained in my hand throughout this curious adventure… My gun reloaded I felt confidence once more in my strength; and determined not to be thwarted in my design of visiting medicine river, but determined never again to suffer my piece to be longer empty than the time she necessarily required to charge her..." (Captain Lewis, 14 June 1805, quoted in Gary Moulton, ed., *The Journals of the Lewis & Clark Expedition*, vol. 4, 292-293.)

Teaching Points:

Commander's Estimate. Lewis' original *commander's estimate* had allocated one day for the portage around the falls. Why was it important for Lewis to immediately begin the process of updating his estimate during his reconnaissance of the Great Falls area?

Complacency. The Corps of Discovery was a military unit moving into unknown territory. The captains and the unit could take pride in what they had accomplished to date. Their primary foe during the last 14 months had been the river itself. What was the significance of Lewis' encounter with the grizzly bear?

Day 1
Stand 6 (Portage Creek)
And
Stand 7 (Willow Run Camp and the Great Portage)

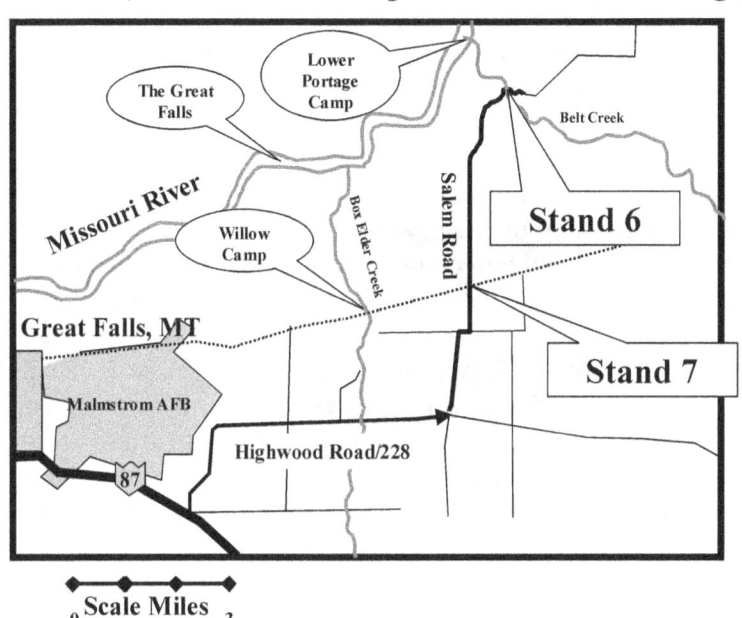

Map 1-6

Stand 6
Portage Creek
(16 June – 4 July 1805)

Directions: Retrace your route back along Giant Springs Road and River Drive. Reset the mileage counter to zero as you pass the Lewis and Clark Interpretive Center. Then, at 1.7 miles, turn left on 25th Street and continue about 20 blocks until you reach 10th Avenue (also US 89/87). At 10th Avenue, turn left and continue east out of Great Falls. At approximately 8.7 miles, turn left on Highwood Road/228. Then, at approximately 14.8 miles (mile marker 6), turn left on Salem Road (gravel). Follow Salem Road to approximately mile 21, where you should cross over the Belt Creek Bridge. Carefully turn around and come back over the bridge and park just past the guardrail looking north into the creek bottom.

Orientation (See Visual 1-5, Appendix D): The creek today is called Belt Creek. The captains referred to it as Portage Creek. The Lower Portage Camp is approximately 1 mile down the creek where it joins with the Missouri River. The Great Falls are 6 miles upstream from the camp. The slopes back up the road to the southwest compose the area represented by the display at the interpretive center showing the corps dragging a dugout canoe uphill.

Situation: The captains reunited on 16 June and established the lower portage camp 6 miles downriver from the falls. They were anxious to begin the planning and execution of the portage. However, they first had to solve a more immediate problem; Sacagawea was seriously ill. The Corps of Discovery was in danger of losing its only means of communicating with the Shoshone, Sacagawea's people, who lived at the headwaters of the Missouri. The Shoshone were critical to Lewis' plan. They had the horses the corps needed to cross the mountains, and Sacagawea would be an important asset in obtaining the horses.

Today's scholars believe that Sacagawea suffered from a chronic pelvic inflammatory disease, probably caused by a gonorrheal infection. Clark had, without success, tried to cure her by repeatedly administering the accepted scientific method of bleeding. He had also experimented with Peruvian bark and laudanum. He handed over his critically ill patient to Lewis on the 16th. Lewis discontinued the bleeding but continued with the doses of Peruvian bark and laudanum. He also encouraged her to drink sulfur water from a nearby spring. Her condition improved significantly over the next three days.

The captains discussed the portage situation on the evening of the 16th. They decided that the portage would have to be made on the south side. They also determined that, to lessen the load for the portage, the corps needed to cache more supplies along with the white pirogue. Their plan was to use the iron-frame boat, the *Experiment*, at the completion of the portage. During their discussion, they received some bad news from the scouts that had been sent out earlier. The scouts reported that the terrain was cut by two deep ravines and was therefore impractical for the portage. Lewis, always the realist, stated: "Good or bad we must make the portage."

The two captains examined the nearby creek the next morning. Both agreed that their canoes could be brought up the creek and then taken up the ravine to the top of the plains. They announced their decision to portage on the south bank and named the stream Portage Creek. The captains divided their efforts over the next three days. Lewis remained in the camp to care for Sacagawea and prepare the equipment for movement. He also had the men cut down the only large tree in the area to make cart wheels. His plan was to mount the canoes on the cart wheels for the portage. Clark led a small group of men to survey the route from 17 to 20 June and determined the portage route to be 17¾ miles in length.

The captains met again to discuss the situation on the evening of 20 June. They decided to continue with a division of labor. Clark was to oversee the portage, and Lewis was to oversee preparation of the *Experiment* at the termination point

Vignette 1 "...in the evening the men who had been sent out to examine the country and made a very unfavorable report. they informed us that the creek just above us and two deep ravines still higher up cut the plain between the river and mountain in such a manner, that in their opinions a portage for the canoes on this side was impracticable. go[o]d or bad we must make the portage. notwithstanding this report I am still convinced from the view I had of the country the day before yesterday that a good portage may be had on this side at least much better than on the other, and much nearer also..." (Captain Lewis, 16 June 1805, quoted in Gary Moulton, ed., *The Journals of the Lewis & Clark Expedition*, vol. 4, 300.)

Vignette 2 "...all appear perfectly to have made up their minds, to Succeed in the expedition or perish in the attempt. we all believe that we are about to enter on the most perilous and dificuelt part of our Voyage, yet I See no one repineing; all appear ready to meet those difficulties which await us with resolution and becomeing fortitude..." (Captain Clark, 20 June

1805, quoted in Gary Moulton, ed., *The Journals of the Lewis & Clark Expedition*, vol. 4, 319.)

Teaching Point: **Team Building.** US Army Field Manual (FM) 22-100, *Army Leadership*, states that as the team becomes more experienced and enjoys more successes, it becomes more cohesive and that a cohesive team accomplishes the mission much more efficiently than a group of individuals. Describe and discuss the status of the Corps of Discovery as a team at the commencement of the great portage.

Stand 7
Willow Run Camp and the Great Portage
(21 June – 4 July 1805)

Directions: Reset your mileage counter to zero and retrace your route back along Salem Road. At approximately 4 miles, stop where an abandoned railroad line crosses the road.

Orientation (See Visual 1-5, Appendix D): The portage route came up the draw along the same path that the road follows. Approximately 1 mile back, the route cut diagonally across the prairie in the direction of the farm complexes situated to the West along the railroad line. The most distant farm complex marks the vicinity of what was the expedition's Willow Run Camp. There is a large coulee between the two farms. The captains referred to the coulee as Willow Run; today it is called Box Elder Creek. The portage route then cut diagonally across the prairie toward the far left water tower on the horizon. From there, the route goes down the slope to the Missouri River and the Upper Portage Camp.

Situation: The captains recorded 22 June 1805 as the start of the Corps of Discovery's portage around the Great Falls. The men had already pulled the waterlogged dugout canoes up Portage Creek and allowed them to dry out. On the 21st, Lewis moved one canoe up from the Portage Creek ravine to the top of the plains. This first mile of the land portage was the most difficult terrain on the route. Moving a canoe and its baggage load out of the ravine onto the plains consumed a full day. In the first load, Lewis had the frame for the iron boat and the supplies needed to set up camp at the far end of the portage. Soon after sunrise on the 22nd, the men were ready to begin the difficult pull around the falls. They harnessed themselves to the canoe and started out across the plains. Captain Clark led the way; he had earlier surveyed the route and marked it with stakes. Over the next few days, he made slight modifications to the route to better take advantage of the terrain.

    That first morning they pulled the initial canoe 6 miles to Willow Creek. Because of the large amount of game in the area, the ground was extremely rough. During wet weather, the antelope and buffalo had churned up the ground with their hoofs. The upturned ground had dried rock hard in the summer sun, making the pull very difficult. They had been able to go around the head of two creek ravines between Portage Creek and Willow Creek. At Willow Creek, however, they had to pass through the ravine. Fortunately, Clark had found a fairly gentle route into and out of the ravine. They reached Willow Creek at about noon and established a rest camp. It was the only area between Portage Creek and the Upper Portage Camp that had firewood and water. Over the course of the portage, the corps continued to use Willow Creek as a designated rest and maintenance halt. They rested the men at Willow Creek, repaired a broken axle, and then resumed hauling the canoe after lunch. The next phase of the route, from Willow Run Camp to the Upper Portage Camp, was another 10 3/4 miles. It was far less challenging than the first 7 miles. The path was relatively flat for the first several miles, then sloped gently downhill to the Missouri River. Upon reaching the Missouri River, Lewis established the Upper Portage Camp on White Bear Island. Clark rested the men there that evening, then returned with them to Portage Creek the next day to begin the process all over again.

The portage was the Corps of Discovery's most difficult undertaking to date. It took them 11 days of backbreaking labor to move all six dugouts and the baggage across the plains to the Upper Portage Camp. On the open plains they had no cover from the elements. At times it seemed that nature conspired against them. They faced extremes of heat and cold. Occasionally the weather cooperated, and the men were able to hoist sails on the crude canoe wagons and actually sail the boats across the plains. At other times, though, they were assailed by violent storms of rain, wind and hail. The successful portage of the falls was a great testament to the men's determination and the leadership skills of their officers and NCOs.

Vignette 1: "having determined to go to the upper part of the portage tomorrow; in order to prepare my boat and receive and take care of the stores as they were transported, I caused the Iron frame of the boat and the necessary tools my private baggage, and Instruments to be taken as a part of this load; also the baggage of Joseph Fields, Sergt. Gass, and John shields, whom I had selected to assist me in constructing the leather boat…" (Captain Lewis, 21 June 1805, quoted in Gary Moulton, ed., *The Journals of the Lewis & Clark Expedition*, vol. 4, 323.)

Vignette 2: "…the men has to haul with all their Strength wate & art, maney times every man all catching the grass & knobes & Stones with their hands to give them more force in drawing on the Canoes & Loads, and notwithstanding the Coolness of the air in high presperation and every halt, those not employed in reparing the Course; are asleep in a moment, maney limping from the Soreness of their feet Some become fant for a fiew moments, but no man Complains all go Cheerfully on - to State the fatigues of this party would take up more of the journal than other notes which I find Scercely time to Set down..." (Captain Clark, 23 June 1805, quoted in Gary Moulton, ed., *The Journals of the Lewis & Clark Expedition*, vol. 4, 328-329.)

Vignette 3: "it is worthy of remark that the winds are sometimes so strong in these plains that the men informed me that they hoisted a sail in the canoe and it had driven her along on the truck wheels. this is really sailing on dry land..." (Captain Lewis, 25 June 1805, quoted in Gary Moulton, ed., *The Journals of the Lewis & Clark Expedition*, vol. 4, 332.)

Vignette 4: "... a torrent of rain and hail fell more violent than ever I saw before, the rain fell like one voley of water falling from the heavens and gave us time only to get out of the way of a torrent of water which was Poreing down the hill in the rivin with emence force tareing every thing before it takeing with it large rocks & mud, ... on arrival at the Camp on the willow run - met the party who had returned in great Confusion to the run leaveing their loads in the Plain, the hail & wind being So large and violent in the plains, and them naked, they were much brused, and Some nearly killed one knocked down three times, and others without hats or any thing on their heads bloodey & Complained verry much; I refreshed them with a little grog..." (Captain Clark, 29 June 1805, quoted in Gary Moulton, ed., *The Journals of the Lewis & Clark Expedition*, vol. 4, 342-343.)

Teaching Point: **The Human Dimension.** To fully appreciate the *human dimension* of leadership, you must understand two key elements: leadership itself and the people you lead. How did the captains demonstrate their understanding of the human dimension of leadership during the great portage?

Day 1
Stand 8
Upper Portage Camp

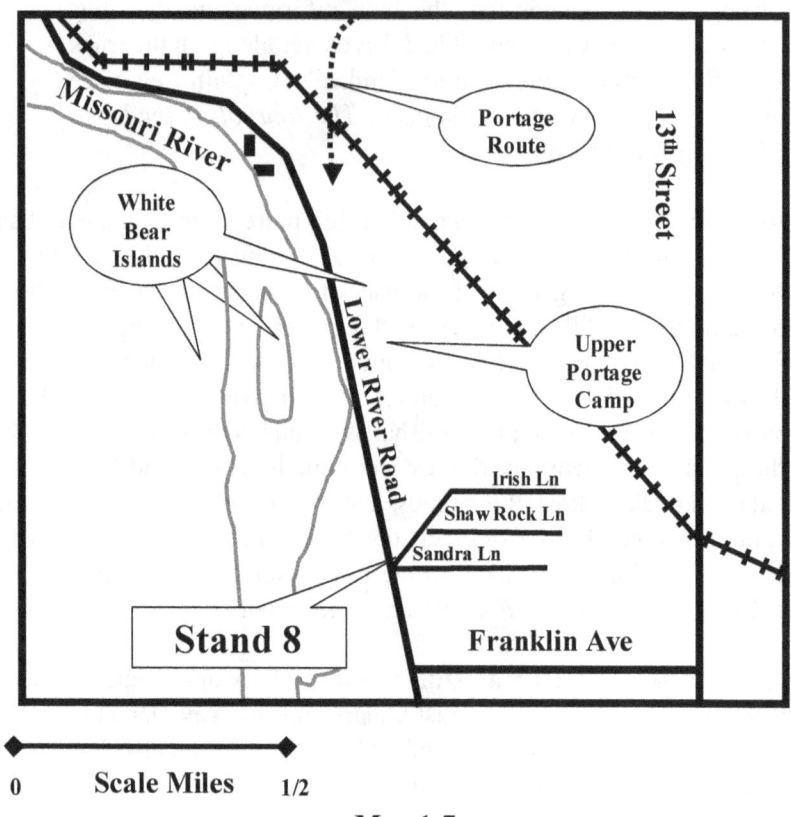

Map 1-7

Stand 8
The Upper Portage Camp
(20 June to 15 July 1805)

Directions: Retrace your route to Great Falls along Salem Road, Highwood Road/228, and US 87. Continue east along US 87/10th Avenue into Great Falls. Turn left on 26th Street South. Then turn right on 33rd Avenue South. Soon after turning, there is a large draw leading down to the Missouri River. This is the final leg of the portage route. Next turn left on 13th Street South. At Franklin Avenue turn right. When you reach the stop sign/junction with Lower River Road, reset the mileage counter to zero. At approximately 0.17 miles, turn right and park in the residential area.

Orientation (See Visual 1-5 & 6, Appendix D): The Missouri River is to the west beyond the tree line. The river has changed significantly since the Corps of Discovery was here in 1805. At that time the river channels formed three small islands. The captains referred to them collectively as the White Bear Islands. The field just ½ mile north of this location was the southern tip of the eastern island. It was there that Lewis established the Upper Portage Camp. The draw, three-quarters of a mile to the north, is where the portage route came down from the upper plains to the river.

Situation: While Clark supervised the portage, Lewis moved to White Bear Island with a small group of men and supervised the construction of the iron-frame boat. Lewis was very excited about his boat and made numerous journal entries about it. Sometimes he referred to the boat as his "favorite boat." The Iron frame was 36 feet long, 4 feet in beam, and 26 inches deep. It probably resembled a large bark canoe common to the Great Lakes region and should have been capable of hauling several tons of supplies. The men referred to the boat as the *Experiment* and shared Lewis' confidence in the design. Clark's feelings about the boat are not well documented. He rarely mentioned the boat and may not have shared everyone else's confidence that the *Experiment* would be successful.

Work on the boat was slow and frustrating. Lewis' original idea for the boat, conceived at Harpers Ferry in 1803, was to use small straight sticks and birch bark to strengthen the hull. He then hoped to use elk skin sealed with pine pitch to waterproof the hull. Unfortunately, most of these materials were not available on the Great Plains, and Lewis had to experiment to find substitutes. The men searched the area, but, unable to find many straight sticks, they had to substitute whatever wood they could find. They expended much effort shaving and notching sticks together to make them suitable. Lewis was also unsuccessful in his search for anything similar to birch bark. They resorted to willow bark, which was a poor substitute. With great difficulty, the men collected the willow bark and then had to soak it in an attempt to make it pliable enough to conform to the shape of the hull. Next, the hunters failed to attain a sufficient number of elk skins to cover the boat hull. Lewis wanted to use elk skin because the elk's short hair made it easy to work and it cured into a tough and flexible hide. Lewis decided to use buffalo hides to make up the difference. The buffalo were very plentiful, but their hides were difficult to cure because of the long, shaggy hair. The end result was that with Lewis' ingenuity and perseverance, and the soldiers' hard work, they made the substitutes of crooked sticks, willow bark, and buffalo hides meet the initial requirements of the iron boat design.

At this point, Lewis had solved three of the four problems with the *Experiment* and was confident that the boat would meet the needs of the Corps of Discovery. However, he was also growing impatient and wanted to finish the portage, launch the boat, and get back on the river. He even allowed himself, on 2 July 1805, to be distracted from work on the boat and devoted more than 200 words in his journals to the scientific discovery of the pack rat. Occasionally, the island's namesake, the *white bears* (grizzly bears), interrupted work on the boat as well. They became so troublesome by 2 July that Lewis mounted a successful expedition against them and pushed them off the island.

Overall, the captains were very pleased with what they had accomplished and decided to allow the men to celebrate the nation's 29th birthday. They were the first US citizens to enter today's Montana. They had named the Yellowstone, Milk, and Marias Rivers; met and defeated in combat the region's most fearsome predator, the grizzly bear; finished the portage around the Great Falls; and would soon be on the river again. To celebrate, the captains issued each man a gill of whiskey, the last of their supply. They also allowed the cooks to prepare a grand dinner of bacon, beans, dumplings, and buffalo beef.

Lewis also recorded a key decision in his journal that evening. During the previous winter, while still at Fort Mandan, the captains had planned to send a second return party home from the Great Falls. The second return party would have carried the current collection of scientific specimens and journals. Their new concerns about the unknown path ahead and whether the Indian nations yet to be encountered would be friendly or hostile led them to forego sending the second group back. They reasoned that they needed all their men (and rifles) for future challenges. They were also concerned about morale. The captains had molded the Corps of Discovery into a cohesive unit. The morale of the team was high, and they were worried that any dividing of the team could adversely affect its morale. The absence of any recorded rumors concerning whether the men knew of the plan or its abandonment speaks highly of the unit's discipline.

The corps, with the exception of the *Experiment*, was ready to resume its journey on 5 July 1805. All that remained to done was to have Lewis finish sealing the boat's hull. Lewis was concerned about the delay but confident that the boat would be a success. One major unsolved deficiency remained—the lack of pine pitch to seal the hull. Lewis first tried to extract tar from pine logs and sticks found floating down the river. He worked at his "Tar-Kiln" from 1-4 July, producing much charcoal but not one drop of tar (pine pitch). He then switched to a mixture of tallow, charcoal, and beeswax as a sealant. This seemed to work well enough, and Lewis was ready to launch his boat on 9 July 1805. At first, Lewis' great experiment was successful. Unfortunately, the seams failed when a storm came up, causing the boat to sink. Lewis was extremely disappointed. Clark, the realist, immediately set the men to work building two more dugout canoes. It appears that he had sent scouts to find suitable trees earlier, perhaps anticipating that the *Experiment* might fail. The corps resumed its journey on 15 July 1805 with eight dugout canoes and significantly less cargo than they had hoped to carry. Without the cargo-carrying capacity of the *Experiment*, the captains had been forced to cache many of the supplies that had been laboriously hauled across the plains.

Vignette 1: "I found that Sergt. Gass and Shields had made but slow progress in collecting timber for the boat; they complained of great difficulty in getting streight or even tolerably straight sticks of 4 ½ feet long. we were obliged to make use of the willow and box alder, the cottonwood being too soft and brittle. I kept one of them collecting timber while the other shaved and fitted them." (Captain Lewis, 24 June 1805, quoted in Gary Moulton, ed., *The Journals of the Lewis & Clark Expedition*, vol. 4, 330.)

Vignette 2: "I begin to be extremely impatient to be off as the season is now waisting a pace nearly three months have now elapsed since we left Fort Mandan and not yet reached the Rocky Mountains I am therefore fully perswaded that we shall not reach Fort Mandan again this season if we even return from the ocean to the Snake Indians..." (Captain Lewis, 30 June 1805, quoted in Gary Moulton, ed., *The Journals of the Lewis & Clark Expedition*, vol. 4, 344.)

Vignette 3: "In the evening, the most of the corps crossed over to an island, to attack and rout its monarch, a large brown bear, that held possession and seemed to defy all that would attempt to besiege him there. Our troops, however, stormed the place, gave no quarter, and its commander fell. Our army returned the same evening to camp without having suffered any loss on their side…" (Patrick Gass, 2 July 1805, quoted in Gary Moulton, ed., *The Journals of the Lewis & Clark Expedition*, vol. 10, 108.)

Vignette 4: "Our work being at an end this evening, we gave the men a drink of sperits, it being the last of our stock, and some of them appeared a little sensible of it's effects the fiddle was plyed and they danced very merrily untill 9 in the evening when a heavy shower of rain put an end to that part of the amusement tho' they continued their mirth with songs and festive jokes and were extreemely merry untill late at night. we had a very comfortable dinner, of bacon, beans, suit dumplings & buffaloe beef &c. in short we had no just cause to covet the sumptuous feasts of our countrymen on this day…" (Captain Lewis, July 04, 1805, quoted in Gary Moulton, ed., *The Journals of the Lewis & Clark Expedition*, vol. 4, 362.)

Vignette 5: "Capt. C completed a draught of the river from Fort Mandan to this place which we intend depositing at this place in order to guard against accedents. not having seen the Snake Indians or knowing in fact whether to calculate on their friendship or hostility … we have conceived our party sufficiently small and therefore have concluded not to dispatch a canoe with a part of our men to St. Louis as we had intended early in the spring. We fear also that such a measure might possibly discourage those who would in such case remain, and might possibly hazard the fate of the expedition. we have never once hinted to any one of the party that we had such a scheme in contemplation, and all appear perfectly to have made up their minds to succeed in the expedition or perish in the attempt. we all believe that we are now about to enter on the most perilous and difficult part of our voyage, yet I see no one repining; all appear ready to met those difficulties which wait us with resolution and becoming fortitude…" (Captain Lewis, 4 July 1805, quoted in Gary Moulton, ed., *The Journals of the Lewis & Clark Expedition*, vol. 4, 359-361.)

Vignette 6: "the boat in every other rispect completely answers my most sanguine expectation; she is not yet dry and eight men can carry her with the greatest ease; she is strong and will carry at least 8,000 lbs with her suit of hands; her form is as complete as I could wish it." (Captain Lewis, 5 July 1805, quoted in Gary Moulton, ed., *The Journals of the Lewis & Clark Expedition*, vol. 4, 363.)

Vignette 7: "...launched the boat, she lay like a perfect cork on the water. Five men would carry her with the greatest ease... just at this moment a violent wind commenced and blew so hard that we were obliged to unload the canoes again... the wind continued violent untill late in the evening, by which time we discovered that a greater part of the composition had separated from the skins and left the seams of the boat exposed to the water and she leaked in such manner that she would not answer. I need not add that this circumstance mortifyed me not a little; and to prevent her leaking without pitch was impossible with us ... therefore the evil was irraparable... I therefore relinquished all further hope of my favorite boat and ordered her to be sunk in the water...and I bid adieu to my boat..." (Captain Lewis, 9 July 1805, quoted in Gary Moulton, ed., *The Journals of the Lewis & Clark Expedition*, vol. 4, 368-369.)

Vignette 8: "At 10 A.M., we once more saw ourselves fairly under way much to my joy and I believe that of every individual who compose the party..." (Captain Lewis, 15 July 1805, quoted in Gary Moulton, ed., *The Journals of the Lewis & Clark Expedition*, vol. 4, 382.)

Teaching Points:

Organizational Climate. The captains recognized the importance of a healthy *organizational climate*. During the great portage, what examples and lessons do the captains provide on how to promote a good organizational climate?

Technology. Technological advances have the potential of greatly increasing the operational capabilities of military units. Two significant items of new technology with the Corps of Discovery were the military rifle and the iron boat, *Experiment*. The military rifle was new technology in 1805. Both captains had served in rifle companies in the Legion of the United States and now readily accepted the rifle as an important resource for the Corps of Discovery. Without the rifle the ability of the corps to sustain itself through hunting would have been significantly less. In regards to the *Experiment*, the iron frame boat, Clark seemed to have been skeptical of its value. However, Lewis invested much faith and effort into the boat. The end result was that the failure of the *Experiment* cost the corps six to 10 days of valuable time. What is the military's relationship with new technology today?

Note on Lodging: CSI recommends group lodging at the end of day one in Great Falls, Montana. Great Falls offers numerous hotel and motel accommodations. Some offer reduced rates for large groups.

Day 2
Gates of the Mountains to the Three Forks
(16 to 30 July 1805)

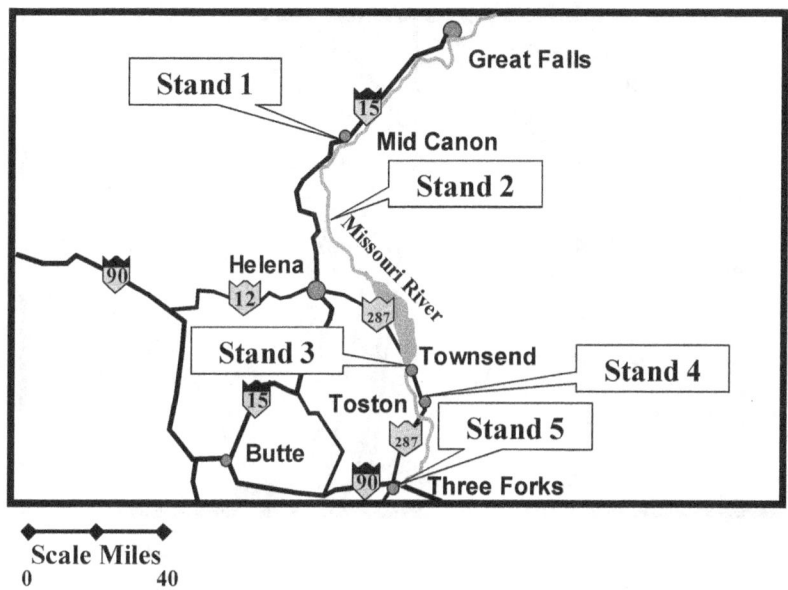

Map 2-1

Begin the day at Great Falls, MT

Stand 1, Under Way Again (Mid Canon, MT)

Stand 2, The Gates of the Mountains (Exit 209, North of Helena—Boat Ride to the Gates of the Mountains View Point)

Stand 3, The Search for the Shoshone Indians (Townsend, MT)

Stand 4, Command and Morale (Toston Dam Park—The Little Gates of the Mountains, Toston, MT)

Stand 5, The Three Forks of the Missouri (Fort Rock Overlook, Three Forks Park)

End the day at Three Forks, MT

Day 2
Stand 1 (Under Way Again)

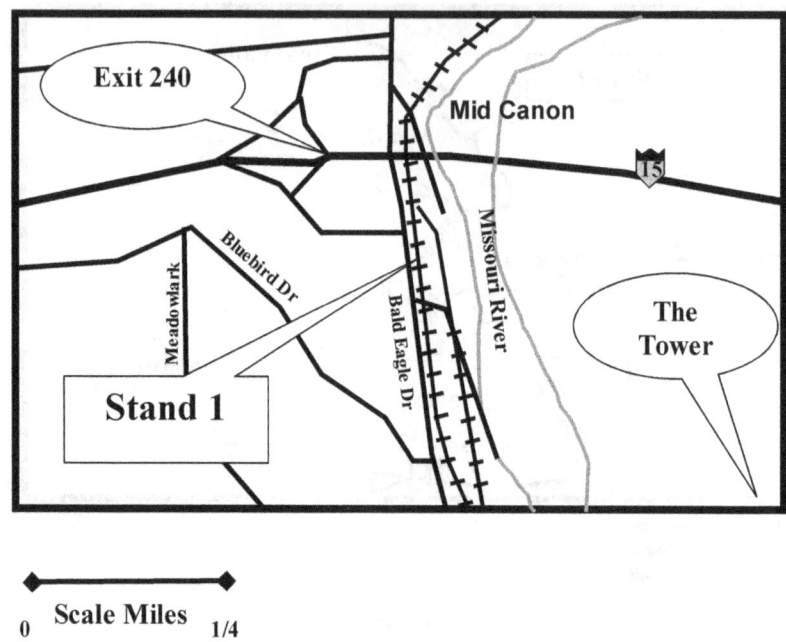

Map 2-2

Stand 1
Under Way Again
(15 – 18 July 1805)

Directions: Take Interstate 15 south from Great Falls, and then take Exit 240 at Mid Canon. Turn right (south) on Cooper Lane and pass underneath Interstate 15. Park beside the road and orient the group on the high ground to the southeast.

Orientation (See Visual 2-1, Appendix D): The river route that the Corps of Discovery followed closely parallels the modern-day interstate. The highway distance back to Great Falls is approximately 40 miles; the distance along the water route was somewhat farther because of the bends and turns in the river. The corps camped here at present-day Mid Canon on 17 July 1805.

Situation: The Corps of Discovery departed the Great Falls area on 15 July 1805. Lewis walked ahead to lighten the load for the canoes and to hunt game for the main group. Clark followed with the heavily loaded canoes. Soon after leaving the Great Falls, the captains named the Smith River for President Jefferson's secretary of the Navy, Robert Smith. On 16 July, Lewis again pushed ahead and passed through what he referred to as the first range of the Rocky Mountains. That evening he camped near present-day Mid Canon, Montana, on a bend in the river. In his journal he noted a rock summit that he called "the tower." Clark and the main body caught up with Lewis the next morning. That evening the captains discussed the situation. They were confident that the Shoshone were nearby because of the numerous Indian signs in the area. However, they were concerned that the daily firing of their hunters would frighten the Shoshone, who could possibly mistake the corps for a Blackfeet raiding party. They therefore decided to send an advance party ahead of the canoes. The two captains reasoned that a small advance party would appear less threatening to the Shoshone and would more likely be able to make contact with the Indians.

Vignette 1: "early this morning we passed about 40 little booths formed of willow bushes to shelter them from the sun; they appeared to have been deserted about 10 days; we supposed that they were the snake Indians. they appeared to have a number of horses with them -. this appearance gives me much hope of meeting with these people shortly…" (Captain Lewis, 16 July 1805, quoted in Gary Moulton, ed., *The Journals of the Lewis & Clark Expedition*, vol. 4, 386.)*

Vignette 2: "the current of the missouri below these rappids is strong for several miles, tho' just above there is scarcely any current, the river very narrow and deep abot 70 yds. wide only and seems to be closely hemned in by the mountains on both sides, the bottoms only a few yards in width… at this place there is a large rock of 400 feet high wich stands immediately in the gap which the missouri makes on its passage from the mountains; it is insulated from the neighboring mountains by a handsome little plain which surrounds its base on 3 sides and the Missouri washes it's base on the other, leaving it on the Lard. [left side] as it descends. this rock I called the tower. it may be ascended with some difficulty nearly to it's summit, and from it

---

* All vignettes retain the enigmatic writing of the journalists. See the introduction to Section III for an explanation of the editorial principles used with the journal entries.

there is a most pleasing view of the country we are now about to leave..." (Captain Lewis, 16 July 1805, quoted in Gary Moulton, ed., *The Journals of the Lewis & Clark Expedition,* vol. 4, 387.)

Vignette 3: "as we were anxious now to meet with the Sosonees, or snake Indians as soon as possible in order to obtain information relative to the geography of the country and also if necessary, some horses we thought it better for one of us either Capt. C. or myself- to take a small party and proceed on up the river, some distance, before the canoes, in order to discover them, should they be on the river before the daily discharge of our guns, which was necessary in procuring subsistence for the party, should allarm and cause them to retreat to the mountains and conceal themselves, supposing us to be their enemies who visit them usually by way of this river. accordingly, Capt. Clark set out this morning after breakfast with Joseph Field, Pots, and his servant York... (Captain Lewis, 18 July 1805, quoted in Gary Moulton, ed., *The Journals of the Lewis & Clark Expedition,* vol. 4, 398.)

Teaching Point: The military decision-making process (**MDMP**). Accomplishing the Army's mission requires leaders who are imaginative, flexible, and daring. How does the captains' leadership during this phase of the journey demonstrate their understanding of the MDMP?

Day 2
Stand 2 (Gates of the Mountains)

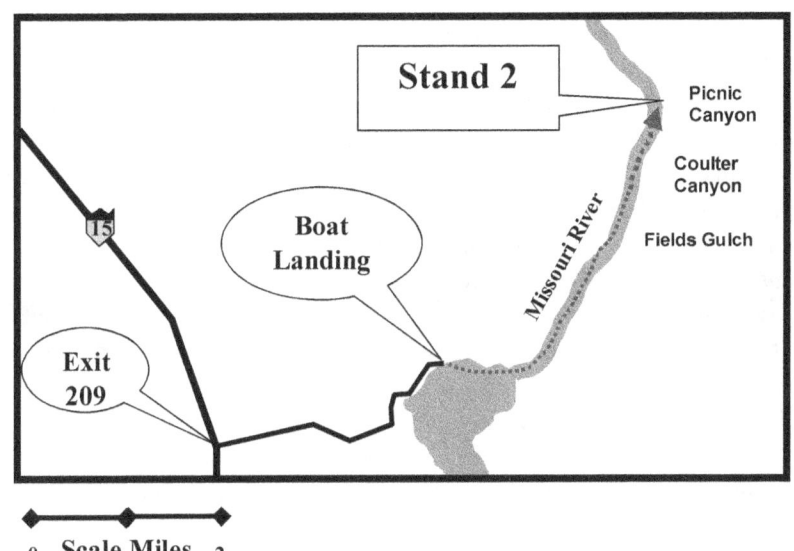

Map 2-3

**Stand 2
Gates of the Mountains
(19–20 July 1805)**

Directions: Continue south on Interstate 15 to Exit 209. Then follow the signs to the Gates of the Mountain Boat Tour.

Orientation (See Visual 2-1, Appendix D): The Corps of Discovery passed through here, moving from the north to the south. The area that Lewis referred to as The Gates of the Mountains is not visible from the boat dock area. However, from the docks you can see the river's exit from the mountain canyon. The Missouri River dams have significantly changed the appearance of the area by creating Upper Lake Holter. The dams have raised the water level inside the canyon but that stretch of the river still appears much as it did in 1805. (Instructor Note: This stand may be executed with or without the boat tour of the Gates of the Mountain. If done without the boat tour, position the group at the edge of the lake in view of where the river exits from the mountains into the lake. If possible, take the group on the boat tour to view the actual Gates of the Mountain at the north end of the river canyon and conduct the discussion at the Picnic Canyon boat stop. Details for coordinating the boat tour are located in Section V of this handbook.)

Situation: On 18 July, the Corps of Discovery continued to push up the Missouri. Clark moved ahead with a small advance party consisting of York and Privates Joseph Field and John Potts. His group moved cross-country, staying roughly parallel to the river. He made only about 20 miles that day because of the mountainous terrain. Lewis followed with the main body in the canoes. He named the Dearborn River for the secretary of war and Ordway's Creek for Sergeant Ordway. Like most of the names the corps applied to smaller creeks and streams, Ordway's Creek did not carry forward to today. It is now known as Little Prickly Pear Creek. That evening Lewis' group camped near present-day Craig, Montana. They set out early the next morning, and Lewis allowed the sergeants to take charge of the canoes while he walked along the shore. It was hard going for the men in the canoes; mosquitoes, strong currents, and rapids hindered their progress. Lewis also seemed to be concerned about the discouraging sight of the high mountains always looming to the west. He knew the corps would soon have to turn toward those mountains. He probably hoped for a water passage through the mountains, but he wanted to find the Shoshone and their horses to ensure a successful crossing. That evening the corps reached the "most remarkable cliffs," which he named the *Gates of the Rocky Mountains*. Clark had proceeded along a route that took him to the west of the Gates. His return route in 1806 also bypassed the Gates. Thus he never saw this remarkable site.

Vignette: "whever we get a view of the lofty summits of the mountains the snow presents itself, altho' we are almost suffocated in this confined vally with heat… this evening we entered much the most remarkable cliffs that we have yet seen. these clifts rise from the waters edge on either side perpendicularly to the hight of (about) 1200 feet. every object here wears a dark and gloomy aspect. the tow[er]ing and projecting rocks in many places seem ready to tumble on us. the river appears to have forced it's way through this immence body of solid rock for the distance of 5 3/4 miles and where it makes it's exit below has thrown on either side vast collumns of rocks mountains high… from the singular appearance of this place I called it the *gates of the rocky mountains*…" (Captain Lewis, 19 July 1805, quoted in Gary Moulton, ed., *The Journals of the Lewis & Clark Expedition*, vol. 4, 402-403.)

Teaching Point:

The Team. *Team* identity comes out of mutual respect among its members and trust between leaders and subordinates. That bond between leaders and subordinates likewise springs from mutual respect as well as from discipline (FM 22-100, page 3-2). Which Army values did the captains best model, by their actions, to build the team?

Day 2
Stand 3 (The Search for the Shoshone Indians)

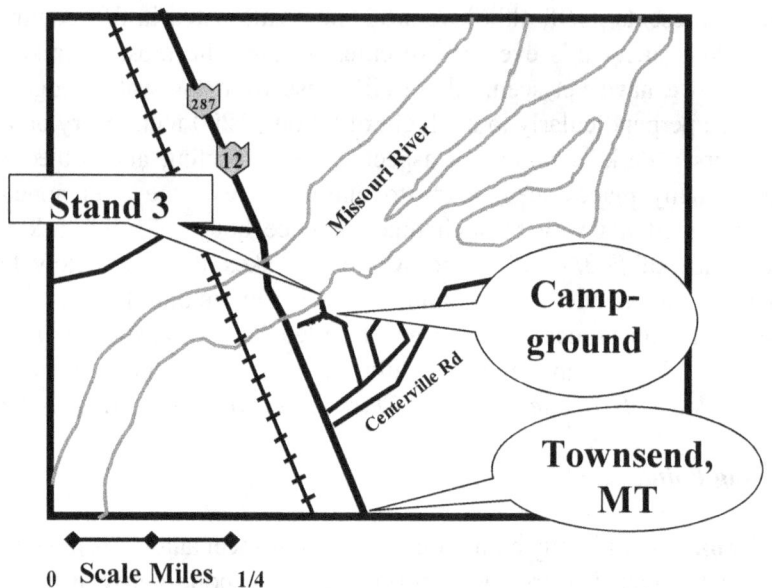

Map 2-4

Stand 3
The Search for the Shoshone Indians
(20 - 23 Jul 1805)

Directions: Return to Interstate 15 and go south toward Helena, MT. At Helena, take Highway 12/287 south toward Townsend, MT. Immediately after crossing the Missouri River, turn right into the campground on the northern edge of Townsend. Park the vehicles and move the group to the boat ramp just to the east of the highway bridge.

Orientation (See Visual 2-2, Appendix D: This location is approximately 110 miles south of the Great Falls area. The distance for the corps was much greater, considering the bends and turns in the river. Here the river looks much as it did in 1805, shallow with numerous channels. The Corps of Discovery passed this location from the right (northeast) to the left (southwest). It took the corps nine days of difficult labor to pole and drag the canoes to this point. The corps camped near here at the north edge of town on 23 July 1805.

Situation: On 20 July 1805, Lewis led his group beyond The Gates of the Mountains and entered a beautiful, intermountain valley. He was making slow but steady progress along the river. Lewis continued to be very anxious about finding the Shoshone Indians and was troubled that day when he observed a large fire 7 miles to the west. He believed that Shoshone scouts had detected either his group or Clark's advance party and then deliberately set the fire as a warning for the tribe to retreat into the mountains. Clark had also seen the fire and reached the same conclusion. Both captains independently decided upon the same course of action. The situation was critical; winter was coming on, and the Corps of Discovery needed to get over the mountains. The captains needed horses from the Indians to get over the mountains, and it appeared that the Indians were retreating from them to avoid contact. Their only choice was to press forward and take measures to make their groups look less threatening. Lewis displayed flags, a sign of peace, on the canoes and ensured that Sacagawea could easily be seen since war parties rarely contained women. Clark decided to leave gifts at his camps, hoping to convince the Indians he was not a threat.

Both Lewis' canoe party and Clark's advance party were severely challenged by the terrain. The men worked hard to pull the canoes along by hand through the low water, with the rocky bottom cutting and bruising their feet. The river was not only going the wrong way, but it also seemed to have no end. Although food was not yet a problem, the easiest source of meat, the buffalo, was no longer available, and to make matters worse all the whiskey was gone. Clark's advance party had similar problems and was also plagued by prickly pear thorns that made walking difficult. The captains were worried about the men's morale slipping. On 22 July, Sacagawea provided a morale boost when she recognized landmarks and assured Captain Lewis that her home country and the Missouri's headwaters were not far away. The two groups merged on the 22nd, and that evening the captains discussed the need for a major overland expedition to search for the Shoshone. Lewis was concerned about Clark's cut and bruised feet. Interestingly, many years later, during the editing of the journals, there was some concern and disagreement over the wording of the decision to allow Clark to lead the advance party. Clark insisted that he "determined to go," instead of Lewis's wording of "I readily consented." Stephen Ambrose, in his book *Undaunted Courage*, stated it was "more a disagreement over the right word to describe the decision-making process than a fight over the question of who was in command." The end result was that Clark led the overland expedition. It appears the captains were so confident in their ability to handle the Indians that they gave very little thought to what they would actually do when they made contact with the Shoshone. Clark took three heavily armed men with him but did not take the Shoshone interpreter, Sacagawea.

Vignette 1: "The misquetors verry troublesom my man York nearly tired out, the bottoms of my feet blistered. I observe a Smoke rise to our right up the Valley of the last Creek about 12 miles distant, The Cause of this Smoke I can't account for certainly, tho' think it probable that the Indians have heard the Shooting of the Partey below and Set the Prairies or Valey on fire to allarm their Camps; Supposing our party to be a war party comeing against them, I left Signs to Shew the Indians if they Should come on our trail that we were not their enemeys. Camped on the river, the feet of the men with me So Stuck with Prickley pear & cut with the Stones that they were Scerseley able to march at a Slow gait this after noon." (Captain Clark, 20 July 1805, quoted in Gary Moulton, ed., *The Journals of the Lewis & Clark Expedition*, vol. 4, 409-410.)

Vignette 2: "Set out early this morning and passed a bad rappid where the river enters the mountain, about 1 m. from our camp of last evening the Clifts high and covered with fragments of broken rocks. the current strong; we employed the toe rope principally, and also the poles, as the river is not now so deep but reather wider and much more rapid our progress was therefore slow and laborious..." (Captain Lewis, 21 July 1805, quoted in Gary Moulton, ed., *The Journals of the Lewis & Clark Expedition*, vol. 4, 411.)

Vignette 3: "The Indian woman recognizes the country and assures us that this is the river on which her relations live, and that the three forks are at no great distance. this peice of information has cheered the sperits of the party who now begin to console themselves with the anticipation of shortly seeing the head of the missouri yet unknown to the civilized world..." (Captain Lewis, 22 July 1805, quoted in Gary Moulton, ed., *The Journals of the Lewis & Clark Expedition*, vol. 4, 416-417.)

Vignette 4: "altho' Captain C. was much fatiegued his feet yet blistered and soar he insisted on pursuing his rout in the morning nor weould he consent willingly to my releiving him at that time by taking a tour of the same kind. finding him anxious I readily consented to remain with the canoes..." (Captain Lewis, 22 July 1805, quoted in Gary Moulton, ed., *The Journals of the Lewis & Clark Expedition*, vol. 4, 417.)

Vignette 5: "I determined to proceed on in pursute of the Snake Indians on tomorrow..." (Captain Clark, 22 July 1805, quoted in Gary Moulton, ed., *The Journals of the Lewis & Clark Expedition*, vol. 4, 418.)

Teaching Points:

Learning Organizations. The Army is a *learning organization*, one that harnesses the experience of its people and organizations to improve the way it does business. Based on their experiences, learning organizations adopt new techniques and procedures to get the job done more efficiently or effectively. Was the Corps of Discovery a learning organization, and did the captains ask, "How can I do this better"?

Selfless Service. FM 22-100 defines s*elfless service* as doing what's right for the nation, the Army, your organization, and your people—and putting these responsibilities above your own interests. How did Clark's insistence on leading the overland expedition demonstrate the Army value of selfless service?

Day 2
Stand 4 (Command and Morale)

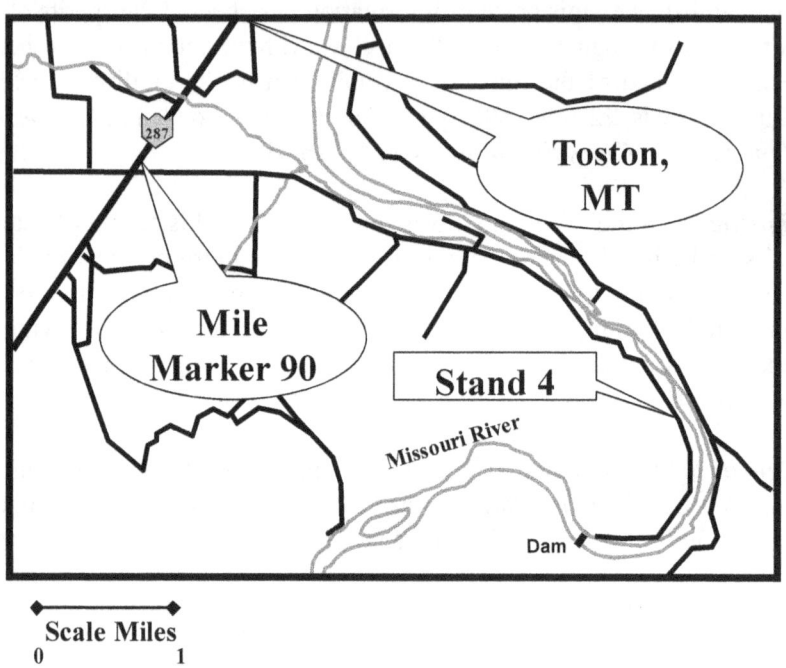

Map 2-5

Stand 4
Command and Morale
(24–25 Jul 1805)

Directions: Continue south on Highway 287 towards Toston, Montana. Pass by Toston and watch for mile marker 90. Then turn left on a gravel road towards Toston Dam and proceed for approximately 4 miles. Watch for a Lewis and Clark marker on the left side of the road and park the group at the picnic area.

Orientation (See Visual 2-2, Appendix D: The river here flows from the right (south) to the left (north). Townsend, Montana (the previous stand), is located approximately 15 miles to the north. The distance along the river, which closely parallels the route driven, is approximately 20 miles. It took the Corps of Discovery two days to cover the distance. The corps camped here under the bluffs on 25 July 1805.

Situation: Lewis departed the vicinity of today's Townsend, Montana, on 24 July 1805. The passage up the river against the strong current was difficult and labor intensive. Because the corps was moving into the mountains, Lewis was concerned they would encounter another set of falls or rapids. He feared this would require another time-consuming portage. The season was growing late, and he did not believe they could afford the time for another long portage if they wanted to complete the crossing of the mountains before the onset of winter. Prior to this phase of the journey, Lewis had spent very little time in the canoes; most of the time he walked along the shore. However, to boost the men's morale, he now decided to participate in the heavy labor of poling the canoes forward. Despite the laborious process of moving up the river, he believed the Corps of Discovery was making good progress through the Rocky Mountains. He recorded that the Gates of the Rocky Mountains, which they passed a few days before, was a chain of the Rocky Mountains and that they were now entering into a second grand chain of mountains. The corps camped that night under a high bluff a few miles south of present day Toston, Montana. Clark's advance party camped more than 25 miles ahead of the corps at the Three Forks of the Missouri.

Vignette 1: "I fear every day that we shall meet with some considerable falls or obstruction in the river notwithstanding the information of the Indian woman to the contrary who assures us that the river continues much as we see it. I can scarcely form an idea of a river running to great extent

87

through such a rough mountainous country without having it's stream intersepted by some difficult and dangerous rappids or falls..." (Captain Lewis, 24 July 1805, quoted in Gary Moulton, ed., *The Journals of the Lewis & Clark Expedition*, vol. 4, 422.)

Vignette 2: "the men complain of being much fortiegued, their labor is excessively great. I occasionally encourage them by assisting in the labour of navigating the canoes, and have learned to *push a tolerable good pole...*" (Captain Lewis, 24 July 1805, quoted in Gary Moulton, ed., *The Journals of the Lewis & Clark Expedition*, vol. 4, 423.)

Vignette 3: "...the valley appeared to termineate and the river was again hemned in on both sides with high caiggy and rocky clifts... two rapids near the large spring we passed this evening were the worst we have seen since that we passed on entering the rocky Mountain; they were obstructed with sharp pointed rocks, ranges of which extended quite across the river...S. 75° E. 1 ½ to a bluff on Stard [right]. here the river again enters the mountains. I believe it to be a second grand chain of the rocky Mots... South ½ to a Clift of rocks in a Lard. bend; opst. to which we encamped for the night under a high bluff." (Captain Lewis, 25 July 1805, quoted in Gary Moulton, ed., *The Journals of the Lewis & Clark Expedition*, vol. 4, 426-428.).

Teaching Points:

Commander's Estimate. Lewis had very little information available to him on the width and height of the Rocky Mountain chains, the last great barrier before reaching the Columbia River. At this point in the expedition, he believed that they were passing through a water-level pass in the "second grand chain of the Rocky Mountains." They were actually only entering the eastern-face foothills of the Rocky Mountains. What might the consequences be for updating an estimate of the situation based on a wrong assumption?

Morale. The most important intangible element of the human dimension of leadership is *morale*. It's a measure of how people feel about themselves, their team, and their leadership. FM 22-100 states that high morale comes from good leadership, shared hardship, and mutual respect (page 3-3). How do the actions of the captains during this phase of the expedition exemplify building high morale in a unit?

Integrity. FM 22-100 states that people of *integrity* consistently act according to principles—not just by what might work at the moment. Did the captains make their principles known and consistently act in accordance with them?

Day 2
Stand 5 (The Three Forks of the Missouri)

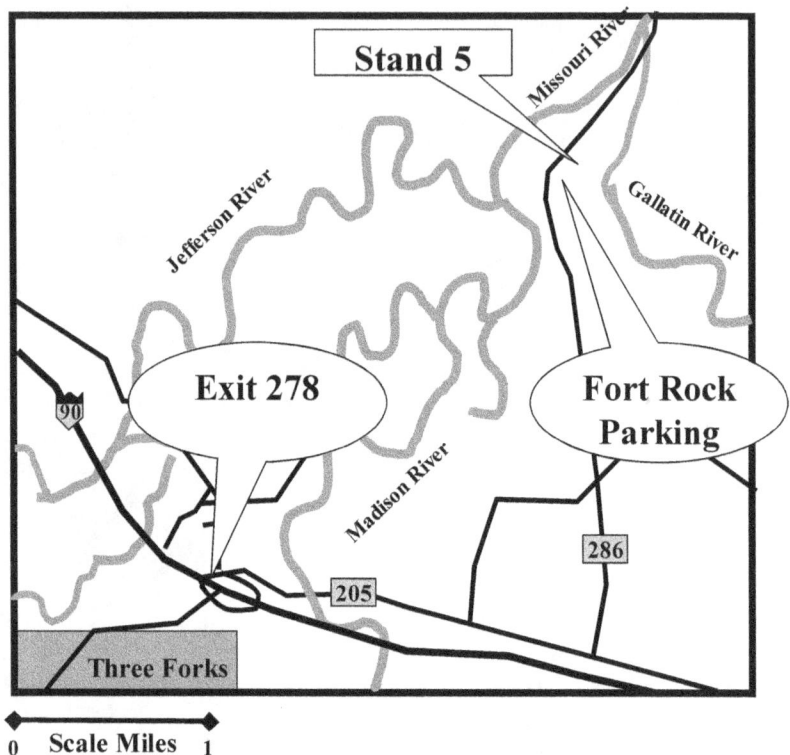

Map 2-6

Stand 5
The Three Forks of the Missouri
(25–30 July 1805)

Directions: Continue south on Highway 287 to Interstate 90, and then go east on Interstate 90. At Exit 278 follow Route 205 to the east. Soon after getting on Route 205, take Route 286 north to the Missouri Headwaters State Park. Then pull into the first turnout to the right for the Fort Rock area and park. Take the walking path to the northeast high point looking out over the three forks.

Orientation (See Visual 2-3, Appendix D): From this location you can look to the southwest and see the forks of the Jefferson and Madison Rivers. The Jefferson River is farthest to the right, with the Madison River to the left. The Gallatin River is to the rear (east).

Situation: Clark arrived at the Three Forks of the Missouri on 25 July 1805. He reasoned that the right fork was the main channel and the one most likely to continue on to the mountains. He also realized that he was several days ahead of Lewis and decided to use the time to explore the area. Clark was confident that the Shoshone Indians were nearby and, therefore, developed his exploration plan to both confirm that the right fork was the correct route and to search for the elusive Indians. He left a note for Lewis and proceeded up the north fork. That evening he camped northwest of present-day Willow Creek. The next day, he allowed two men to remain in camp to rest; Charbonneau's ankle had given out and Joseph Field's feet were sore. Clark pushed ahead with Privates Robert Frazer and Reubin Field. His group headed west toward a mountaintop to get a view of the river valley and the surrounding area. From the top of the overlook, he confirmed his belief that the right fork continued to the mountains but saw no signs of the Shoshone Indians. He decided to double back, pick up the two invalids and explore the middle fork. That evening he camped southeast of present-day Willow Creek. On the 27th, he moved east toward the middle fork and then down the middle fork to link up with Lewis back at the Three Forks.

On the 26th and 27th, Lewis continued his struggle up the Missouri with the main body. He was very concerned about fatigue and worried that the men had reached their breaking point. Fortunately, they arrived at the Three Forks the morning of 27 July before the men collapsed from exhaustion. Lewis found Clark's note and decided to set up camp and wait for Clark's return. He directed the NCOs to care for the equipment and rest the men while he explored the area. During his exploration he noted a handsome site for a future fortification, today's Fort Rock. Clark rejoined the main body that afternoon.

The Corps of Discovery remained in camp the next day to rest. Lewis noted in his journal that Captain Clark was sick; he was probably suffering from exhaustion. The two captains did take the time to name the three rivers. They named the right fork (the main channel), the Jefferson River. They named the middle fork the Madison River for Secretary of State James Madison. They called the left fork the Gallatin River, for Albert Gallatin, secretary of the Treasury.

The captains also updated their estimate of the situation. They were both worried about finding the Shoshone in time to get over the mountains before winter. The future food situation was questionable. The hunters were still able to keep the corps supplied with food, but each day game was getting harder to find as the corps moved farther west. The most serious issue was the fatigue of the men. Again the captains feared the men were almost at their breaking point with exhaustion. Their analysis of the situation was that the risk was high for continued movement to the west. But, Lewis reasoned, if the Indians could survive in this country, the corps could also survive. Both captains were determined to continue west. They decided another overland expedition should push far to the front again. This time Lewis would lead and allow Clark to remain with the canoes and recuperate. The corps continued to rest at the forks on the 29th and then departed the area on the morning of 30 July. Lewis pushed ahead with a small advance party and Clark led the main body with the canoes.

Vignette 1: "a fine morning we proceeded on a fiew miles to the three forks of the Missouri those three forks are nearly of a Size, the North fork appears to have the most water and must be Considered as the one best calculated for us to ascend middle fork is quit as large about 90 yds. wide. The South fork is about 70 yds wide & falls in about 400 yards below the midle fork... I wrote a note informing Capt Lewis the rout I intended to take, and proceeded on up the main North fork thro' a vallie..." (Captain Clark, 25 July 1805, quoted in Gary Moulton, ed., *The Journals of the Lewis & Clark Expedition*, vol. 4, 428.)

Vignette 2: "We set out at an early hour and proceeded on but slowly the current still so rapid that the men are in a continual state of their utmost exertion to get on, and they begin to weaken fast from this continual state of violent exertion..." (Captain Lewis, 27 July 1805, quoted in Gary Moulton, ed., *The Journals of the Lewis & Clark Expedition*, vol. 4, 433.)

Vignette 3: "about 9 oClock we Came or arived at the 3 forks of the Missourie which is in a <wide> valley in open view of the high Mountains which has white Spots on it which has the appearance of snow. ... the plain on N. Side of the forks has lately been burned over by the natives... Camped on the point which is a Smoth plain. a large Camp of Indians has been encamped here Some time ago. our Interrupters wife was taken prisoner at this place 3 or 4 years ago by the Gross vauntous Indians. ... at this Camp we unloaded all the canoes & conclude to rest & refresh ourselves a day or too ...-" (Private Whitehouse, 27 July 1805, quoted in Gary Moulton, ed., *The Journals of the Lewis & Clark Expedition*, vol. 11, 242-243.)

Vignette 4: "between the middle and S.E. forks near their junctions with the S.W. fork there is a handsom site for a fortification. it consists of a limestone rock of an oblong form; it's sides perpendicular and about 25 ft high except at the extremity towards the middle fork where it ascends gradually and like the top is covered with a fine terf of greensword. the top is level and contains about 2 Acres." (Captain Lewis, 27 July 1805, quoted in Gary Moulton, ed., *The Journals of the Lewis & Clark Expedition*, vol. 4, 434.)

Vignette 5: "we begin to feel considerable anxiety with rispect to the Snake Indians. if we do not find them or some other nation who have horses I fear the successful issue of our voyage will be very doubtfull, or at all events much more difficult in it's accomplishment. we are now several hundred miles within the bosom of this wild and mountanous country, where game may rationally be expected shortly to become scarce and subsistence precarious without any information with rispect to the country, not knowing how far these mountains continue, or wher to direct our course to pass them to advantage or intersept a navigable branch of the Columbia, or even were we on such an one the probability is that we should not find any timber within these mountains large enough for canoes, if we judge from the portion of them through which we have passed. however, I still hope for the best, and intend taking a tramp myself in a few days to find these yellow gentlemen if possible. my two principal consolations are that from our present position it is impossible that the S.W. fork can head with the waters of any other river but the Columbia, and that if any Indians can subsist in the form of a nation in these mountains with the means they have of acquiring food we can also subsist... (Captain Lewis, 27 July 1805, quoted in Gary Moulton, ed., *The Journals of the Lewis & Clark Expedition*, vol. 4, 436-437.)

Teaching Points:

Agile and Adaptive Leadership. The Lewis and Clark expedition offers numerous examples of *agile and adaptive leadership*. The captains' consistent ability to remain flexible and to adapt strengths and weaknesses to the task at hand made the journey possible. In what ways do the captains' actions in this phase of the expedition demonstrate agile and adaptive leadership?

Honor. FM 22-100 states that *honor* provides the "morale compass" for character and personal conduct in the Army. How do the actions of the officers and NCOs of the Corps of Discovery demonstrate the Army Value of honor?

Note on Lodging: CSI recommends group lodging at the end of day two in Three Forks, Montana. Three Forks offers limited, but adequate hotel and motel accommodations.

Day 3
The Jefferson River to the Shoshone Indians
(30 July to 24 August 1805)

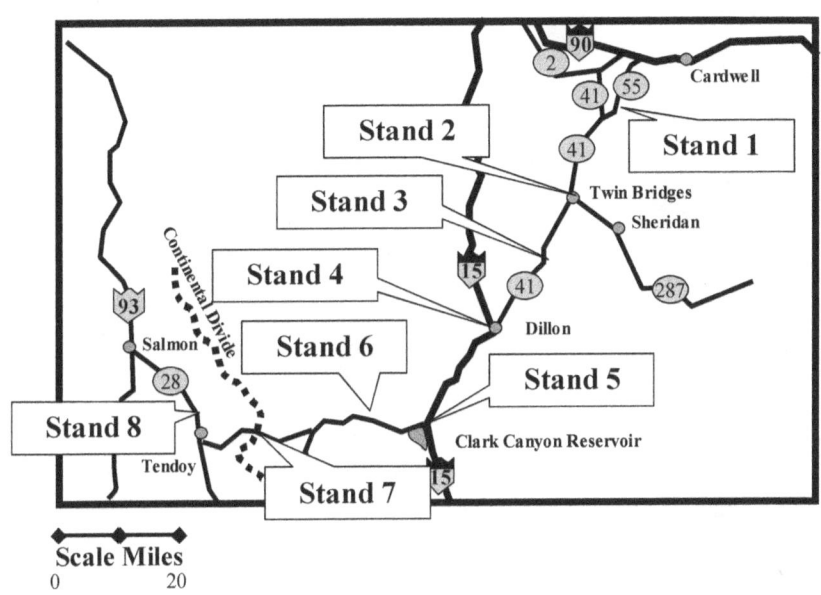

Map 3-1

Begin the day at Three Forks, MT

Stand 1, The Endless River (near Waterloo, MT)

Stand 2, The Forks of the Jefferson (Twin Bridges, MT)

Stand 3, Beaverhead Rock (south of Twin Bridges, MT)

Stand 4, Clark Overlook (Dillon, MT)

Stand 5, Camp Fortunate (Camp Fortunate Overlook south of Dillon, MT)

Stand 6, Failed Contact with the Shoshone (Grant, MT)

Stand 7, Lemhi Pass
7A: Headwaters of the Missouri (east of Lemhi Pass, west of Grant, MT)
7B: Lemhi Pass (west of Grant, MT)
7C: Headwaters of the Columbia (West of Lemhi Pass)

Stand 8, The Shoshone Indians (north of Tendoy, ID)

End day at Salmon, ID

Day 3
Stand 1 (The Endless River)

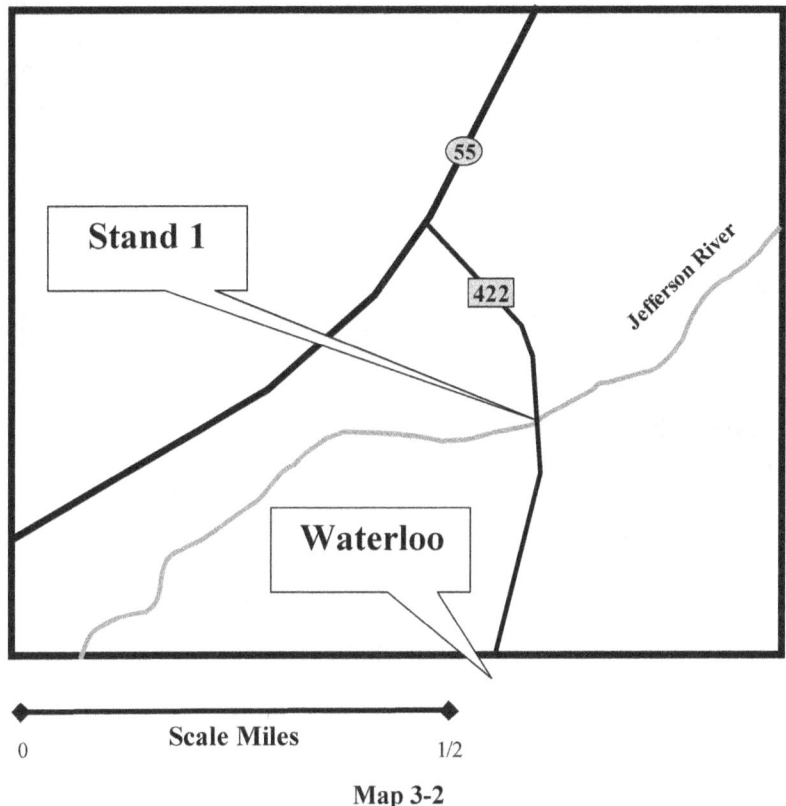

Map 3-2

Stand 1
The Endless River
(30 July to 3 August 1805)

Directions: At Three Forks, Montana, go west on Highway 2 and then take Highway 55 south at Whitehall, Montana. Watch for mile marker 3 and then turn left on Road 422 to Waterloo. Park the vehicles before crossing the bridge. Walk to the northeast corner of the bridge and orient to the southeast.

Orientation (See Visual 3-1, Appendix D): We are currently 41 miles to the west of the Three Forks. The Corps of Discovery traversed this section of the river between 30 July and 4 August 1805. The river channel today is much like it was in 1805.

Situation: The Corps of Discovery departed the Three Forks on 30 July 1805. While exploring the area Lewis lost track of the canoes and ended up camping alone that night. The next morning he was unsure whether he was ahead of the canoes or behind them. He decided, incorrectly, that he was behind the main body and attempted to catch up with the canoes. Fortunately, he made contact with one of the hunters, who informed him the canoes were behind them. The next morning Lewis moved out with Sergeant Gass, Drouillard, and Charbonneau on an overland expedition to find the Shoshone. Meanwhile, Clark struggled up the Jefferson with the main body of the corps. His group had to contend with low water, strong currents, and countless bends and curves in the river. It took Clark's group five days to move the 41 miles from the Three Forks to the vicinity of present-day Waterloo, Montana. Clark had a sore ankle and was not able to help with the poling and dragging of the canoes. He spent most of the time hunting on the shore and kept the group supplied with fresh meat. The NCOs took charge of the canoe movement and, at times, had to double up canoe crews to drag the boats over the shoals. The journals provide few details on how Clark and the NCOs motivated the soldiers of the corps to continue. However, the leadership challenge was probably very significant considering the tremendous physical effort required to maintain westward movement. The corps camped the evening of 3 August 1805 near today's Parson Bridge on Montana Highway 422. Lewis' advance party was 14 miles to the south in the vicinity of the forks of the Jefferson.

Vignette 1: "The river so rapid that the greatest exertion is required by all to get the boats on…" (Captain Clark, 1 August, quoted in Gary Moulton, ed., *The Journals of the Lewis & Clark Expedition*, vol. 5, 29.) They made 13 miles that day.*

Vignette 2: "we proceeded on with great dificuelty from the rapidity of the current & rapids, abt. 15 miles..." (Captain Clark, 2 August 1805, quoted in Gary Moulton, ed., *The Journals of the Lewis & Clark Expedition*, vol. 5, 34.)

Vignette 3: "the river more rapid and Sholey than yesterday... we are oblige to haul over the canoes sholey in maney places where the islands are noumerous and bottom sholey...we encamped on an Island avove a part of the river which passed thro a rocky bed enclosed on both sides with thick willow current & red buries... (Captain Clark, 3 August 1805, quoted in Gary Moulton, ed., *The Journals of the Lewis & Clark Expedition*, vol. 5, 38-39.)

Vignette 4: "passed verry rapid water we have to double man the canoes and drag them over the Sholes and rapid places. we have to be in the water half of our time... the River gitting more rapid the rapids longer..." (Sergeant Ordway, 3 August 1805, quoted in Gary Moulton, ed., *The Journals of the Lewis & Clark Expedition*, vol. 9, 195.)

Teaching Point:

Loyalty. Brigadier General S.L.A. Marshall, in *Men Against Fire*, stated: "Loyalty is the big thing, the greatest battle asset of all. But no man ever wins the loyalty of troops by preaching loyalty. It is given to him as he proves his possession of the other virtues (FM 22-100, 2-3)." Did the soldiers of the Corps of Discovery demonstrate *loyalty* to their unit and their leaders? How did the captains and their NCOs win the loyalty of their men?

---

* All vignettes retain the enigmatic writing of the journalists. See the introduction to Section III for an explanation of the editorial principles used with the journal entries.

Day 3
Stand 2 (The Forks of the Jefferson)

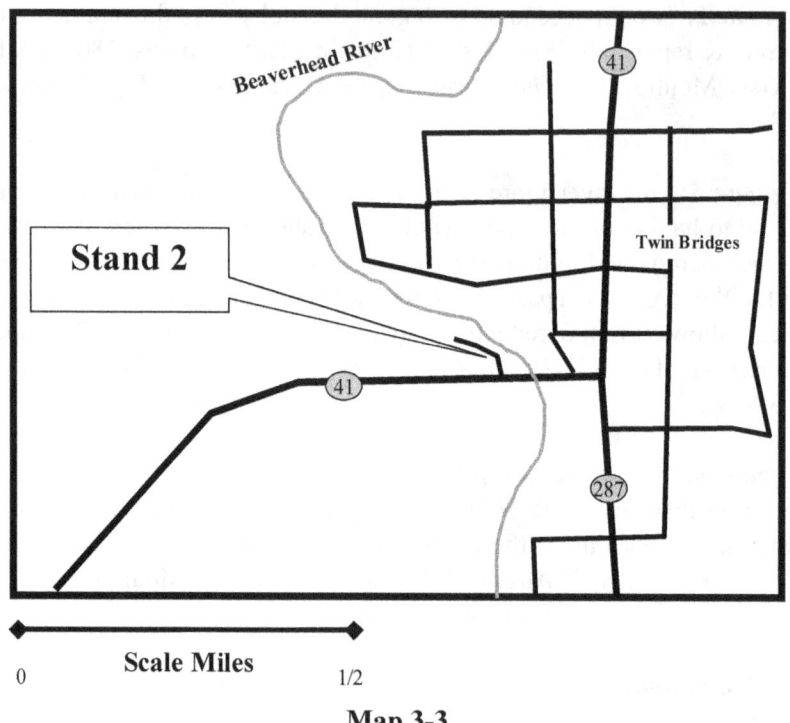

Map 3-3

Stand 2
The Forks of the Jefferson
(3 to 8 August 1805)

Directions: Continue south on Highway 55 until it merges with Highway 41. Then continue south on Highway 41 to Twin Bridges, Montana. At Twin Bridges, follow Highway 41 across the bridge and immediately turn into the rest area on the right side of the road.

Orientation (See Visuals 3-2, 3-3, and 3-4, Appendix D): Both the geography and the names of the forks of the Jefferson have changed significantly since 1805. The river to the front is today's Beaverhead. The captains referred to the river as the Jefferson. To the northwest is today's Big Hole River, which Lewis called the Wisdom; and to the east is today's Ruby, which Lewis called the Philanthropy. Today the forks of the two major rivers, the Beaverhead/Jefferson and Big Hole/Wisdom, are 1 1/8 miles to the north. In 1805 the junction was ¾ mile to the south. You are currently located at a bend of the river with the water to the front flowing momentarily to the west. Just downstream, the river bends again and resumes its general course to the northeast.

Situation: While Clark's group struggled up the Jefferson, Lewis' advance party forged ahead, hoping to find the Shoshone Indians. The advance party camped just short of the forks of the Jefferson on 3 August 1805. The next morning the advance party arrived at the forks. Lewis decided the center fork was the main channel and the course for the Corps of Discovery to follow. His analysis was that the eastern fork veered too far to the south, not the correct route to the mountains. The western fork was a larger branch of the river and flowed directly toward the mountains. However, because it flowed much colder than the center branch, he reasoned that the center fork must come a greater distance, making it the main channel. Lewis decided to spend time exploring the area to allow Clark to catch up. He left a note for Clark to take the center fork and used the remainder of the day to explore. He first examined the eastern fork and then backtracked to the western fork to camp for the evening. The next day he moved cross-country to a high ground overlook. There he confirmed his original estimate that the center fork was the main channel, but he saw no sign of the Shoshone Indians. He then moved to the center fork and camped for the evening planning to move back to the river junction the following morning to link up with Captain Clark.

Captain Clark reached the junction on 5 August. Unfortunately, Lewis' note was gone. More than likely a beaver had carried it away because it was on a green willow branch. In the absence of Lewis' note, Clark selected the western fork. He had also ruled out the eastern fork because it veered too far to the south. However, he chose the western fork because it moved in the most westerly direction. He led his group up the western fork and then camped for the evening. On 6 August Lewis moved back to the junction to wait for Clark, not realizing Clark had already passed to the west. Meanwhile, Clark continued his movement up the western fork. Fortunately he made contact with Drouillard, the corps' designated hunter. Drouillard informed Clark that he should be on the middle fork.

Unfortunately, in the process of reversing course, the men overturned three of the canoes and drenched many of the valuable supplies. The noise of recovering their spilled items and drying out the equipment attracted Lewis to Clark's location. Reunited, the entire Corps of Discovery camped at the forks to rest and to allow the provisions time to dry. The captains named two tributaries for two of Jefferson's virtues. They called the eastern fork the Philanthropy River; today it is called the Ruby River. They named the western fork the Wisdom River; today it is the Big Hole River. The captains continued to call the center fork the Jefferson (today's Beaverhead River).

On 7 August the corps rested and dried out equipment. The captains decided, because of their reduced supply stocks, to cache one canoe. It meant the weary men had one less canoe to drag and pole upriver, and it provided more hunters to search for scarce game. The captains were ready to proceed on the next morning, but one of the hunters, Private Shannon, was missing. They were very concerned about Shannon; he had also been lost in late 1804 for over two weeks and nearly starved to death. The next morning, 8 August 1805, they remained in the area of the forks to search for Shannon. That afternoon they detailed Private Reubin Field to remain behind to continue the search, and the balance of the corps resumed its journey.

Vignette 1: "we encamped this evening after sunset having traveled by estimate 23 miles. from the width and appearance of the valley at this place I conceived that the river forked not far above me and therefore resolved the next morning to examine the adjacent country more minutely." (Captain Lewis, 3 August 1805, quoted in Gary Moulton, ed., *The Journals of the Lewis & Clark Expedition*, vol. 5, 36.)

Vignette 2: "we passed a handsome little river which meanders through this valley; it is about 30 yds wide, affords a considerable quantity of water and appears as if it might be navigated some miles... I now changed my rout to S.W. passed a high plain which lies between the valleies and returned to the South valley, in passing which I fell in with a river about 45 yds. wide... still continuing down ... and at the distance of three miles further arrived at it's junction with a river 50 yds wide which Comes from the S.W. and falling into the South valley runs parallel with the middle fork about 12 miles before it forms a junction... the middle fork is gentle and possesses about 2/3rds as much water as this stream. It's course so far as I can observe it is about S.W. and from the opening of the valley I believe it still bears more to the West above... it's water is much warmer then the rapid fork and it's water more turbid; from which I conjecture that it has it's sources at a greater distance in the mountains and passes through an opener country than the other..." (Captain Lewis, 4 August 1805, quoted in Gary Moulton, ed., *The Journals of the Lewis & Clark Expedition*, vol. 5, 41-42.)

Vignette 3: "...called the bold rapid and clear stream *Wisdom*, and the more mild and placid one which one which flows in from the S.E. *Philanthrophy*, in commemoration of two of those cardinal virtues, which have so eminently marked that deservedly selibrated character through life."(Captain Lewis, 6 August 1805, quoted in Gary Moulton, ed., *The Journals of the Lewis & Clark Expedition*, vol. 5, 54.)

Vignette 4: "I am fearful he is lost again. this is the same man who was separated from us 15 days as we came up the Missouri [in South Dakota] and subsisted 9 days of that time on grapes only." (Captain Lewis, 6 August 1805, quoted in Gary Moulton, ed., *The Journals of the Lewis & Clark Expedition*, vol. 5, 53-54.) [Note: Shannon rejoined the corps on 9 August.]

Teaching Point:

Army Values and Taking Care of Soldiers. FM 22-100 states that *Taking Care of Soldiers* means creating a disciplined environment where soldiers can learn and grow. The field manual goes on to state that leaders take care of soldiers when they treat them fairly, refuse to cut corners, share their hardships, and set examples. How do the captains' decisions and actions in their struggle up the Jefferson River demonstrate today's Army values and specifically exemplify taking care of soldiers?

Day 3
Stand 3 (Beaverhead Rock)

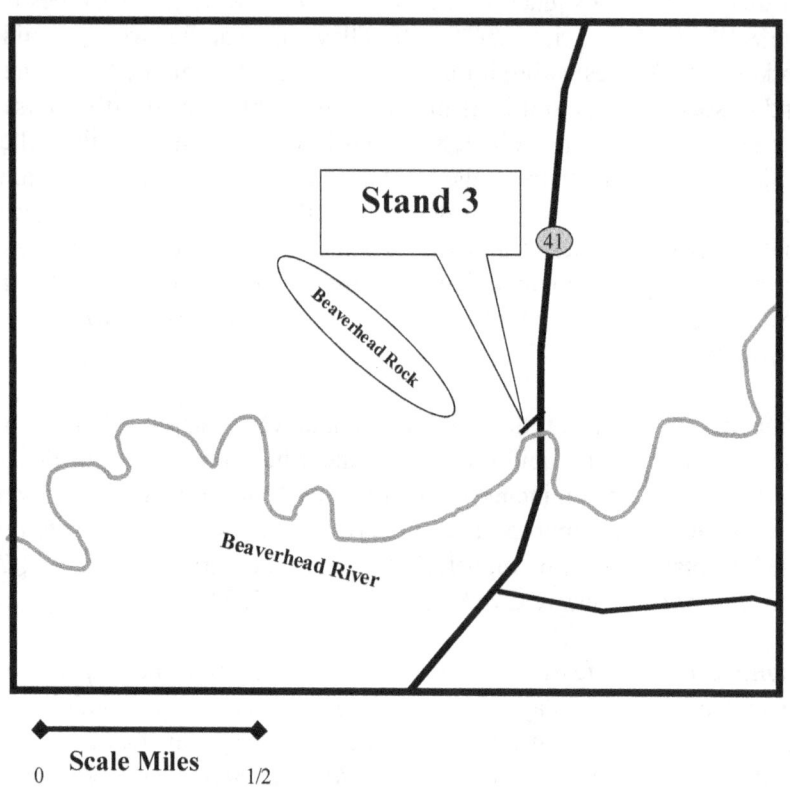

Map 3-4

Stand 3
Beaverhead Rock
(8 – 11 August 1805)

Directions: Continue south on Highway 41. At mile marker 15, watch for the turnout just north of the bridge over the Beaverhead River and park the vehicles.

Orientation (See Visual 3-4, Appendix D): The large rock formation to the northwest is called Beaverhead Rock. Just to the south is the Beaverhead River (referred to by the captains as the Jefferson River). The river today looks much like it did in 1805. The route just driven closely parallels the river route taken by the Corps of Discovery. The camp at the forks is 13 miles to the northeast.

Situation: This section of the river was extremely difficult for the Corps of Discovery. The men continued to pull, drag, and pole the canoes upriver against a strong current. The shallow water and numerous bends and turns in the river created additional challenges. Although they were making several miles of movement along the river, their actual progress to the west was minimal. The men's morale and energy, due to the heavy labor and slow progress, continued to decline daily. Sacagawea provided a needed morale boost when she recognized the mountain chain to the west and stated that the homeland of her people was not very distant. Sacagawea's observations boosted morale but did not solve the problem of finding the Shoshone and getting over the mountains before the winter.

    The captains discussed the situation that evening in camp. Lewis seemed almost desperate to find the Shoshone. The captains decided that Lewis would push ahead with an overland expedition to find the Indians. Clark, though more experienced in dealing with Native Americans, was not able to lead the advance party because of an abscess on his ankle. Lewis pushed ahead on 9 August with Drouillard and Privates McNeal and Shields. Clark and his group continued to struggle upriver with the canoes, only averaging about 4 or 5 miles a day. On 10 August, Clark noted a remarkable cliff, today's Beaverhead Rock. The next day Clark noted in his journal that the corps had traveled 3,000 miles by river since leaving St. Louis.

Vignette 1: "the Indian woman recognized the point of a high plain to our right which she informed us was not very distant from the summer retreat of her nation on a river beyond the mountains which runs to the west... she assures us that we shall either find her people on this river or on the river immediately west of it's source; which from it's present size cannot be very distant..." (Captain Lewis, 8 August 1805, quoted in Gary Moulton, ed., *The Journals of the Lewis & Clark Expedition*, vol. 5, 59.)

Vignette 2: "as it is now all important with us to meet with those people as soon as possible, I determined (to leave the charge of the party, and the care of the lunar observations to Capt. Clark; and) to proceed tomorrow with a small party to the source of the principal stream of this river and pass the mountains to the Columbia; and down that river untill I found the Indians; in short it is my resolution to find them or some others, who have horses if it should cause me a trip of one month. for without horses we shall be obliged to leave a great part of our stores, of which, it appears to me that we have a stock already sufficiently small for the length of the voyage before us." (Capt Lewis, 8 August 1805, quoted in Gary Moulton, ed., *The Journals of the Lewis & Clark Expedition*, vol. 5, 59.)

Vignette 3: "we proceeded on passed a remarkable clift point on the Stard. Side about 150 feet high, this Clift the Indians call the *Beavers* head..." (Captain Clark, 10 August 1805, quoted in Gary Moulton, ed., *The Journals of the Lewis & Clark Expedition*, vol. 5, 66.)

Vignette 4: "passed a large Island which I call the 3000 mile Island as it is Situated that distance from the mouth of the Missouri by water..." (Captain Clark, 11 August 1805, quoted in Gary Moulton, ed., *The Journals of the Lewis & Clark Expedition*, vol. 5, 72.)

Teaching Point:

Problem Solving. The draft FM 5-0, *Planning*, identifies seven steps in the *problem solving* process: (1) Problem Definition; (2) Information Gathering; (3) Course of Action (COA) Development; (4) COA Analysis; (5) COA Comparison; (6) Decision; and (7) Execution and Assessment. Using these modern criteria, evaluate the captains' decision to send an advance party in search of the Shoshone Indians.

Day 3
Stand 4 (Clark Overlook)

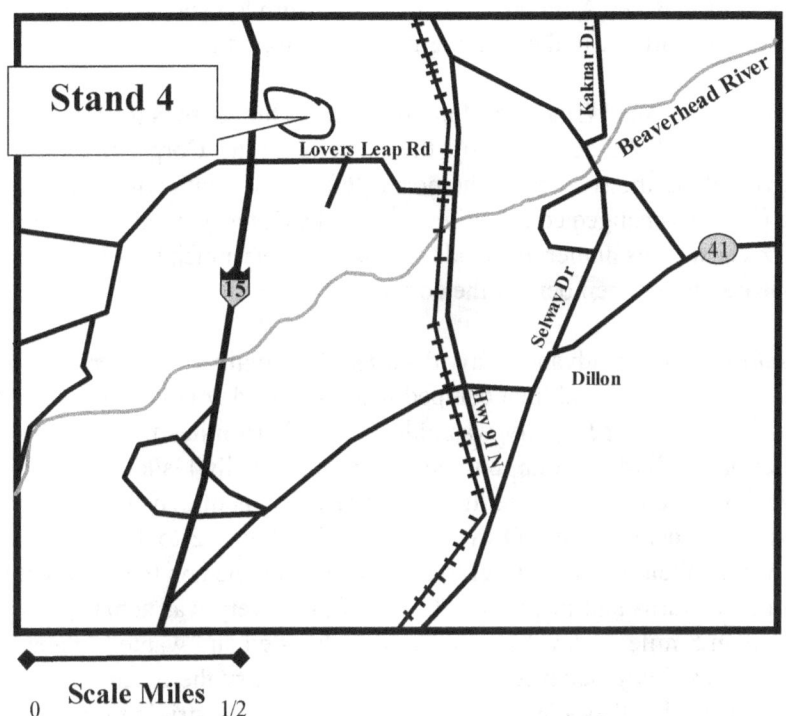

Map 3-5

Stand 4
Clark Overlook
(9 to 13 August 1805)

Directions: Continue south on Highway 41 into Dillon. In Dillon turn right (west) on Frontage Road/Old US 91. At .6 miles the road passes over the Beaverhead River. After crossing the bridge, turn left and cross the railroad tracks and park. Take the walking path to the top of the rock outcrop.

Orientation (See Visual 3-5, Appendix D): To the south is the Beaverhead River (called the Jefferson by the captains). The Corps of Discovery moved along the river from the north (left) to the south (right). Although the river has changed course slightly since 1805, the general appearance of the river with its numerous bends and turns is very much how it must have appeared to the members of the corps.

Situation: Lewis' advance party departed the vicinity of Beaverhead Rock on 9 August 1805 and then camped near present-day Dillon that evening. His lightly equipped party was able to march 14 miles that day. On the other hand, Clark's group, burdened with the heavily loaded canoes, took five days to cover the same distance. The journals of Private Whitehouse and Sergeants Gass and Ordway speak of making 12 to 15 miles a day. However, their estimates refer to the distance traveled on the river, with its numerous turns and bends. The Corps of Discovery was actually making less than 5 miles a day. The men were exhausted and wanted to abandon the canoes. They believed that, if allowed to carry the essential supplies on their backs, they could make better progress by striking out on land. Clark realized that their essential on-hand supplies exceeded their present on-land haul capabilities. The captains were determined to hold onto the canoes until the supplies could be transferred to horses. Today we know few of the details other than that the "men complained very much" and that Clark had to "pacify them." It must have been a tremendous leadership challenge for Clark and the NCOs to keep the men moving.

On 13 August, Clark's group passed through the area occupied by present-day Dillon. There Clark climbed a small rocky hill known today as Clark's Overlook. He probably hoped to see an end to the *endless* river. What he saw was the long and winding course of the river and, in the far distance, a gap in the mountains. After Clark rejoined the canoes, his contingent continued to work its way upriver until evening, when the men camped about 2 miles south of the overlook.

Vignette 1: "We set out early (Wind N E) proceeded on passed Several large Islands and three Small ones, the river much more Sholey than below which obliges us to haul the Canoes over those sholes which Suckceed each other at Short intervales emencely laborious men much fatigued and weakened by being continualy in the water drawing the Canoes over the sholes encamped on the Lard side men complain verry much of the emence labour they are obliged to undergo & wish much to leave the river. I pacify them…" (Captain Clark, 12 August 1805, quoted in Gary Moulton, ed., *The Journals of the Lewis & Clark Expedition*, vol. 5, 75-76.)

Vignette 2: "This morning Capt. Clark set out early having previously dispatched some hunters ahead. it was cool and cloudy all the forepart of the day. at 8 A.M they had a slight rain. they passed a number of shoals over which they were obliged to drag the canoes; the men in water 3/4ths of the day, the[y] passed a bold runing stream 7 yards wide on the Lard. side just below a high point of Limestone rocks. this stream we call McNeal's Creek after Hugh McNeal one of our party… S. 30° W. 4 … The river very crooked and bends short. (Captain Lewis, 13 August 1805, quoted in Gary Moulton, ed., *The Journals of the Lewis & Clark Expedition*, vol. 5, 83-84.)

Teaching Point:

Honor. *Honor* holds Army values together while, at the same time, is a value itself. How did Captain Clark demonstrate the Army value of honor during the difficult movement up the Jefferson River? How did the soldiers of the Corps of Discovery demonstrate honor?

Day 3
Stand 5 (Camp Fortunate)

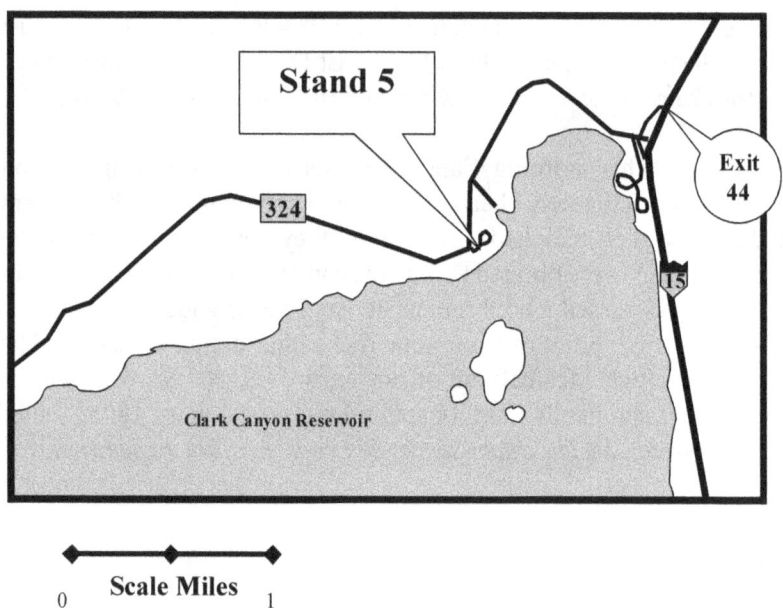

Map 3-6

Stand 5
Camp Fortunate
(9 - 24 August 1805)

Directions: From Dillon, take Interstate 15 south to exit 44 and then turn right on Route 324. At approximately 1.5 miles, turn into the Camp Fortunate Overlook.

Orientation (See Visuals 3-5 & 3-6, Appendix D): The Clark Canyon Reservoir has significantly changed the lay of the land. In 1805 this hill overlooked the forks of the Beaverhead/Jefferson River. The left-hand fork flowed to the east of the large rock island to the front, and the west fork passed between our current location and the island to the west. Barely discernable Indian roads followed both forks.

Situation: Lewis found an Indian trail, which he called a road, to the southwest of present-day Dillon. He followed the road past "Rattlesnake Cliffs" and arrived at the forks of the Jefferson River on 10 August 1805. The Indian road divided and followed both branches of the Jefferson. One fork, today's Horse Prairie Creek, led to the west. The other fork, known today as the Red Rock River, flowed from the southwest. He considered both forks to be non-navigable and decided that this would be the point where the Corps of Discovery switched from a waterborne to a land expedition. He was uncertain which path to follow, so he sent scouts to examine each trail to determine which was the most used by the Indians. Lewis decided to follow the south fork based on the information provided to him by the scouts. He left a note for Clark recommending that he wait at the forks for his return. Lewis was very careful to choose a dry willow branch to prevent the same mishap that occurred at the previous fork in the river. After less than 2 miles on the road, Lewis changed his mind. He found little evidence of significant use and no sign that horses had been down the road. As a result Lewis decided to return to the western track. He sent Drouillard back to the forks with a second note for Captain Clark and then proceeded up the western fork. Lewis remained on the west side of the divide from 12 to 15 August 1805 (see Day 4 for additional details about Lewis' actions on the west side of the divide), then returned to the forks on the 16th to link up with Captain Clark.

    Clark arrived at the forks on 17 August. The reunited corps established a camp, which the captains called Camp Fortunate. They used the camp to rest and reorganize the corps in preparation for the transition from waterborne movement to land movement. Camp Fortunate was also the

111

location of the initial negotiations conducted with the Shoshone for horses (See Day 4, Stand 3 for more details on the negotiations).

On the evening of 17 August, the captains discussed the situation and adopted their familiar strategy of dividing tasks and responsibilities. They decided that Clark would lead 11 men with tools over the mountain to examine the western rivers (see Day 4, Stand 4 for more details on the Salmon River Reconnaissance). Lewis would remain at Camp Fortunate and prepare the equipment for transport over the mountains.

Lewis stayed at Camp Fortunate from 17 to 24 August 1805. During that period he selected necessary equipment for transport by packhorses and established a cache for the excess. He did not anticipate getting the number of horses he needed and wanted to lighten the load for the available horses. Lewis also celebrated his 31st birthday, 18 August 1805, by trading with the Indians and reflecting upon his life. His horse trading that day was very successful; he and the men used pieces of their uniforms, knives, and other small articles to get horses. His reflections on life were a combination of moody thoughts about his past accomplishments and a determination to do better in the future. He decided on 24 August that he needed to move the corps to the west side of the divide and there barter for more horses at the main Shoshone village. Lewis led the corps west from Camp Fortunate that day at noon. He had about a dozen horses and a mule, all heavily laden with supplies. He estimated the corps would require at least 25 horses to successfully traverse the mountains.

Vignette 1: "we continued our rout along the Indian road which led us sometimes over the hills and again in the narrow bottoms of the river till at the distance of fifteen Ms. from rattle snake Clifts we arrived at a handsome open and leavel vally where the river divided itself nearly into two equal branches; here I halted and examined those streams and readily discovered from their size that it would be vain to attempt the navigation of either any further… I was now determined to pursue that which appeared to have been the most traveled this spring. in the meantime I wrote a note to Capt. Clark informing him of the occurrences which had taken place, recommending it to him to halt at this place untill my return… accordingly I put up my note on a dry willow pole at the forks, and set out up the SE fork, after proceeding about 1 ½ miles I discovered that the road became so blind that it could not be that which we had followed to the forks of Jefferson's river, neither could I find the tracks of the horses which had passed early in the spring along the other; I therefore determined to return and examine the other myself, which I did, and found that the same horses had passed up the West fork which was reather largest, and more in the direction that I wished to pursue; I therefore did not hesitate about changing my rout but determined to take the western road. I now wrote a second note to Capt C. informing him of this change and sent Drewyer to put it with the other at the forks and waited untill he returned..." (Captain Lewis, 10 August 1805, quoted in Gary Moulton, ed., *The Journals of the Lewis & Clark Expedition*, vol. 5, 64-65.)

Vignette 2: "... it was mutually agreed that he (Capt. Clark) should set out tomorrow morning with eleven men furnished with axes and other necessary tools for making canoes, their arms accoutrements and as much of their baggage as they could carry... In the mean time I was to bring on the party and baggage to the Shoshone Camp, calculating that by the time I should reach that place that he would have sufficiently informed himself with rispect to the state of the river . . . as to determine us whether to prosicute our journey from thence by land or water.... The sperits of the men were now much elated at the prospect of geting horses." (Captain Lewis, 17 August 1805, quoted in Gary Moulton, ed., *The Journals of the Lewis & Clark Expedition*, vol. 5, 113.)

Vignette 3: "This day I completed my thirty first year, and conceived that I had in all human probability now existed about half the period which I am to remain in this Sublunary world. I reflected that I had as yet done but little, very little indeed, to further the hapiness of the human race, or to advance the information of the succeeding generation. I viewed with regret the many hours I have spent in indolence, and now soarly feel the want of that information which those hours would have given me had they been judiciously expended. but since they are past and cannot be recalled, I dash from me the gloomy thought and resolved in future, to redouble my exertions and at least indeavour to promote those two primary objects of human existence, by giving them the aid of that portion of talents which nature and fortune have bestoed on me; or in future, to live for *mankind*, as I have heretofore lived *for myself*." (Captain Lewis, 18 August 1805, quoted in Gary Moulton, ed., *The Journals of the Lewis & Clark Expedition*, vol. 5, 118.)

Vignette 4: "at twelve Oclock we set out and passed the river below the forks, directing our rout towards the cove along the track... most of the horses were heavily laden, and it appears to me that it will require at least 25 horses to convey our baggage along such roads as I expect we shall be obliged to pass in the mountains. I had now the inexpressible satisfaction to find myself once more under way with all baggage and party..." (Captain

Lewis, 24 August 1805, quoted in Gary Moulton, ed., *The Journals of the Lewis & Clark Expedition*, vol. 5, 158.)

Teaching Points:

Respect. In the Army, *respect* means recognizing and appreciating the inherent dignity and worth of all people. The captains fostered a climate in which everyone was treated with dignity and respect. How did the captains' efforts foster the Army value of respect contribute to the development of a more disciplined and cohesive Army unit?

Facilities. The captains and their NCOs recognized the importance of providing adequate *facilities* for their men. In most cases, the unit "camped out." However, the captains established temporary and semi-permanent facilities based on mission requirements. They established camps to rest and regroup in preparation for different phases of the operation. Examples of semi-permanent camps included Fort Mandan for the winter of 1804 and Fort Clatsop for the winter of 1805. Examples of temporary camps include Camp Fortunate and Camp Travelers' Rest. Evaluate the captains' decision to establish Camp Fortunate (17-24 August 1805).

Day 3
Stand 6
(Failed Contact with the Shoshone Indians)

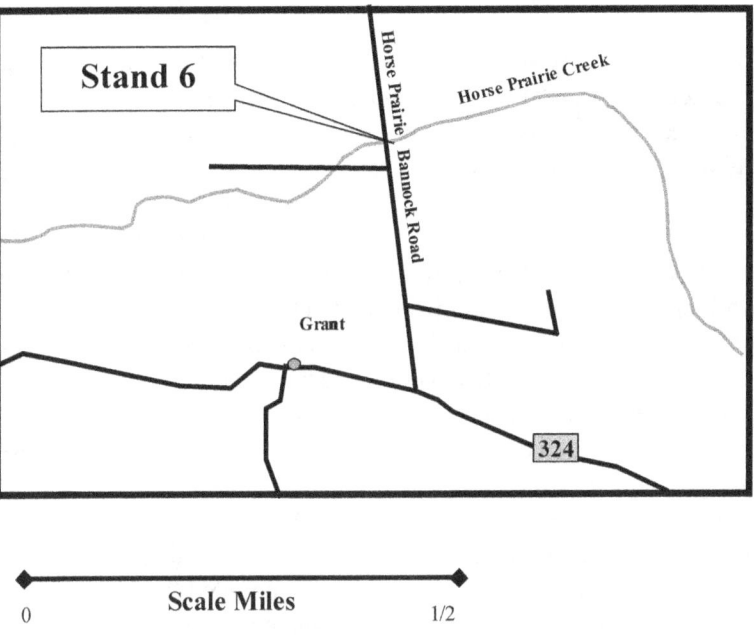

Map 3-7

Stand 6
Failed Contact with the Shoshone Indians
(10 – 12 August 1805)

Directions: Continue west on Route 324 about 11 miles and, just short of Grant, Montana, turn right (north) on Horse Prairie Bannock Road. Travel approximately 1 mile and park short of the small bridge.

Orientation (See Visual 3-7, Appendix D): Captain Lewis and his advance party entered this valley on 10 August 1805. His group moved along the small creek from east to west. Lewis referred to the creek as the west fork. Today it is called Horse Prairie Creek.

Situation: Lewis passed by the forks and the future location of Camp Fortunate on 10 August. He left a note for Clark to wait there for him to return and then continued to move west. That evening his group camped at the base of a prominent hill just to the east of today's Grant, Montana. He believed the Corps of Discovery had already passed through two grand chains of the Rockies and had ascended to a great height along the gradual river valleys. Lewis was confident he was nearing the top of the Rocky Mountains, and the Columbia River was just ahead.

Lewis set out early the next morning. He had Drouillard and Private Shields on each flank searching for signs of the Indian road. They had covered about 5 miles when Lewis spotted a mounted Indian. The captains had been trying to contact these Indians since mid July 1805, and in that time they had sent five overland expeditions ahead to search for them. Lewis had commanded three and Clark two. In each case, the advance party had consisted of four or five well-armed men. The Shoshone interpreter, Sacagawea, had not been a member of any of the expeditions. There is no record that the captains ever interviewed Sacagawea about how best to make first contact, although they did ask her for the Shoshone word for "White Men." There is also no record that the captains discussed how to conduct the initial meeting. In more modern terms they did not wargame or rehearse the contact. Stephen E. Ambrose stated in *Undaunted Courage* that Lewis "… just blundered ahead on the unshakable and unacknowledged assumption that he was such an expert in handling Indians that when he met a Shoshone he would know instinctively what to do."

Lewis advanced to within 200 paces of the Indian and made the sign for friendship. The Indian was wary of the two white men moving on his flanks and retreated from them. Lewis yelled what he thought was the Shoshone word for friendship and signaled for his men to halt. Drouillard obeyed, but unfortunately Shields did not see the signal and continued to advance. The Indian feared a trap and galloped off into the brush. Lewis, very disappointed in the failed contact, vented his frustration upon the unfortunate Private Shields.

After failing to relocate the lone Indian, Lewis resumed his westward trek, again following the west fork and the Indian trail. His group camped that evening about 17 miles to the west of today's Grant, Montana. Despite his failure to meet the Indians he was diligently seeking, Lewis awoke the next morning confident he would soon find a passage over the mountains and drink from the Columbia River.

Vignette 1: "the mountains do not appear very high in any direction tho' the tops of some of them are partially covered with snow. this convinces me that we have ascended to a great hight since we have entered the rocky Mountains, yet the ascent has been so gradual along the vallies that it was scarcely perceptable by land. I do not believe that the world can furnish an example of a river running to the extent which the Missouri and Jefferson's rivers do through such a mountainous country and at the same time so navigable as they are. if the Columbia furnishes us such another example, a communication across the continent by water will be practicable and safe." (Captain Lewis, 10 August 1805, quoted in Gary Moulton, ed., *The Journals of the Lewis & Clark Expedition*, vol. 5, 65.)*

Vignette 2: "he [the Indian] remained in the same stedfast poisture untill I arrived in about 200 paces of him when he turned his hose about and began to move off slowly from me; I now called to him as loud a voice as I could command repeating the word *tab-ba-bone*, which in their language signifyes *white man*. But loking over his sholder he still kept his eye on Drewyer and Sheilds who wer still advancing neither of them haveing segacity enough to recollect the impropriety of advancing when they saw me thus in parley with the Indian. I now made a signal to these men to halt, Drewyer obeyed but Shields who after wards told me that he did not obseve the signal still kept on ... I believe he would have remained untill I came up whith him had it not been for Shields who still pressed forward. Whe[n] I arrived within about 150 paces ... he suddonly turned his hose about ... and disapeared in the willow brush in an instant and with him vanished all my hopes of obtaining horses for the preasent... I fet soarely chargrined at the conduct of the men particularly Sheilds to whom

---

* All vignettes retain the enigmatic writing of the journalists. See the introduction to Section III for an explanation of the editorial principles used with the journal entries.

117

I principally attributed this failure in obtaining an introduction to the natives. I now called the men to me and could not forbare abraiding them a little for their want of attention and imprudence on this occasion." (Captain Lewis, 11 August 1805, quoted in Gary Moulton, ed., *The Journals of the Lewis & Clark Expedition*, vol. 5, 69.)

Vignette 3: "I therefore did not dispair of shortly finding a passage over the mountains and of taisting the waters of the great Columbia this evening..." (Captain Lewis, 12 August 1805, quoted in Gary Moulton, ed., *The Journals of the Lewis & Clark Expedition*, vol. 5, 74.)

Teaching Point:

Duty. The Army value of *duty* states that soldiers and DA civilians commit to excellence in all aspects of their professional responsibility so that, when the job is done, they can look back and say, "I couldn't have given any more." Did the captains do their duty in preparation for contact with the Shoshone Indians? What more could they have done?

Day 3
Stand 7
(Lemhi Pass)

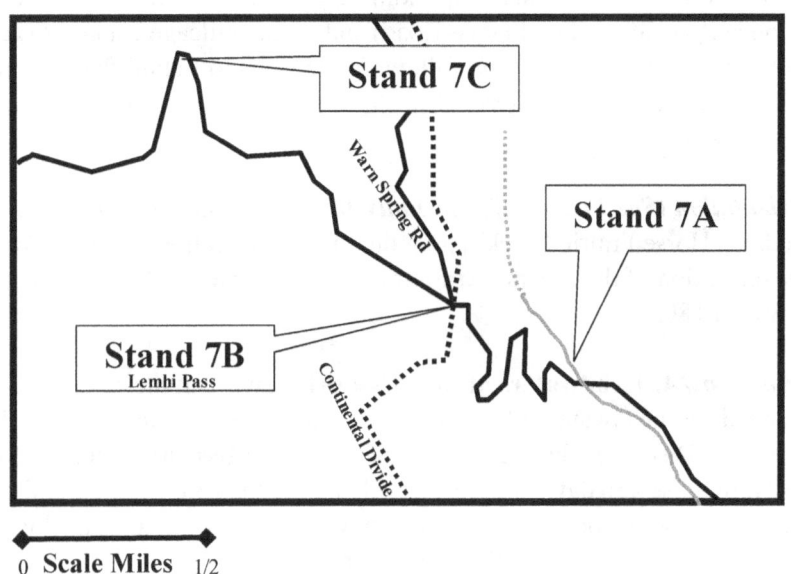

Map 3-8

**Stand 7
Lemhi Pass
(12 August 1805)**

Directions: Return to Route 324 and continue west. Watch for the road sign for Lemhi Pass Road at approximately 22 miles. Turn right on Forest Service Road 3909 (Lemhi Pass Road) and set the mileage counter to zero. Continue west on Road 3909, following the signs to Lemhi Pass. At mile 11.2, pull off to a small turnout to the right just prior to the first major switchback.

Orientation (See Visual 3-7, Appendix D): Lewis followed the west fork (today's Horse Prairie Creek) along the same basic route just taken. With the exception of the few modern intrusions, the terrain today is much like it was in 1805.

Situation 7A: **Headwaters of the Missouri.** Lewis and the advance party reached the headwaters of Horse Prairie Creek on 12 August 1805. The Corps of Discovery had followed the "endless Missouri" since 14 May 1804. In those 456 days, they had traveled more than 3,000 miles, and now Lewis had the opportunity to drink from what he believed to be the highest and most distant source of the great river.

Vignette 1: "at the distance of 4 miles further the road took us to the most distant fountain of the waters of the mighty Missouri in surch of which we have spent so many toilsome days and wristless nights. thus far I had accomplished one of those great objects on which my mind has been unalterably fixed for many years, judge then of the pleasure I felt in allying my thirst with this pure and ice cold water which issues from the base of a low mountain... two miles below McNeal had exultingly stood with a foot on each side of this little rivulet and thanked his god that he had lived to bestride the mighty & heretofore deemed endless Missouri..." (Captain Lewis, 12 August 1805, quoted in Gary Moulton, ed., *The Journals of the Lewis & Clark Expedition*, vol. 5, 74.)

Directions: Continue west along Lemhi Pass Road to the top of the Continental Divide. Park the vehicle at the top of the mountain and walk to an overview looking to the west.

Orientation: The road up the mountain closely approximates the route taken by Lewis. The view to the west is one of the few along the Lewis and Clark route that has changed very little since the time Lewis first gazed upon it.

Situation 7B: **Lemhi Pass.** After drinking from a source of the Missouri, Lewis ascended what he believed to be the final ridge of the Continental Divide. He still hoped to find Jefferson's Northwest Passage. Although he did not record exactly what he expected to see from the top of the pass, it seems likely that he expected the west face of the divide to resemble the east face, just as the west and east faces of the Appalachian Mountains closely resemble each other. The accepted theory of the day postulated a vast plain to the west with a large river flowing to the Pacific. His disappointment, although not recorded, must have been significant, for all he saw from the top of the pass was a succession of snow-covered mountains extending westward as far as the eye could see.

Vignette 2: "after refreshing ourselves we proceeded on to the top of the dividing ridge from which I discovered immence ranges of high mountains still to the West of us with their tops partially covered with snow..." (Captain Lewis, 12 August 1805, quoted in Gary Moulton, ed., *The Journals of the Lewis & Clark Expedition*, vol. 5, 74.)

Directions: Continue westward on the Idaho side of the Continental Divide on the road toward Tendoy, ID. At mile marker 27.5, park the group near the spring coming out of the rocks on the right side of the road.

Orientation: Lewis and his advance party's route down the west face closely approximated the route just driven. However, from this point on, the road differs greatly from the route followed by Lewis. Lewis moved to the north of the high ground to our west. The road will move along the south face of the spur.

Situation 7C: **Headwaters of the Columbia.** If he was disappointed in what he saw from the top of the pass, Lewis neither recorded his thoughts nor dwelled upon the subject. Following established operating procedures for the Corps of Discovery, he "proceeded on." He crossed over the Continental Divide and moved down the west face of the mountain. About three-quarters of a mile down the slope, he found a spring flowing from the side of the mountain, celebrated his first drink from the headwaters of the Columbia River, and then continued to the west in search of the Shoshone Indians.

Vignette 3: "I now descended the mountain about ¾ of a mile which I found much steeper that on the opposite side, to a handsome bold running Creek of cold Clear water [today's Horseshoe Bend Creek]. here I first tasted the water of the great Columbia river..." (Captain Lewis, 12 August 1805, quoted in Gary Moulton, ed., *The Journals of the Lewis & Clark Expedition*, vol. 5, 74.)

***Teaching Point:* Personal Courage and Will.** *Will* is a mental attribute of *personal courage*. It is the inner drive that compels soldiers and leaders to keep going when they are exhausted, hungry, afraid, cold, and wet—when it would be easier to quit (FM 22-100, 2-11). In what ways does Lewis' reaction to his discovery of Lemhi Pass demonstrate the mental attribute of will? Have the soldiers of the corps demonstrated the mental attribute of will during the journey?

Day 3
Stand 8
(The Shoshone Indians)

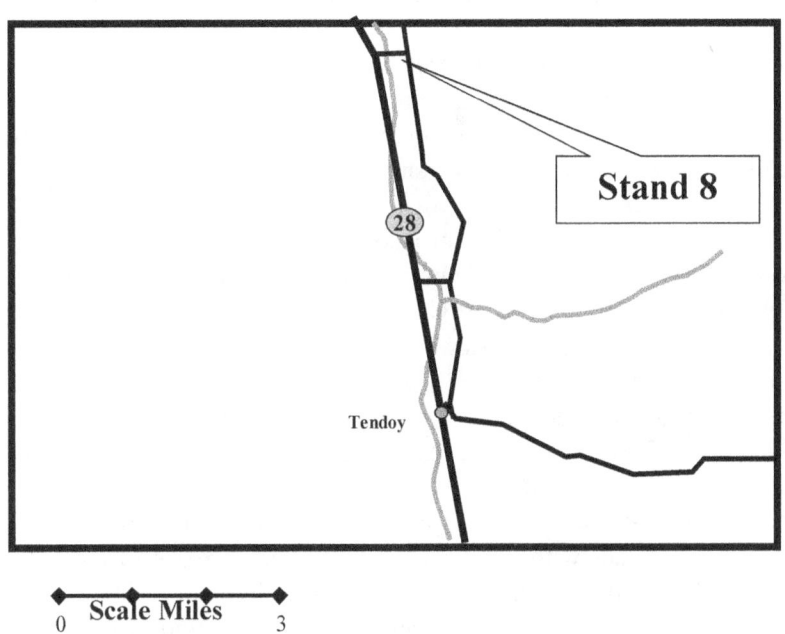

Map 3-9

Stand 8
The Shoshone Indians
(12 -30 August 1805

Directions: Continue west on the road toward Tendoy, ID. Near Tendoy, turn right at the first stop sign. Follow this road for approximately 4.9 miles and stop at the monument marking the location of the Shoshone village.

Orientation (See Visual 3-8, Appendix D): You have crossed over the Continental Divide into today's Lemhi River Valley. Clark called the river the East Fork of Lewis' River in honor of his co-captain. This valley was a traditional village site for the Shoshone Indians.

Situation: Lewis crossed Lemhi Pass on 12 August 1805 and continued westward. He was moving into Indian territory with only four armed men. Clark and the main body of the Corps of Discovery were four days behind and well beyond supporting Lewis if he got into a fight. Lewis was not sure if the Shoshone would be friendly or hostile. However, he did know that at least one frightened Indian had spotted his group and would probably warn the village. He wanted to find the village before the Shoshone dispersed into the mountains and thus was determined to forge ahead with his small group and make contact. Lewis probably reviewed in his mind the failure of the last contact with the Shoshone and was anxious to try again. It appears that he did develop some basic procedures to follow upon next meeting the Indians and that he had reviewed them with his men. About 4 miles northeast of today's village site marker, he spotted two Indian women, a man, and some dogs. This time he was determined not to make the same mistake as had been made previously; he ordered the men to stop. All stopped and placed their packs and weapons on the ground. Lewis then unfurled the 15-star American Flag and shouted, *tab-ba-bone,* "white man" in Shoshone. Unfortunately, despite Lewis' preparations for contact, the plan did not work, and the Indians fled into the brush. Lewis and the men followed them over broken terrain and soon came face to face with three Shoshone women. One ran away into the brush. However, the oldest woman and a young girl stayed meekly on the ground. They probably feared that these strangers were an enemy raiding party and expected to be killed. Lewis, a Virginia gentleman, extended his hand and helped the old woman up from the ground. He showed her his white skin under his shirt; his exposed skin was as brown as the Indians' due to constant exposure to the sun. Lewis had Drouillard calmed the women with sign language and asked them to call back the one who had run away. He was afraid she would warn the village and that the tribe would disappear into the mountains. Lewis then provided the women with gifts and persuaded them to escort him and his men to the village.

The women led Lewis' group toward the village, and they had only proceeded about 2 miles when 60 mounted warriors rushed up at full gallop. Lewis handed his gun to one of the men and had them halt. He then held the American Flag and advanced with the Indian women toward the charging Indians. The intervention of the elderly Shoshone woman saved Lewis' group from annihilation. She explained to the leading warrior, Chief Cameahwait, that Lewis' group was friendly and showed her gifts to the mounted warriors. The warriors dismounted and graciously greeted the strangers. The combined group then returned to the Indian village. The Shoshone were a poor but generous people. The more numerous and better-armed Blackfeet Indians had forced them away from the game-rich plains into the mountains. They had little food but willingly shared what they had with the explorers.

During his stay at the Shoshone village, Lewis saw that the nearby river, today's Lemhi River, would provide easy passage and hoped that the corps would be able to float canoes all the way to the Pacific. However, through sign language he discovered some bad news. Chief Cameahwait revealed that the river merged downstream with a larger river, today's Salmon River. The larger river was too rough to be successfully navigated. Equally disappointing was the news that the mountains also blocked any land route parallel to the river. It wasn't all bad news, though; Lewis counted over 700 horses at the Indian camp, and the Indians fed the group salmon for dinner. The corps needed the horses to transport men and supplies over the mountain, and the salmon indicated they were close to the Pacific Ocean.

On 14 August the men participated in an Indian hunting expedition. At the same time, Clark and the main body were struggling up the Jefferson River and were currently southwest of modern-day Dillon, Montana. That day Lewis convinced Cameahwait to return with him to meet Clark at the forks and to help bring the corps over the mountain. Cameahwait agreed to bring 30 horses to accomplish the tasks. Lewis intentionally delayed their departure by one day to allow Clark time to get to the meeting place. The next day, the Shoshone decided they did not want to go back with Lewis. They feared that Lewis was working in cooperation with the Blackfeet Indians and would lead them into an ambush. With his basic understanding of the warrior ethos of the western tribes, Lewis was able to shame them into going back with him.

The combined group departed the village toward the divide on 15 August. The majority of the Indians still feared Lewis was working with the

Blackfeet and refused to cross the mountains. However, Chief Cameahwait managed to convince a small group, 16 warriors and three women, to continue eastward with the white men. They crossed over the divide and camped along today's Horse Prairie Creek. The next day, Lewis sent Drouillard and Shields to hunt and provide food for the combined group. Fearing the warriors would scare off the game, Lewis asked Cameahwait to keep the warriors in camp. This unfortunately led the Shoshone to believe that Lewis was trying to coordinate with a nearby Blackfoot war party. The suspicion continued that morning until Drouillard killed a deer. The famished Indians devoured the kill raw and, at least for the moment, forgot their mistrust of the white men. Their suspicions returned when they neared the agreed meeting place. Cameahwait, still wary of a trap, had the Indians and white men trade articles of clothing. This, combined with the already rustic appearance of Lewis and his men, made them almost indistinguishable from the Indians. Lewis was "mortified" when they reached the forks and Clark was not there. He feared the Indians would lose faith and flee. To allay Cameahwait's fears, Lewis handed him his rifle. He also deceived Cameahwait into believing that the note he had left for Clark was a note from Clark asking them to wait there for his impending arrival. Lewis, desperate to find Clark, sent Drouillard to look for him. Cameahwait, still mistrustful of the white men, sent along a young brave to keep an eye on Drouillard. That evening Lewis was so preoccupied with the failure to link up with Clark and their need to successfully negotiate with the Shoshone that he had trouble sleeping.

Clark finally arrived at the forks on 17 August 1805. They began the initial negotiations that day. Lewis' wise forethought in having included Sacagawea in the expedition became immediately apparent. Their first advantage in having Sacagawea with them was that she filled their obvious need for a translator. Their negotiations followed a particularly complicated sequence of translation. In the chain of translation, the Shoshone first spoke to Sacagawea in Shoshone; then Sacagawea spoke to Charbonneau in Hidatsa; next Charbonneau spoke to Private Francois Labiche in French; and, finally, Labiche spoke to the captains in English. Their second advantage was in the fortuitous happenstance of Sacagawea being the long-lost sister of the Shoshone chief, Cameahwait. This alone was probably one of the most significant factors contributing to the success of the negotiations.

Lewis estimated that the corps required at least 25 horses to successfully traverse the mountains. To obtain these horses, he negotiated with the Shoshone in two phases. He conducted phase one, from 17 to 24 August, at Camp Fortunate. In this phase, he secured about a dozen horses. In the second phase, 25 to 30 August, the corps moved to the west side of the divide and negotiated at the main Shoshone village. The corps eventually departed the Shoshone village on 30 August 1805 with a herd of 29 horses. Interestingly, Lewis' insightful observations of the Shoshone during the negotiations foretold the difficulties the United States would have in the late 19th century with the tribes of the West. He recognized the important role that warfare played in their culture and the obstacle this would be in establishing a lasting peace with the various tribes.

Vignette 1: "we had not continued our rout more than a mile when we were so fortunate as to meet with three female savages. the short and steep ravines which we passed concealed us from each other untill we arrived within 30 paces. a young woman immediately took to flight, an Elderly woman and a girl of about 12 years old remained. I instantly laid by my gun and advanced towards them. they appeared much allarmed but saw that we were too near for them to escape by flight they therefore seated themselves on the ground, holding down their heads as if reconciled to die which they expected no doubt would be their fate; I took the elderly woman by the hand and raised her up repeated the word *tab-ba-bone* and strip up my shirt sleve to sew her my skin; to prove to her the truth of the assertion that I was a white man for my face and hands which have been constantly exposed to the sun were quite as dark as their own. they appeared instantly reconciled, and the men coming up I gave these women some beads a few mockerson awls some pewter looking-glasses and a little paint... I now painted their tawny cheeks with some vermillion which with this nation is emblematic of peace... we had marched about 2 miles when we met a party of about 60 warriors mounted on excellent horses who came in nearly full speed, when they arrived I advanced towards them with the flag leaving my gun with the party about 50 paces behind me... these men then advanced and embraced me very affectionately in their way which is by puting their left arm over you wright sholder clasping your back, while they apply their left cheek to yours and frequently vociforate the word *ah-hi-e, ah-hi-e* that is, I am much pleased, I am much rejoiced. bothe parties now advanced and we wer all carressed and besmeared with their grease and paint till I was heartily tired of the national hug... they seated themselves in a circle around us and pulled off their mockersons before they would receive or smoke the pipe.. I gave him [Chief Cameahwait] the flag which I informed him was an emblem of peace among whitemen and now that it had been received by him it was to be respected as the bond of union between us... I made a hearty meal, and then walked to the river, which I found about 40 yards wide very rapid clear and about 3 feet deep... Cameahwait informed me that this stream discharged itself into another doubly as large at the distance of half a days march which came from the S.W. but he added on further enquiry that there was but little more timber below the junction of those rivers than I saw here, and that the river was confined between inaccessible mountains, was very rapid and rocky insomuch that it was impossible for us to pass either by land or water down this river to the great lake where the white men lived as he had been informed. this was unwelcome information but I still hoped that this account had been exaggerated with a view to detain us among them..." (Captain Lewis, 13 August 1805, quoted in Gary Moulton, ed., *The Journals of the Lewis & Clark Expedition*, vol. 5, 78-81.)

Vignette 2: "the Chief addressed them several times before they would move they seemed very reluctant to accompany me. I at length asked the reason and he told me that some foolish persons among them had suggested the idea that we were in league with the Pahkees [Blackfeet Indians] and had come on in order to decoy them into an ambuscade where their enimies were waiting to receive them. but that for his part he did not believe it. I readily perceived that our situation was not entirely free from danger as the transision from suspicion to the confermation of the fact would not be very difficult in the minds of these ignorant people who have been accustomed from their infancy to view every stranger as an enimy. I told Cameahwait that I was sorry to find that they had put so little confidence in us, that I knew they were not acquainted with white men and therefore could forgive them. that among whitemen it was considered disgracefull to lye or entrap an enemy by falsehood... and that if the bulk of his nation still entertained this opinion I still hoped that there were some among them that were not afraid to die... I soon found that I had touched him on the right string; to doubt the bravery of a savage is at once to put him on his metal..." (Captain Lewis, 15 August 1805, quoted in Gary Moulton, ed., *The Journals of the Lewis & Clark Expedition*, vol. 5, 96-97.)

Vignette 3: "when they arrived where the deer was which was in view of me they dismounted and ran in tumbling over each other like a parcel of famished dogs each seizing and tearing away a part of the intestens which had been previously thrown out by Drewyer who killed it; the scene was such when I arrived that had I not have had a pretty keen appetite myself I am confident I should not have taisted any part of the venison shortly. each one had a piece of some discription and all eating most ravenously. some were eating the kidnies the melt and liver and the blood running from the corners of their mouths, others were in a similar situation with the paunch and guts but the exuding substance in this case from their lips was of a different description. one of the last who attracted my attention particularly had been fortunate in his allotment or reather active in the division, he had provided himself with about nine feet of the small guts one end of which he was chewing on while with his hands he was squezzing the contents out at the other. I really did not untill now think that human nature ever presented itself in a shape so nearly allyed to the brute creation. I viewed these poor starved divils with pity and compassion. I directed McNeal to skin the deer and reserved a quarter, the ballance I gave the Chief to be divided among his people; they devoured the whole of it nearly without cooking..." (Captain Lewis, 16 August 1805, quoted in Gary Moulton, ed., *The Journals of the Lewis & Clark Expedition*, vol. 5, 103.)

Vignette 4: "we now dismounted and the Chief with much cerimony put tippets about our necks such as they temselves woar I redily perceived that this was to disguise us and owed it's origine to the same cause already mentioned. to give them further confidence I put my cocked hat with feather on the chief and my over shirt being of the Indian form my hair deshivled and skin well browned with the sun I wanted no further addition to make me a complete Indian in appearance the men followed my example and we were son completely metamorphosed... when we arrived in sight at the distance of about 2 miles I discovered to my mortification that the party had not arrived... I now determined to restore their confidence cost what it might and therefore gave the Chief my gun and told him that if his enimies were in those bushes before him that he could defend himself with that gun, that for my own part I was not affraid to die and if I deceived him he might make what uce of the gun he thought proper or in other words that he might shoot me... after reading the notes which were the same I had left I told the Chief that when I had left my brother Chief with the party below where the river entered the mountain that we both agreed not to bring the canoes higher up than the next forks of the river above us wherever this might happen...that this note was left here today and that he informed me that he was just below the mountains and was coming on slowly up, and added that I should wait here for him... my mind was in reallity quite as gloomy all this evening as the most affrighted indian but I affected cheerfullness to keep the Indians so who were about me... I slept but little as might be well expected, my mind dwelling on the state of the expedition which I have ever held in equal estimation with my own existence, and the fait of which appeared at this moment to depend in a great measure upon the caprice of a few savages who are ever as fickle as the wind..." (Captain

Lewis, 16 August 1805, quoted in Gary Moulton, ed., *The Journals of the Lewis & Clark Expedition*, vol. 5, 104-106.)

Vignette 5: "Capt. Clark arrived with the Interpreter Charbono, and the Indian woman, who proved to be a sister of the Chif Cameahwait. the meeting of those people was really affecting, particularly between Sah-cah-gar-we-ah and an Indian woman, who had been taken prisoner at the same time with her, and who had afterwards escaped from the Minnetares and rejoined her nation... accordingly about 4 P. M. we called them together and through the medium of Labuish, Charbono and Sah-cah-gar-weah, we communicated to them fully the objects which had brought us into this distant part of the country, in which we took care to make them a conspicuous object of our own good wishes and the care of our government. we made them sensible of their dependance on the will of our government for every species of merchandize as well for their defence & comfort; and apprized them of the strength of our government and it's friendly dispositions towards them... every article about us appeared to excite astonishment in their minds; the appearance of the men, their arms, the canoes, our manner of working them, the back man york and the segacity of my dog were equally objects of admiration. I also shot my air-gun which was so perfectly incomprehensible that they immediately denominated it the great medicine... the cerimony of our council and smoking the pipe was in conformity of the custom of this nation performed barefoot. on those occasions points of etiquet are quite as much attended to by the Indians as among scivilized nations. To keep indians in a good humor you must not fatiegue them with too much business at one time..." (Captain Lewis, 17 August 1805, quoted in Gary Moulton, ed., *The Journals of the Lewis & Clark Expedition*, vol. 5, 109-112.)

Vignette 6: "I soon obtained three very good horses for which I gave an uniform coat, a pair of legings, a few handkerchiefs, three knives and some other small articles the whole of which did not cost more than about 20$ in the U' States. the Indians seemed quite as well pleased with their bargain as I was. the men also purchased one for an old checked shirt a pair of old leggings and a knife." (Captain Lewis, 18 August 1805, quoted in Gary Moulton, ed., *The Journals of the Lewis & Clark Expedition*, vol. 5, 117.)

Vignette 7: "Among the Shoshones, as well as all the Indians of America, bravery is esteemed the primary virtue; nor can any one become eminent among them who has not at some period of his life given proofs of his possessing this virtue. with them there can be no preferment without some warelike achievement, and so completely interwoven is this principle with the earliest Elements of thought that it will in my opinion prove a serious obstruction to the restoration of a general peace among the nations of the Missouri..." (Captain Lewis, 24 August 1805, quoted in Gary Moulton, ed., *The Journals of the Lewis & Clark Expedition*, vol. 5, 159-160.)

Teaching Point:

Host Nation Support. *Host Nation Support* (HNS) is the civil and military assistance provided by an HN to the forces located in or transiting through that HN's territory. Was HNS an important part of the logistics planning for the expedition, and how critical was HNS to the Corps of Discovery?

Note on Lodging: CSI recommends group lodging at the end of day three in Salmon, Idaho. Salmon offers numerous hotel and motel accommodations. Some offer reduced rates for large groups.

Day 4
Salmon River Reconnaissance to Travelers' Rest
(11 August to 6 September 1805)

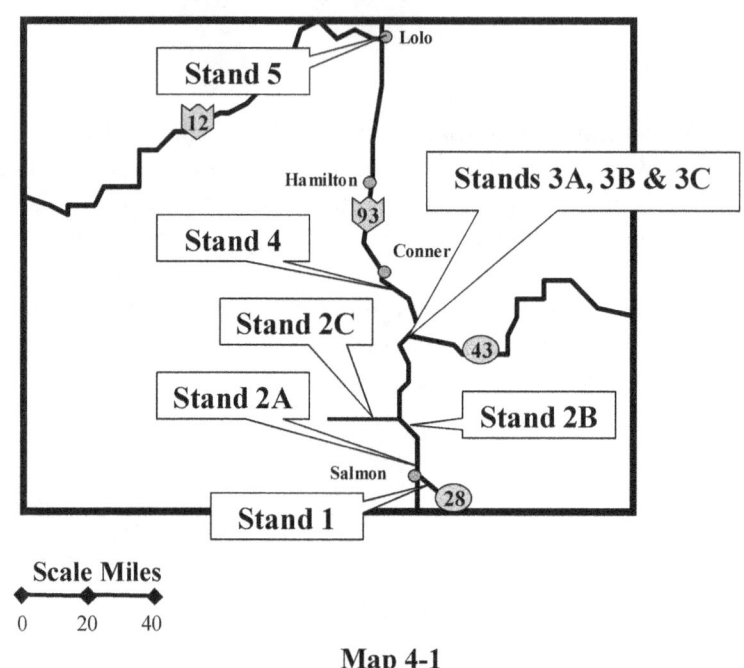

Map 4-1

Begin the day at Salmon, ID

Stand 1: Sacagawea (Sacajawea Interpretive Cultural & Education Center, Salmon, ID)

Stand 2, Salmon River Reconnaissance
2A: Lewis' River – The Confluence of the Lemhi and Salmon Rivers (Salmon, ID)
2B: Tower Rock (Tower Rock Recreation Site)
2C: Clark's Decision (Squaw Creek Ranger Station, west of North Fork, ID)

Stand 3, Lost Trail Pass

3A, Deep Creek (Mile Marker 341.3)
3B, Toby Leads the Way (Mile Marker 346.5)
3C, North Slope (Lost Trail Pass Turnout)

Stand 4, The Salish Indians (Sula, MT)

Stand 5, Travelers' Rest (Travelers' Rest State Park, Lolo, MT)
5A: Westward Bound
5B: Eastward Bound (Optional)

End the day in Lolo, MT

Day 4
Stand 1
(Sacagawea)
Stand 2A
(Lewis' River)

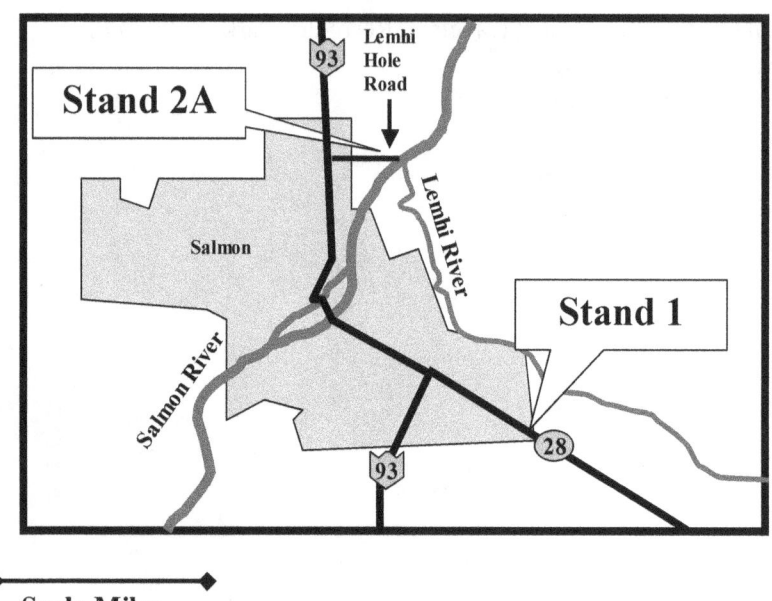

Map 4-2

135

Stand 1
Sacagawea

Directions: On the south edge of Salmon, Idaho, in the vicinity of mile marker 134, turn into the Sacajawea [Sacagawea] Interpretive Cultural and Education Center, Salmon, Idaho.

Situation: Sacagawea was the only woman to accompany the Corps of Discovery to the Pacific Ocean and back. She is second only to the captains in being the most remembered character of the Lewis and Clark expedition. Today, there are 23 statues, a dollar coin, mountains, lakes, and rivers honoring her participation in the exploration. Her accomplishments and contributions to the success of the expedition were numerous. Unfortunately, 20th-century biographers and novelists have distorted her actual role and clouded truth into legend. Significant controversies about this remarkable young woman focus on two areas: the importance of her contributions (was she a guide or an interpreter?) and the spelling and meaning of her name.

She was born about 1788 near present-day Tendoy, Idaho, as a member of the Shoshone Indian Nation. The Shoshone were a seminomadic tribe whose homeland was in today's Lemhi River Valley, Idaho. The tribe frequently ventured to the east to hunt buffalo. It was on one of these hunting forays in 1800 that a war party of Hidatsa Indians kidnapped her near the Three Forks of the Missouri River. The Hidatsa took her to their villages near modern Bismarck, North Dakota. Later they sold her as a slave to Toussaint Charbonneau, a French-Canadian fur trader. He, in time, claimed Sacagawea and another Shoshone woman as his wives. In 1804 the Corps of Discovery, while wintering with the Hidatsa, hired Charbonneau and Sacagawea as interpreters. Prior to the corps' departure from the Hidatsa villages, Sacagawea gave birth to her son Jean-Baptiste Charbonneau, who accompanied the corps all the way to the Pacific and back again.

Sacagawea's contributions to the success of the expedition were significant. On 14 May 1805, she recovered many important papers and supplies from a nearly capsized boat. The loss of the supplies would have been a major problem for the corps, and the destruction of the papers could have been a major loss to scholars studying the Lewis and Clark Expedition. Her actions, especially her calmness, during the crisis earned the compliments of the captains and the men. Other activities, although less dramatic than the capsized canoe, were just as important to the day-to-day survival of the corps in the wilderness. These included teaching the men of the corps how to dig roots, collect edible plants, and pick berries for use as food and sometimes as medicine.

Sacagawea's most essential role was as an interpreter. The Charbonneaus were vital to the captains' plans for obtaining horses from the Shoshone Indians. As discussed earlier, Sacagawea played a significant role in the successful negotiations with the Shoshone to obtain horses. Ironically, her major contribution to the success of the negotiations was not her language skill, but the fortuitous circumstance of being related to the Shoshone chief, Cameahwait. Another vital contribution was her role as an emissary of peace. On numerous occasions the captains placed Sacagawea and her child conspicuously at the front of the corps. They wanted the Indian tribes to see her and know that the corps came in peace. A war party rarely traveled with a woman, especially a woman with a baby.

One of the most significant controversies is the question of whether or not Sacagawea served as a guide. There is no question that, on more than one occasion, she recognized landmarks on the upper Missouri and Jefferson Rivers. These sightings boosted the morale of the men and gave them hope that the rivers were not endless. However, she had never been on the river east of the Three Forks of the Missouri. The Hidatsa, after kidnapping her, took her by horse down the Yellowstone River to their villages. Therefore, she could not have guided the corps along a river she had never traveled upon. She had also never been west of her Lemhi Valley home and could not have served as a guide from the valley west to the Pacific. However, she had significant knowledge of the Big Hole country and the Yellowstone River. She was familiar with this ground and proved to be very valuable to Clark as "a pilot" during the Yellowstone River reconnaissance on the 1806 return trip.

Even the spelling and meaning of Sacagawea's name has become a topic of controversy in the 20th century. The captains, well noted for their creative spelling, were very deliberate and careful in their recording of Indian names and their meaning. They recorded her name as Sah-cah' gah-we-ah 17 times in their journals and on their maps, and each time it was spelled with a *"g"* in the third syllable. They also, on at least three occasions, referred to the meaning of Sacagawea as "bird woman." The spelling of *Sacajawea* can first be attributed to Nicholas Biddle's 1814 two-volume narrative of the journey. He attempted to standardize the spelling of the name to Sah ca gah we a. However, editors changed the 20 May 1805 journal entry to Sacajawea and then consistently spelled it with a "j" throughout the remainder of the two-volume edition of the journals. The spelling of Sacajawea was perpetuated by Grace Hebard in her controversial work *Sacajawea, A Guide and Interpreter of the Lewis and Clark Expedition* and in Eva Emery Dye's novel *The Conquest.* These books also put forth the theory that Sacajawea was a Shoshone word meaning "boat pusher." Both names and meanings have supporters, and it is unlikely that the controversy will ever be definitively resolved one way or the other.

Sacagawea very much deserves to be remembered by history. Her role as an interpreter and emissary of peace significantly contributed to the success of the Lewis and Clark Expedition. The corps would have had difficulty acquiring the horses from the Shoshone without Sacagawea's participation in the negotiations. Her role as an emissary of peace allowed the corps to peaceably trade with numerous Indian tribes and may have prevented a tragic confrontation between the explorers and native warriors. The dispute over her name is unfortunate and should not be allowed to overshadow her contributions. Despite these controversies, Sacagawea, the "bird woman," and Sacajawea, the "boat pusher," both refer to the same remarkable woman, a valuable member of the Corps of Discovery.

Vignette 1: "A French man by name Chabonah, who Speaks the Big Belley language visit us, he wished to hire & informed us his 2 squars were Snake [Shoshone] Indians, we engau him to go on with us and take one of his wives to interpet the Snake language..." (Captain Clark, 4 November 1804, quoted in Gary Moulton, ed., *The Journals of the Lewis & Clark Expedition*, vol. 3, 228.)*

Vignette 2: "...this stream we called Sah-ca-gar me-ah or bird woman's river, after our interpreter the Snake woman..." (Captain Lewis, 20 May 1805, quoted in Gary Moulton, ed., *The Journals of the Lewis & Clark Expedition*, vol. 4, 171.)

---

* All vignettes retain the enigmatic writing of the journalists. See the introduction to Section III for an explanation of the editorial principles used with the journal entries.

Day 4
Stands 2B & 2C
(Salmon River Reconnaissance)

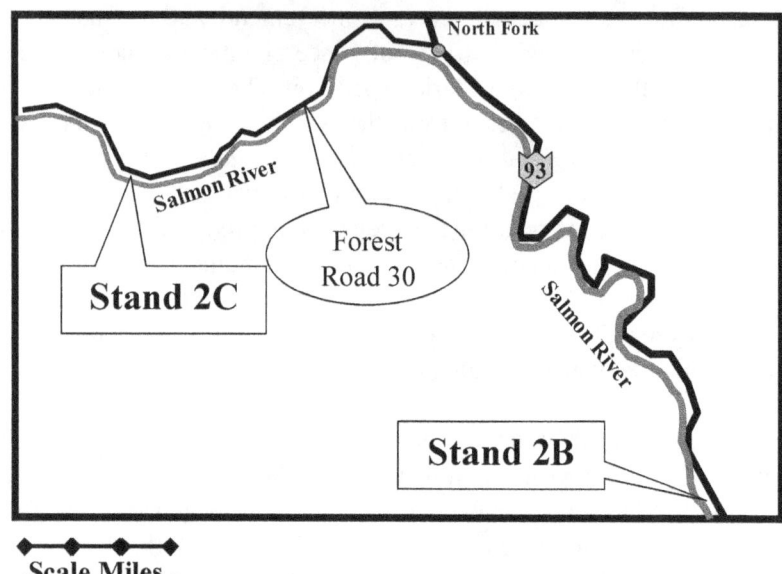

Map 4-3

Stand 2
Salmon River Reconnaissance
(18 –26 August 1805)

Directions: Continue north on Highway 28 into Salmon, Idaho. Pass over the bridge and turn north on Highway 93. Then turn right on Lemhi Hole Road and proceed to the gravel parking lot near the river. Walk through the cattle gate and orient the group to where the Lemhi River flows into the Salmon River.

Orientation (See Visual 4-1, Appendix D): The main river flowing from south to north is today's Salmon River, known to the captains as Lewis' River. The small river flowing into the Salmon from the opposite bank is today's Lemhi River, which the captains called the East Fork of Lewis' River. Today's Highway 28, the route just driven by the group, is the same basic route followed by the Corps of Discovery in 1805 to reach this location.

Situation 2A: Back at Camp Fortunate, Lewis had shared with Clark the intelligence obtained about the west side of the Continental Divide. He had observed that the first major river (today's Lemhi River) was navigable. However, Cameahwait had informed him that the river joined with a larger river, today's Salmon River, which the Indians called "The River of No Return." The Indians insisted it was not navigable and could not be followed on a land route because of the mountainous terrain. The captains discussed the situation and retained their familiar strategy of dividing tasks and responsibilities. They decided that Clark, who wanted to see for himself if the river was navigable, would lead 11 men with tools over the Continental Divide to examine the river. His mission was to determine how the next phase of the journey would be conducted. If he determined the river to be navigable, he had the tools to build canoes. Lewis would remain at Camp Fortunate to barter for horses and prepare the equipment for transport over the divide.

Clark departed Camp Fortunate on 18 August with 11 men. He was confident in his own river skills as well as those of his men and did not accept the Shoshone assessment that the river was not navigable. The reconnaissance group arrived at the Shoshone village in the vicinity of modern-day Tendoy, Idaho, on 20 August. There Clark hired an elderly Indian man to act as a guide. His name was PI-Kee queen-ah (or Swooping Eagle) and he knew more about the way west than anyone else in the village. The captains nicknamed him Toby, which was a simplification of the title given to him by his people when he departed with the Corps of

Discovery, Tosa-tive koo-be, meaning *furnished white-man brains*. Even though the captains rarely mention Toby in their journals, he proved to be a valuable asset to the corps. The group departed the Shoshone village on 21 August and moved down today's Lemhi River. They cut cross-country and reached the main river just north of today's Carmen, Idaho, at Tower Creek. Clark named the stream Lewis River in honor of his co-captain. He then continued to move north following today's Salmon River.

Vignette 1: "I now prevailed on the Chief to instruct me with rispect to the geography of his country. this he undertook very cheerfully, by delienating the rivers on the ground... he placed a number of heeps of sand on each side which he informed me represented the vast mountains of rock eternally covered with snow through which the river passed... the Chief further informed me that he had understood from the perced nosed Indians who inhabit this river below the rocky mountains that it ran a great way toward the seting sun and finally lost itself in a great lake of water which was illy taisted, and where the white men lived... I now asked Cameahwait by what rout the Pierced nosed indians, who he informed me inhabited this river below the mountains, came over to the Missouri; this he informed me was to the north, but added that the road was very bad one as he had been informed by them and that they had suffered excessively with hunger on the rout being obliged to subsist for many days on berries alone as there was no game in that part of the mountains which were broken rockey and so thickly covered with timber that they could scarcely pass... my rout was instantly settled in my own mind... I felt perfectly satisfyed, that if the Indians could pass these mountains with their women and Children, that we could also pass them..." (Captain Lewis, 14 August 1805, quoted in Gary Moulton, ed., *The Journals of the Lewis & Clark Expedition*, vol. 5, 88-91.)

Vignette 2: "I shall in justice to Capt. Lewis who was the first white man ever on this fork of the Columbia Call this Louis's river." (Captain Clark, 21 August 1805, quoted in Gary Moulton, ed., *The Journals of the Lewis & Clark Expedition*, vol. 5, 140.)

Directions: Return to Highway 93 and go north (right). Watch for mile marker 314.9 and park at the Tower Rock Recreation Site on the left side of the road. Orient the group on the red cliffs across the road to the northeast.

Orientation: The red cliffs are one of the many spots along the expedition route that Lewis and Clark enthusiasts can match with journal descriptions of actual terrain. The 21 August 1805 campsite was at the base of the cliffs and adjacent to Highway 93; the interpretive sign marks the spot.

Situation 2B: **Tower Rock.** Clark continued to lead his men down the river, noting the Shoshones' dependency on the salmon and their methods of trapping and spearing. The men used their rifles to shoot the large fish. They dined at lunch that day on a 2 ½-foot salmon. Clark halted the group the night of 21 August 1805 and camped under some reddish bluffs along the river. To this point, Clark was confident that the corps could navigate the river and doubted old Toby's insistence that it was the river of no return.

Vignette 3: "...This Clift is of redish brown Colour. Some Gullies of white Sand Stone and Sand fine & a[s] white as Snow. The mountains on each Side are high, and those on the East ruged and Contain a fiew Scattering pine, those on the West contain pine on ther tops and high up the hollows..." (Captain Clark, 21 August 1805, quoted in Gary Moulton, ed., *The Journals of the Lewis & Clark Expedition*, vol. 5, 140.)

Directions: Continue north on Highway 93 to North Fork, Idaho. At North Fork, take the left turn toward Shoup (Forest Road 30). Continue west for 6 miles and park at the turnout on the left side of the road.

Orientation: The modern road has changed the original lay of the land. Imagine how this valley would look if you took away the forest road and extended the slopes down to the river. Also modern construction has significantly decreased the drainage into the river. In 1805 the river was both deeper and faster.

Situation 2C: **Clark's Decision.** Clark continued to push up the river on 22 August. He doubted the information provided by the Shoshones, and believed that the river, though challenging, was navigable. However, the nature of the river changed when it swung to the west near present day North Fork, Idaho. The rough terrain on both sides of the stream forced the men to ride their horses in the river. At times, the group had to swim the horses around dangerous obstructions. The farther they traveled to the west, the rougher the river became, and Clark finally began to accept old Toby's assessment of the route. Clark decided to leave the majority of his group and the horses behind while he proceeded overland with a smaller group. Toby led Clark over the mountainous terrain to a high point about 3 miles short of present-day Shoup, Idaho. From there, Clark was able to see about 20 miles down the river and admitted that old Toby was correct; the river truly was not a practical route to the Pacific.

Clark was very disappointed that the river route was "impractical." He realized that there was no time to be lost with the season growing late and winter coming on. He rejoined his group and immediately dispatched a messenger, Private Colter, to Lewis with the bad news, urging him to move forward quickly. In the message to Lewis, he outlined three options and offered a recommendation. His recommendation, the first option, was that the Corps of Discovery should abandon the river route, keep the corps together as one group, buy more horses, and hire old Toby as a guide. Toby knew of a route over the mountains used by the Nez Perce Indians to travel east to hunt buffalo on the plains. His second option was to divide the corps into two groups. One group would attempt the river of no return in canoes while the other group attempted to parallel the river route along the mountain ridges. His third option was a variation of option one. His own experience, plus the intelligence from Toby, indicated that game was sparse in the mountains; therefore, food would be a major concern during the crossing. He outlined the possibility of sending a small group back to the Great Falls area to get a supply of buffalo meat. The balance of the corps would then move north to find Toby's Nez Perce trail and wait for the buffalo group to return. The buffalo group, after obtaining a large supply of meat, was to march directly west from the Great Falls and rejoin the main party in the mountains. Prior to dispatching the messenger, Clark must have determined that the third option was impracticable because of the time delay in sending a group all the way back to the Great Falls and he crossed it out. Private Colter joined Lewis on 26 August, 5 miles north of present-day Tendoy, Idaho. Lewis reviewed Clark's options, agreed with his assessment that the first option was the best course of action, and continued efforts to obtain horses from the Shoshone.

Vignette 4: "I determined to delay the party here and with my guide and three men proceed on down to examine if the river continued bad or was practicable..." (Captain Clark, 23 August 1805, quoted in Gary Moulton, ed., *The Journals of the Lewis & Clark Expedition*, vol. 5, 155.)

Vignette 5: "The river from the place I left my party to this Creek is almost one continued rapid, five verry Considerable rapids the passage of either with Canoes is entirely impossible, as the water is Confined between hugh Rocks & the Current beeting from one against another for Some distance below ... at one of those rapids the mountains Close So Clost as to prevent a possibility of a portage... my guide and maney other Indians tell me that the Mountains Close and is a perpendicular Clift on each Side, and Continues for a great distance and that the water runs with great violence from one rock to the other on each Side foaming & roreing thro the rocks in every direction, So as to render the passage of any thing impossible..." (Captain Clark, 23 August 1805, quoted in Gary Moulton, ed., *The Journals of the Lewis & Clark Expedition*, vol. 5, 155-156.)

Vignette 6: "I wrote a letter to Capt Lewis informing him of the prospects before us and information recved of my guide which I thought favorable ...& Stating two plans <for> one of which for us to pursue &c. and despatched one man & horse and directed the party to get ready to march back...

The plan I stated to Capt Lewis if he agrees with me we shall adopt is to procure as many horses (one for each man) if possible and to hire my present guide who I sent on to him to interregate thro' the Intprtr. and proceed on by land to Some navagable part of the *Columbia* River, or to the *Ocean*, depending on what provisions we can procure by the gun aded to the Small Stock we have on hand depending on our horses as the last resort.

a second plan to divide the party one part to attempt this deficuet river with what provisions we had, and the remaindr to pass by Land on hose back...

a third to [send?] one party to attempt to pass the mountain by horses, & the other to return to the Missouri Collect provisions & go up Medison riv..." (Captain Clark, 24 August 1805, quoted in Gary Moulton, ed., *The Journals of the Lewis & Clark Expedition*, vol. 5, 163.)

Vignette 7: "I found it a folly to think of attempting to decend this river in canoes and therefore <determined> to commence the purchase of horses in the morning from the indians in order to carry into execution the design <we had formed of> passing the rocky Mountains... matters being thus far arranged I directed the fiddle to be played and the party danced very merily much to the amusement and gratification of the natives, though I must confess that the state of my own mind at this moment did not well accord with the prevailing mirth as I somewhat feared that the caprice of the indians might suddenly induce them to withhold their horses from us without which my hopes of prosicuting my voyage to advantage was lost; however I determined to keep the indians in a good humour if possible, and to loose no time in obtaining the necessary number of horses..." (Captain Lewis, 26 August 1805, quoted in Gary Moulton, ed., *The Journals of the Lewis & Clark Expedition*, vol. 5, 173.)

Teaching Points:

Integrity. People of *integrity* do the right thing, not because it is convenient or because they have no choice; they choose the right thing because their character permits no less. Was Clark's decision to execute the Salmon River reconnaissance the right thing to do even though the captains had local intelligence that the river was not navigable?

METT-TC. Today's commanders use the factors of Mission, Enemy, Terrain and Weather, Troops and Support Available, Time Available, and Civil Considerations (METT-TC) to assess and visualize the situation. Staff estimates and collaborative information sharing among commanders refine and deepen their situational understanding. Commanders then visualize the operation, describe it within their intent, and direct their subordinates toward mission accomplishment. How do the captains' actions concerning the Salmon River recon demonstrate an effective problem solving and visualization process?

Day 4
Stand 3
(Lost Trail Pass)

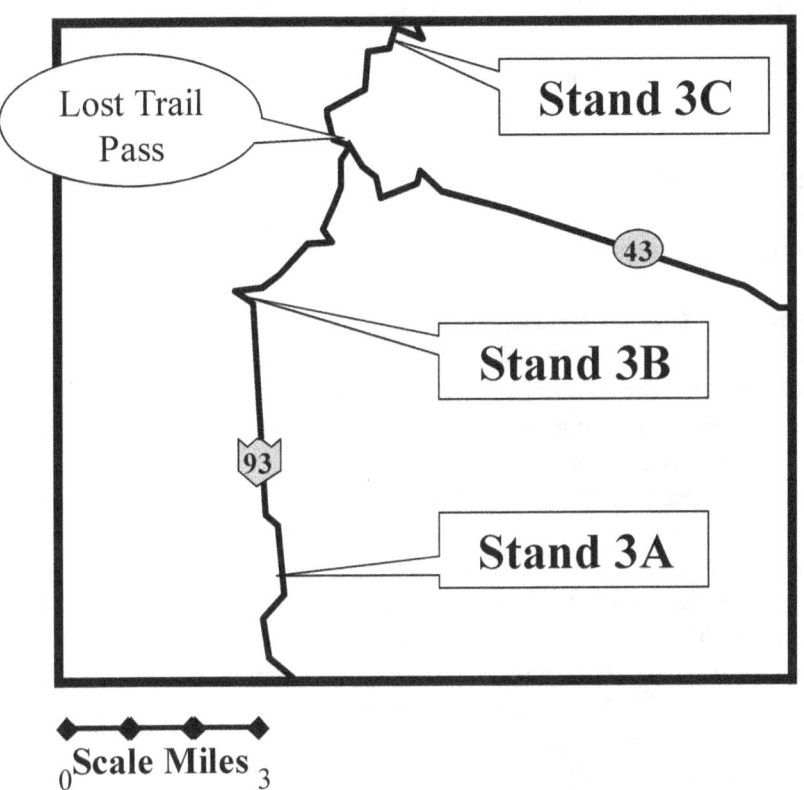

Map 4-4

Stand 3
Lost Trail Pass
(27 August - 4 September 1805)

Directions: Return to Highway 93 and drive north. Watch for mile marker 341 and park at the turnout on the left side of the road.

Orientation (See Visual 4-2, Appendix D): The route just followed along Highway 93 from North Fork to this location is the same route followed by the Corps of Discovery in late August and early September 1805. Of course the road was not here and the corps traveled along the Indian trail that followed the creek. Today the creek is the north fork of the Salmon River. The captains referred to it as Fish Creek.

Situation 3A: **Deep Creek.** On 27 August 1805, the two captains were still separated and taking care of their divided responsibilities. Lewis was at Chief Cameahwait's upper village, about 5 miles north of present-day Tendoy, Idaho, bartering for more horses. Clark was at the lower village on the Lemhi River, about 5 miles east of present-day Salmon, Idaho. He had finished his Salmon River reconnaissance and was waiting for Lewis and the main body of the Corps of Discovery to move up and join him. On 28 August, Clark sent Sergeant Gass to find out what was holding Lewis back. Lewis sent Gass back to Clark, requesting that he come to the upper village and assist him with the horse trading. Lewis was determined to obtained more horses and believed he could still get more from the Shoshone. Clark met Lewis on 29 August and immediately joined in the horse trading. The novelty of the white men's trinkets seemed to have lost much of its perceived value, and the Indians were demanding much higher prices for their horses. Clark set his eye on one particular horse and ended up trading a pistol, 100 lead balls, powder, and a knife for the horse.

On the same day Clark bought his horse, Lewis decided that the corps had obtained all the horses it would probably get from the Shoshone. Both captains were probably competent judges of good horses. However, they had to make the most of what the Shoshone were willing to trade. Most of the horses were not the best the Shoshone had, and many were too young to carry a heavy pack load. The next day, 30 August, the corps departed the Shoshone camp with 29 horses and Toby, Clark's guide from the Salmon River Reconnaissance. There is no record of Sacagawea's good-byes to her brother, Chief Cameahwait, whose hospitality had been of valuable assistance to the corps. Over the next several days, as the members of the corps moved along the established Indian trails, the weather remained good and morale was high. They marched 22 miles on 31 August and another 20 on 1 September.

The situation worsened on 2 September, when it started to rain and the Indian trail veered to the east near present-day Gibbonsville along Dahlonega Creek. The trail crossed to the east face of the Continental Divide and then linked up with another trail that crossed back to the west face of the divide along today's Gibbon Pass route. The captains now faced the dilemma of which route to take to get to the Bitterroot Valley. They could either follow the established trail along its 35-mile detour to the east, with two crossings of the Continental Divide, or abandon the trail and remain west of the Continental Divide, pushing 18 miles straight ahead through rough terrain. They left no record of why they decided to abandon the established trail. It may have been Clark's faith that Toby could lead the way, combined with the captains' total confidence in themselves and in the corps' ability to overcome any obstacle. Another factor could have been the captains' mind-set to "proceed on" to the west and their reluctance to backtrack to the east. The end result was that the corps moved into some of the worst terrain it would encounter during the expedition. The creek they followed was choked with briars and brush, and the men had to use axes and knives to clear a path. To avoid the tangled creek, they tried to angle along the steep, talus slopes that came directly down to the creek banks. The sharp rocks on the slopes cut the feet of the unshod horses, and occasionally the horses lost their footing and rolled down the slopes. One horse was crippled in a fall and another two collapsed from exhaustion. They struggled, making only 13 miles on 2 September through what they called a "dismal swamp." Exhausted, they camped that night along the creek not far from today's historical sign on Highway 93 near mile marker 341.

Vignette 1: "I purchased a horse for which I gave my Pistol 100 Balls Powder & a Knife." (Captain Clark, 29 August 1805, quoted in Gary Moulton, ed., *The Journals of the Lewis & Clark Expedition*, vol. 5, 178.)

Vignette 2: "the mountains on each Side of the Creek is verry Steep and high. the bottoms on the Creek narrow and Swampy a nomber of beaver dams. we Call this place dismal Swamp, and it is a lonesome rough part of the Country. we were obleged to climb Several hills with our horses, where it was So Steep and rockey that Some of the horses which was weak and their feet Sore, that they fell back 3 or 4 fell over backwards and roled to the foot of the hills. we were then obleged to carry the loads up the hills and then load again. one of the horses gave out So that his load was left a little before night. we Came 13 miles this day and Camped in a thicket of pine and bolsom fir timber near the Creek... this horrid bad going where we came up this creek which we Call dismal Swamp was six miles and we are not out of it yet, but our guide tells us that we will git on a plain tomorrow..." (Private Whitehouse, 2 September 1805, quoted in Gary Moulton, ed., *The Journals of the Lewis & Clark Expedition*, vol. 11, 296.)

Directions: Continue north on Highway 93 to mile marker 346.5 and then park at the turnout on the right side of the road.

Orientation: Toby continued to guide the corps up Fish Creek, which parallels the road to this point. At this location, the creek flows down the mountain from the northwest and crosses under the road. In this vicinity, the Corps of Discovery abandoned its route along the creek and moved northward up the ridge.

Situation 3B: **Toby Leads the Way.** The Corps of Discovery resumed its movement about 8 a.m. the next morning and followed the creek to the north. The corps' exact route is unknown and is the subject of much scholarly debate. Somewhere between today's West Fork and where the modern highway ascends out of the Moose Creek Valley, Toby abandoned the creek and led the corps up a steep ridge to the north. The route was once again very challenging to both the men and the horses, which frequently slipped and injured themselves on the sharp rocks. The slopes already had a two-inch layer of snow and the weather now turned against the corps, making the route more treacherous with alternating rain and sleet.

Vignette 3: "we pursued our journey up the creek, which still continued fatiguing almost beyond description..." (Sergeant Gass, 3 September 1805, quoted in Gary Moulton, ed., *The Journals of the Lewis & Clark Expedition*, vol. 10, 136.)

Vignette 4: "hills high & rockey on each Side, in the after part of the day the high mountains closed the Creek on each Side and obliged us to take on the Steep Sides of those Mountains, So Steep that the horses Could screcly keep from Slipping down, Several Sliped & Injured themselves verry much..." (Captain Clark, 3 September 1805, quoted in Gary Moulton, ed., *The Journals of the Lewis & Clark Expedition*, vol. 5, 185-186.)

Directions: Continue north on Highway 93 up and over Lost Trail Pass. Continue to mile marker 346.5 and then park at the turnout on the left side of the road.

Orientation: Orient the group to the west. To the southwest is the high ridge that the Corps of Discovery passed over on 3 Sept. The corps crossed approximately 1.5 miles to the west of where the road tops the divide, then moved north along the east face of the large ridge to your front.

Situation 3C: **The North Slope.** There is considerable historical debate, with at least five major theories, on where the Corps of Discovery crested the ridge and camped on the night of 3 September. Most agree that the corps passed over the ridge somewhere to the west of the current highway crossing, probably in the vicinity of the modern-day ski slopes. It appears that Toby missed the route he was aiming for and crossed the ridge too late in the day to attempt a descent of the north face. He apparently decided to wait until morning to find his way. The corps camped that evening either along the ridge top or, more likely, on the north face. The evening was cold, and the men had very little to eat. Clark personally brought in five pheasants, and the hunters another four. Nine birds and a little corn was not much food for 32 hungry men, one woman, and a baby.

The morning of 4 September was clear and cold for the Corps of Discovery. It remained below freezing the whole day. Although the exact route down the north slope is not known, it appears that the corps backtracked to the top of the mountain and then followed a ridge just to the west of present-day Highway 93 that led into the Bitterroot Valley. The decision to bull straight ahead for 18 miles over the mountain had taken the corps most of three days. They had climbed up and over the present-day Saddle Mountain, which at 8,400 feet, was the highest point crossed by the corps during the expedition. The decision to leave the established trail had cost them three days and exhausted both men and animals.

Vignette 5: "Encamped on a branh of the Creek we assended... This day we passed over emence hils and Some of the worst roade that ever horses passed our horses frequently fell. Snow about 2 inches deep when it began to rain which termonated in a Sleet." (Captain Clark, 3 September 1805, quoted in Gary Moulton, ed., *The Journals of the Lewis & Clark Expedition*, vol. 5, 186.)

Vignette 6: "We then went on about 3 miles over a large mountain, to the head of another creek and encamped there for the night. This was not the creek our guide wished to have come upon; and to add to our misfortunes we had a cold evening with rain." (Sergeant Gass, 3 September 1805, quoted in Gary Moulton, ed., *The Journals of the Lewis & Clark Expedition*, vol. 10, 136.)

Teaching Points:

Contractor and Civilian Support. Today's Army relies heavily on contractors and Department of the Army civilians. Old Toby played a significant role in the Salmon River reconnaissance and a prominent role again in this phase of the journey. Overall, how important a role did contractors and civilians play in the Corps of Discovery?

Integrity. As discussed at the previous stand, the Army value of *integrity* involves doing what is right because that is what is expected of our leaders. In hindsight, we know that the captains' decision to abandon the established trail and push directly north over the mountains was not the correct decision; they would have saved time and resources taking the 35-mile detour to the east. Was the decision to move due north a matter of integrity based on their confidence in themselves and the unit, or was it a matter of arrogance, overconfidence, and refusal to backtrack to the east?

Day 4
Stand 4
(The Salish Indians)

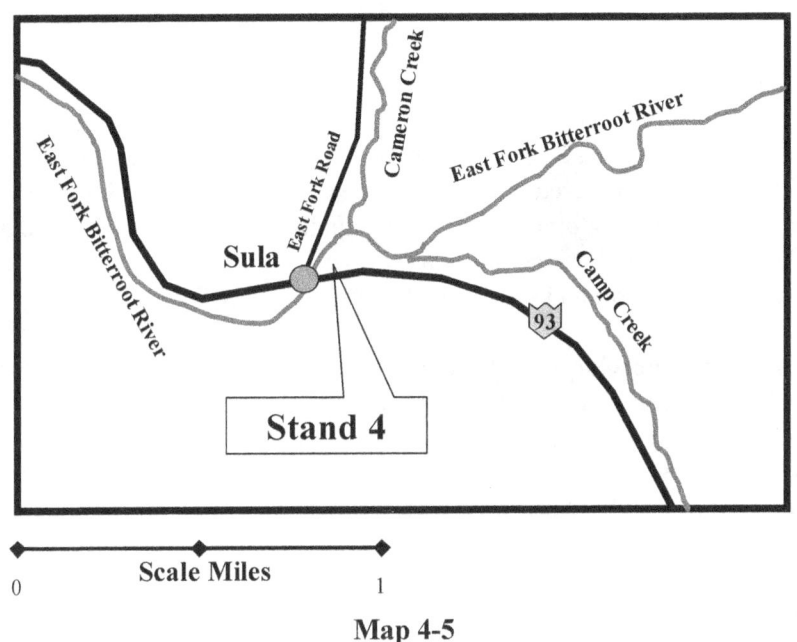

Map 4-5

Stand 4
Salish Indians
(4 - 6 September 1805)

Directions: Continue north along Highway 93 toward Sula, Montana. Park at the historical interpretive signs on the right side of the road.

Orientation (See Visual 4-2, Appendix D): We are currently at the head of the Bitterroot Valley. This location is today called Ross' Hole. It was named for Alexander Ross of the Hudson's Bay Company and his party of 55 fur trappers who used this as a meeting place in the early 1820s. Hole is a trapper name for a broad flat area surrounded by mountains. The Indians who lived here and passed through the area at the time of Lewis and Clark referred to this ground as the "Great Gathering Place."

Situation: The Corps of Discovery entered the beautiful Bitterroot Valley on 4 September 1805. It had just negotiated some of the roughest terrain it would encounter in the journey and was now entering some of the easiest terrain it would traverse. The corps followed present-day Camp Creek, which parallels Highway 93, making substantial progress through the wide valley with its numerous open meadows. The hunters made first contact with the Salish Indians near present-day Sula, Montana, and received a cordial welcome. The Salish extended the same friendly welcome to the captains when they came up with the main body of the corps. The Indian chiefs wanted to talk, but the captains were exhausted from their mountain crossing and delayed the talks until the next day. Clark referred to the Salish as Flat Head Indians, although there is no evidence of any head-flattening practices. They called themselves the Oat-la-shoot (today's spelling), which was their name for the valley's river, the Red Willow. Today the river is called the Bitterroot.

The fifth of September was a cold and leisurely day for the corps. It was also the last date upon which the captains recorded a temperature during the expedition; the last thermometer broke sometime afterward. The men helped the Indians hunt, and the captains bartered with the Indians for more horses. That day they purchased 11 horses and traded seven of their lame animals for stronger horses. As with the Shoshone, the negotiations were complicated and assisted by fortuitous circumstances. Fortunately, there was a young Shoshone Indian boy with the Salish. The translation chain had the boy speaking to the Salish and then to Sacagawea in Shoshone, Sacagawea speaking to Charbonneau in Hidatsa, Charbonneau to Private

Labiche in French, and Labiche to the captains in English.

The captains continued to barter with the Salish on 6 September and also carefully recorded much of the Salish vocabulary. For a short time, they theorized that the Salish might be the legendary lost tribe of Welsh Indians, which supposedly came to the Americas in 1170. They later dropped any idea that the Salish could be descendants of the Welsh. That morning they purchased two more horses plus three colts for use as emergency rations. The corps now had approximately 40 horses and three colts, enough to carry their supplies and for most to ride. At noon the corps and the Indians departed the area; the corps went to the north and the Indians to the south.

Vignette 1: "Prosued our Course down the Creek to the forks about 5 miles where we met a part of the <Flat Head> [Tushepau] Nation of 33 lodges about 80 men 400 Total and least 500 horses, those people recved us friendly, threw white robes over our Sholders & Smoked in the pipes of peace, we Encamped with them & found them friendly but nothing but berries to eate a part of which they gave us, those Indians are well dressed with Skin Shirts & robes..." (Captain Clark, 4 September 1805, quoted in Gary Moulton, ed., *The Journals of the Lewis & Clark Expedition*, vol. 5, 187.)

Vignette 2: "we assembled the Chiefs & warriers and Spoke to them (with much dificuety as what we Said had to pass through Several languajes before it got into theirs, which is a gugling kind of languaje Spoken much thro the through [throat])... I purchased 11 horses & exchanged 7 for which we gave a fiew articles of merchendize. those people possess ellegant horses... They Call themselves Eoote-lash-Schute [Oat la shoot]..." (Captain Clark, 5 September, quoted in Gary Moulton, ed., *The Journals of the Lewis & Clark Expedition*, vol. 5, 188-189.)

Vignette 3: "The Indian dogs are so hungry and ravenous, that they eat 4 or 5 pair of our mockasons last night... They are a very friendly people; have plenty of robes and skins for covering, and a large stock of horses, some of which are very good; but they have nothing to eat but berries, roots and such articles of food. This band is on its way over to the Missouri or Yellow-stone river to hunt buffaloe. They are the whitest Indians I ever saw..." (Sergeant Gass, 5 September 1805, quoted in Gary Moulton, ed., *The Journals of the Lewis & Clark Expedition*, vol. 10, 138.)

Teaching Points:

Civil Affairs. *Civil Affairs* activities establish, maintain, influence, or exploit relations among civil authorities and the civilian populace in an area of operations to facilitate military operations. Evaluate the captains' dealings with the Shoshone and Salish Indians.

Selfless Service. General of the Army Omar N. Bradley stated: "The Nation today needs men who think in terms of service to their country and not in terms of their country's debt to them." During this phase of the expedition—over the divide, the Salmon River reconnaissance, and Lost Trail Pass—how did the actions of the captains and their men demonstrate the Army value of selfless service to their country?

Day 4
Stands 5A & B
(Over the Mountains)

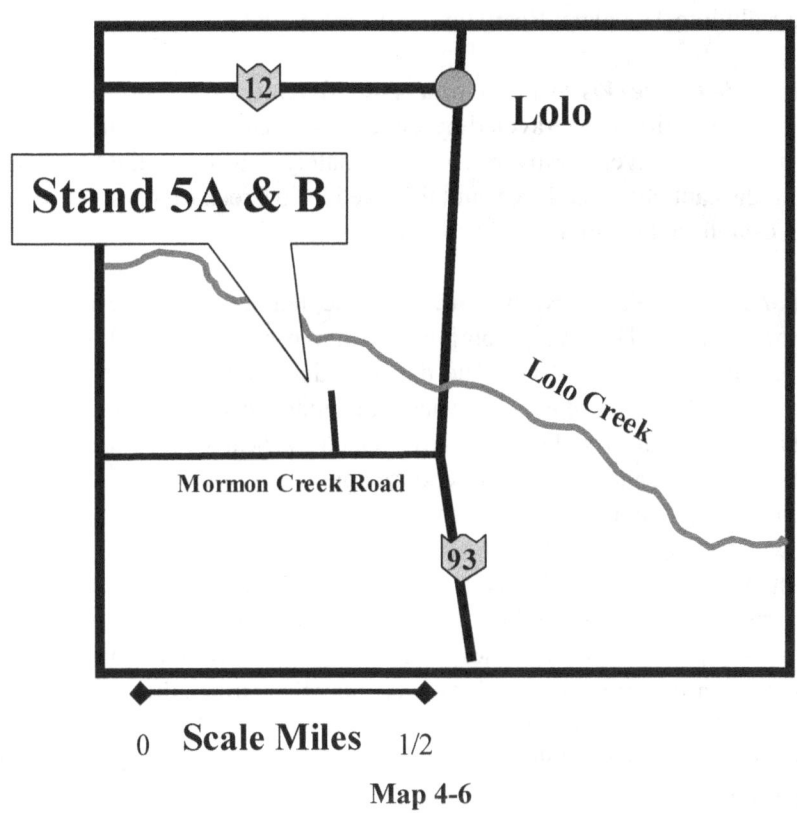

Map 4-6

Stand 5
Travelers' Rest
(9-10 September 1805)

Directions: From Hamilton, Montana, go north on US 93. At the southern outskirts of Lolo, Montana, turn right onto Mormon Creek Road. Then turn right into Travelers' Rest State Park.

Orientation (See Visuals 4-3 and 4-4, Appendix D): US 93 closely approximates the route traveled by the Corps of Discovery as it followed the Bitterroot River northward. Approximately 1 mile southeast of this point, the captains turned west and followed Lolo Creek to this spot, where they established camp in the flats below.

Situation 5A: **Westward Bound.** On 7 September 1805, the members of the Corps of Discovery continued to move northward following the present-day Bitterroot River. The day was dark and rainy, but they still managed to travel more than 22 miles. The hunters had significant success, bringing in two deer and several birds that day. A hearty meal that evening boosted morale, and Private Whitehouse noted in his journal his trust in the two captains. Their good spirits must have been somewhat dampened by the constant sight of the high mountains to the west, knowing they would eventually have to turn westward and cross them. They made 23 miles over relatively easy ground on 8 September and also added to their herd with the capture of two lame horses and a colt. They camped that evening near present-day Stevensville, Montana. On 9 September, the corps moved north to the vicinity of today's Lolo, Montana. That day Toby provided Clark with excellent intelligence for the future return trip to the east. He stated that, by following today's Clark Fork River and then the Blackfoot River, they would reach an excellent pass over the Continental Divide and then down to the Missouri River. Using Toby's information, the captains made a correct assessment of the route and determined it would return them to the vicinity of the Great Falls. It had taken the corps 53 days to get from the Great Falls to this point. Toby believed it would only take four days to get back to the Missouri River; it actually took Lewis' party nine days on the 1806 return trip.

On 9 September, the captains established a camp along a small creek that they called Travelers' Rest (today's Lolo Creek) near present-day Lolo, Montana. The captains chose the location, a well-used Indian campsite, based on advice from Toby. It was here the corps would leave the Bitterroot Valley and follow an Indian trail to the west over the mountains. The captains used the camp to make their final plans and preparations for the crossing. The men used the good weather to clean and repair their equipment. Taking advantage of the plentiful supply of game in the area, the captains also had the hunters add to their food supply. On 10 September, the hunters returned with fresh meat and were accompanied by three Indians they had encountered while hunting. The three Indians were searching for 25 horses stolen by the Shoshone. Lewis mistakenly called them "Flatheads," as with the Salish, but they were actually Nez Perce from the west side of the mountains. For Lewis, this was most important and irrefutable proof that the mountains could be crossed. The Nez Perce also provided additional intelligence to the captains. They insisted the mountains could be crossed in six days, which probably greatly encouraged the captains. It gave them hope that perhaps the Bitterroot Mountains were not as daunting as they appeared. The Indians also spoke of three other routes back to the Missouri River, each shorter than the route taken by the corps. Lewis may have mentally reviewed his orders from Jefferson instructing him to find "the most direct & practicable water communication across the continent." However, rather than taking time then to backtrack and confirm these alternate routes, the captains decided to complete their westward trek first and then explore the alternate routes on the return journey. One of the three Nez Perce also agreed to join them and help guide the corps back over the mountains. The corps remained at Travelers' Rest until 11 September. The party departed the camp at about 3 p.m., determined at last to cross over the mountains, their last major obstacle before reaching the rivers that flowed into the Pacific.

Vignette 1: "Our party seemed revived at the success that the hunters had met with, however in all the hardships that they had yet undergone they never once complained, trusting to Providence & the Conduct of our Officers in our difficulties..." (Private Whitehouse, 7 September 1805, quoted in Gary Moulton, ed., *The Journals of the Lewis & Clark Expedition*, vol. 11, 305.)

Vignette 2: "...encamped on a large creek which falls in on the West as our guide informes that we should leave the river at this place and the weather appearing settled and fair I determined to halt the next day rest our horses and take some scelestial Observations. we called this Creek *Travelers Rest...*" (Captain Lewis, 9 September 1805, quoted in Gary Moulton, ed., *The Journals of the Lewis & Clark Expedition*, vol. 5, 192.)

Teaching Points:

Operational Pause. FM 3-0, *Operations*, states an *operational pause* is a deliberate halt taken to extend operational reach or prevent culmination. Evaluate the captains' decision to pause at Travelers' Rest.

The Team. *Team* identity comes out of mutual respect among its members and trust between leaders and subordinates. The bond between leaders and subordinates likewise springs from mutual respect as well as from discipline (FM 22-100, 3-2). What does Private Whitehouse's journal entry for 7 September tell us about the Corps of Discovery as a team?

Situation 5B: **Eastward Bound.** The Corps of Discovery returned to Travelers' Rest on 30 June 1806 after a six-day crossing of the Bitterroot Mountains. Once again they used the site to rest and prepare for the next phase of the operation. It was also the site where they executed what may have been the captains' most controversial decision during the expedition. They had conceived a plan at Fort Clatsop over the previous winter to split the corps into multiple detachments to explore more ground on the return trip. At Travelers' Rest they rested for two days and finalized plans for dividing the expedition. The plan called for Captain Lewis to explore the Marias River and Captain Clark to explore the Yellowstone River. The NCOs would conduct supporting missions to recover the canoes and caches, portage equipment around the Great Falls, and move the horses to the Mandan villages.

From 3 July 1806 to 12 August 1806, the corps split into multiple detachments. Lewis departed Travelers' Rest with nine men, five Nez Perce guides, and 17 horses. He moved down the Bitterroot River to present-day Missoula, Montana, and then up the Big Blackfoot River. He then traveled along an Indian trail over the Continental Divide and followed the Sun River to the upper portage camp on the Missouri. At the upper portage camp, Lewis split his group into two detachments, one commanded by himself and the other by Sergeant Gass. The Gass Detachment, consisting of Sergeant Gass and Privates Frazer, Thompson, Werner, Goodrich, and McNeal, remained at the upper portage camp and prepared the cache for the portage around the falls. Lewis' Detachment, which included Drouillard and the Field brothers, moved cross-country to the Marias River to determine if the river continued north into the British fur trading grounds. Lewis followed the Marias River to present-day Cut Bank, Montana, where he decided the river did not continue north and so turned back to the Missouri.

Meanwhile, Clark departed Travelers' Rest with the main body of the corps. He followed the Bitterroot River toward Ross' Hole. He disregarded the previous route over Lost Trail Pass and followed the established Indian trail through the Salmon River valley to today's Gibbon Pass and into the Big Hole country. Clark arrived back at Camp Fortunate on 8 July 1806 and recovered the cache and canoes. Clark used the canoes to float down the Beaverhead River to the Jefferson River and then on to the Three Forks. Meanwhile, Sergeant Pryor and his six men herded the horses along parallel to the river. At the Three Forks, Clark divided his group into three detachments. He directed Sergeant Ordway and his nine men to take the canoes down the Missouri to the upper portage camp, where they were to link up with the Gass Detachment and continue on to the confluence of the Marias and Missouri Rivers. Clark ordered Sergeant Pryor to take three men and the remaining 26 horses cross-country to the Mandan villages. They were to negotiate with the Mandans and the Northwest Fur Company, using the horses as trading material. The goal was to persuade key Indian leaders to return with the corps to meet with President Jefferson. Clark took the Charbonneau family and five men to explore the Yellowstone River.

All the detachments had mixed success, with the exception of the Pryor Detachment. Not long after they departed from Clark, Crow Indians raided Pryor's camp and stole all the horses. Sergeant Pryor recovered from the mishap by directing his men to build bullboats from willow branches and buffalo skins. He then floated his detachment down the Yellowstone until he met Clark at the confluence of the Yellowstone and Missouri Rivers on 8 August 1806. Sergeant Ordway's group took the canoes down the Missouri to the upper portage camp. There he linked up with the Gass Detachment, and the combined group executed a portage around the falls. The two sergeants then moved the group to the confluence of the Missouri and Marias Rivers to wait for the Lewis Detachment. Clark's Detachment explored the Yellowstone River and arrived at the Missouri River on 3 August. There, he established a camp to wait for the remainder of the corps.

To the north, the Lewis Detachment experienced difficulty soon after turning back toward the Missouri River. On 26 July they encountered a group of young Blackfeet Indians and camped with them that night. The next morning, the Indians attempted to steal several rifles and horses. In the resulting scuffle, Private Reubin Field killed one Indian with a knife and Lewis mortally shot another. Lewis now found himself in the middle of hostile Blackfoot territory with no help within supporting distance. He decided the best course of action was to flee. He and his men rode 120 miles in 24 hours. Miraculously, they reached the Missouri River just as Ordway's and Gass's Detachments were floating by. The combined groups then floated down the river to link up with Clark at the Yellowstone River. Lewis' misfortune continued when Private Cruzatte accidentally shot him in the buttocks during a hunting accident. The Corps of Discovery reunited again on 12 August, not far from the confluence of the Yellowstone and Missouri Rivers.

Vignette 3: "All arrangements being now compleated for carrying into effect the several scheemes we had planed for execution on our return, we saddled our horses and set out I took my leave of my worthy friend and companion Capt. Clark and the party that accompanyed him. I could not avoid feeling much concern on this occasion although I hoped this separation was only momentary..." (Captain Lewis, 3 July 1806, quoted in Gary Moulton, ed., *The Journals of the Lewis & Clark Expedition*, vol. 8, 83.)

Vignette 4: "... and now (thanks to God) we are all together again in good health, except Captain Lewis, and his wound is not serious..." (Sergeant Gass, 12 August 1806, quoted in Gary Moulton, ed., *The Journals of the Lewis & Clark Expedition*, vol. 10, 266.)

Teaching Points:

Risk Management. *Risk Management* is the process of identifying, assessing, and controlling risk arising from operational factors, and the making of informed decisions that balance risk cost with mission benefits. Evaluate the captains' decision to split the corps, sending different detachments on multiple routes with multiple missions.

Collective Confidence. FM 22-100 states that *collective confidence* comes from winning under challenging and stressful conditions. In what ways does the captains' decision to split into four detachments demonstrate collective confidence?

Note on Lodging: CSI recommends group lodging at the end of day four in Lolo, Montana. Lolo offers numerous hotel and motel accommodations. Some offer reduced rates for large groups.

Day 5
The Challenge of the Rocky Mountains
(7 September to 7 October 1805)

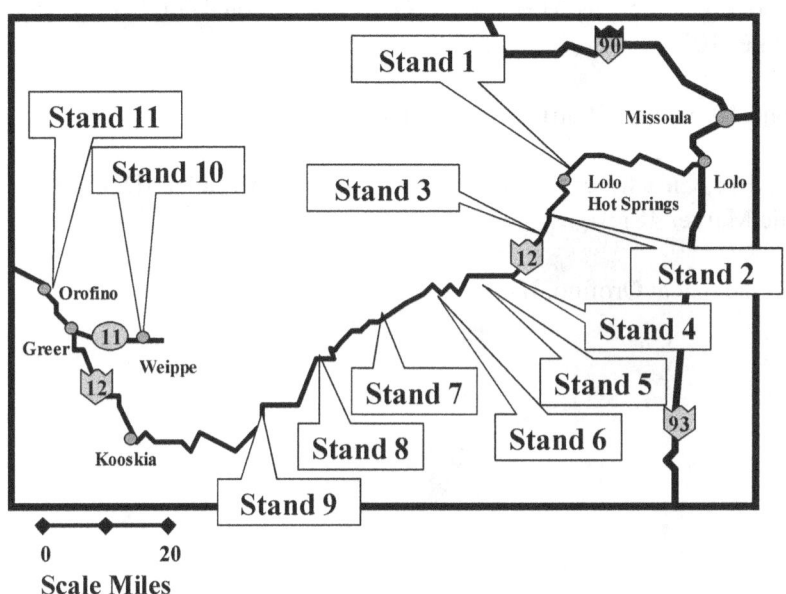

Map 5-1

Begin the day in Lolo, MT

Stand 1, Howard Creek (Interpretive Turnout, US 12, Mile Marker 9.5)

Stand 2, Packer Meadow (Lolo Pass Visitor Center, US 12)

Stand 3, Road not Taken (Interpretive Turnout, US 12, Mile Marker 172)

Stand 4, Colt Killed Camp (US 12, Powell Ranger Station)

Stand 5, Whitehouse Pond and Snow Bank Camp (Wendover Campground, US 12, Mile Marker 159)

Stand 6, Lonesome Cove Camp (Colgate Licks, US 12)

Stand 7, Sinque [Sink] Hole Camp (Eagle Mountain Pack Bridge, Mile Marker 136)

Stand 8, Sherman Peak (Fish Creek, US 12, Mile Marker 121)

Stand 9, Horse Steak Meadow (APGAR Recreation Area, US 12, Mile Marker 105)

Stand 10, Weippe Prairie (Weippe, ID)

Stand 11, Clearwater River (Canoe Camp Park, Ahsahka, ID, US 12, Mile Marker 48)

End the day at Orofino, ID

Day 5
Stand 1
(Howard Creek)

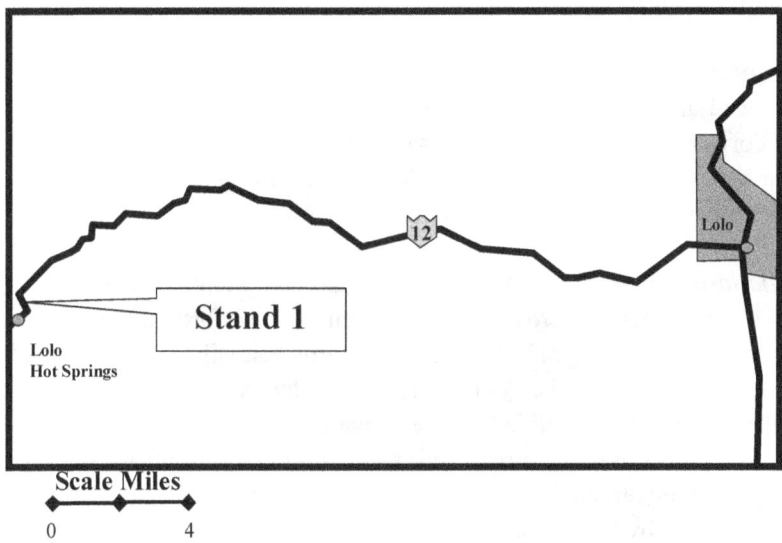

Map 5-2

Stand 1
Howard Creek
(11 - 12 September 1805)

Directions: From Lolo, go west on US 12 to mile marker 9.5. Park at the interpretive sign pullout on the left side of the road and orient the group toward the cleared field and Lolo Creek to the west.

Orientation (See Visual 5-1, Appendix D): The Corps of Discovery followed an Indian trail that closely approximates today's US 12. It took the corps two days to travel the same route you have just followed. The area today is much like it was in 1805 and is still very much uninhabited. The modern highway was not completed until 1962.

Situation: The captains planned to depart Travelers' Rest the morning of 11 September and cross over the mountains. Unfortunately, two of the horses strayed the night before, and the corps lost valuable time searching for the missing animals. While waiting for the expedition to get ready to move, the Nez Perce guide became impatient and quietly disappeared into the woods. He may have returned over the mountains ahead of the corps or, more likely, rushed on to join his two companions in searching for the horses stolen by the Shoshone.

The corps finally left Travelers' Rest at 3 p.m. with 40 horses and three colts. The men had accumulated extra food for the planned, six-day crossing and counted the colts as emergency rations. However, their feeding plan depended heavily upon supplementing their limited food supply with game the hunters could kill. They moved from Travelers' Rest along an established Indian trail to the vicinity of present-day Anderson Gulch. It is interesting to note that although the Indian trail was little more than a well-worn footpath, the captains referred to it as a road. The fact that the hunters saw no game that day foreshadowed hungry times ahead for the corps.

The corps' departure went much better on 12 August; it was able to begin moving around 7 a.m. Continuing to follow the Indian road, which stayed on higher ground, allowed the corps to avoid the dense brush along the creek. The road's frequent ups and downs over the steep terrain quickly tired the men and horses. The captains continued to push forward till approximately 8 p.m. and camped for the night near present-day Spring Gulch (the location of Stand 2). Some of the party had straggled and did not reach the campsite until 10 p.m.

Vignette 1: "The loss of 2 of our horses detained us util'. 3 oClock. P.M. our *Flathead* Indian being restless thought proper to leave us and proceed on alone..." (Captain Clark, 11 September 1805, quoted in Gary Moulton, ed., *The Journals of the Lewis & Clark Expedition*, vol. 5, 199.)*

Vignette 2: "Set out at 7 oClock & proceeded on up the Creek... at 2 miles assended a high hill & proceeded through a hilley and thickly timbered Countrey for 9 miles & on the Right of the Creek, passing Several branches from the right of fine clear water and Struck at a fork [Grave Creek] at which place the road forks, one passing up each fork... The road through this hilley Countrey is verry bad passing over hills & thro' Steep hollows, over falling timber continued on & passed Some most intolerable road on the Sides of the Steep Stony mountains, which might be avoided by keeping up the Creek which is thickly covered with under groth & falling timber ... Crossed a mountain 8 miles with out water & encamped on a hill Side on the Creek after Decending a long Steep mountain..." (Captain Clark, 12 September 1805, quoted in Gary Moulton, ed., *The Journals of the Lewis & Clark Expedition*, vol. 5, 201.)

Teaching Point:

Assessing the Situation. The captains planned an estimated six days for crossing the Bitterroot Mountains. They based their plan on the anticipated cooperation of the Nez Perce guide. Their six-day plan also depended heavily upon hunting successfully and foraging to supplement food supplies for the men and horses. Today our commanders use the factors of METT-TC to *assess the situation*. Using those METT-TC factors, update the captains' estimate of the situation after two days in the mountains.

---

* All vignettes retain the enigmatic writing of the journalists. See the introduction to Section III for an explanation of the editorial principles used with the journal entries.

Day 5
Stand 2
(Packer Meadow)
and
Stand 3
(The Road Not Taken)

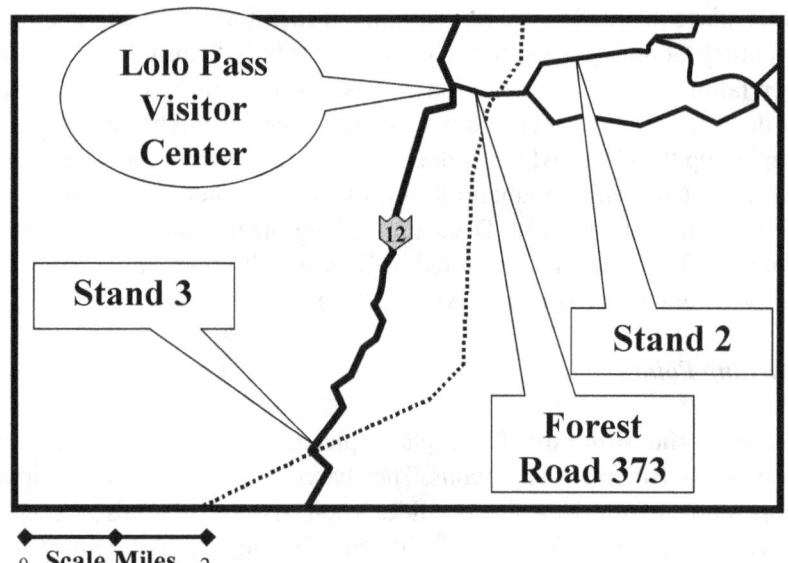

Map 5-3

Stand 2
Packer Meadow
(13 September 1805)

Directions: Continue west on US 12 to the top of the pass. At the Lolo Pass visitor center, go east for one mile on Forest Road 373.

Orientation (See Visual 5-2, Appendix D): These glades are among the few remaining spots along the Lewis and Clark Trail that still look much the same as they did when the captains first saw them. The Corps of Discovery entered the meadow at the northeast end and then followed the creek to the west. The camp was at the southwest end of the meadow.

Situation: On the morning of 13 September 1805, the Corps of Discovery again encountered difficulty collecting the horses. Lewis' horse and another had strayed from the Howard's Creek camp. The captains decided that, instead of delaying the whole group, Lewis and four privates would remain behind to search for the animals. Clark proceeded on with the main body and, later that morning, came upon some hot springs. Unfortunately Toby was confused by the multiple trails leading into and out of the hot springs and initially took the wrong trail. This caused the party to make a treacherous 3-mile detour to get back on the main trail. Clark was concerned about Lewis and decided to stop for lunch to allow time for Lewis to catch up. Lewis and the four privates rejoined the group during lunch but without the strays. The captains decided to continue westward but did send their two best hunters back to find the lost animals. They pushed over the top of the mountain ridge that serves today as a border between Montana and Idaho. At the top they found a beautiful open glade with a clear mountain stream running through it, a perfect campsite with easy access to water, firewood, and grass. The captains established a camp at the lower end of the meadow and named the creek Glade Creek (known today as Pack Creek).

Vignette 1: "a Short distance passed a Warm Spring, which nearly boiled where it Issued out of the rocks a Short distance below the natives has dammed it up to bathe themselves in, and the water in that place is considerable above blood heat. it runs out in Sundry places and Some places cooler than others. Several of us drank of the water, it has a little sulfur taste and very clear. these Springs are very beautiful to See, and we think them to be as good to bathe in &c. as any other ever yet found in the United States..." (Private Whitehouse, 13 September 1805, quoted in Gary Moulton, ed., *The Journals of the Lewis & Clark Expedition*, vol. 11, 312-313.)

Vignette 2: "as Several roads led from these Springs in different derections, my Guide took a wrong road and took us out of our rout 3 miles through intolerable rout, after falling into the right road I proceeded on thro tolerabl rout abt. 4 to 5 miles and halted to let our horses graze as well as waite for Capt Lewis who has not yet Come up… after he came up, and we proceeded over a mountain to the head of the Creek which we left to our left and at 6 miles from the place I nooned it, we fell on a Small Creek from the left which Passed through open glades Some of which ½ mil wide, we proceeded down this Creek about 2 miles to where the mountains Closed on either Side crossing the Creek Several times & Encamped…" (Captain Clark, 13 September 1805, quoted in Gary Moulton, ed., *The Journals of the Lewis & Clark Expedition*, vol. 5, 203.)

Teaching Points:

NCOs. The role of the NCO in the US Army has evolved over time. Today the NCOs are the backbone of the Army. They train, lead, and take care of enlisted soldiers. In short, the NCOs conduct the Army's daily business. The 13th of September was the second time strayed horses had interfered with the unit's movement. Did Lewis make the correct decision to stay behind with four men to look for the horses? Should he have detailed the responsibility to an NCO?

Value of the Staff Ride. The stand at Packer Meadow provides the opportunity to discuss staff riding in general. A private company planned to log this land in 1997. Through the modern miracle of e-mail, several Lewis and Clark activists were able to mobilize state agencies and sway public opinion to prevent the logging. Over the next two years, they raised money and purchased the land. They then donated the ground to the Idaho Department of Parks and Recreation, saving this historical piece of ground for future generations to enjoy. Much of what we have done today could be done in a classroom or briefing environment. Evaluate the linking of historical events with the actual terrain used in the staff ride methodology.

Stand 3
The Road Not Taken
(14 September 1805)

Directions: Continue west on US 12 to the vicinity of mile marker 172. Park the group at the interpretive sign pullout on the right side of the road.

Orientation (See Visual 5-2, Appendix D): The main Indian road crossed today's US 12 at this location and continued to the southwest toward the Nez Perce homeland. A secondary trail branched off the main trail about 1 mile to the east and then paralleled the modern highway down to the Lochsa River. The Salish Indians used the secondary trail to get to fishing areas on the river.

Situation: Toby led the Corps of Discovery out of the Packer Meadow Camp the morning of 14 September 1806. He continued to lead them along the Indian road with the intention of remaining on the trail that crossed over the mountains to the Nez Perce homeland. Unfortunately, he missed a turn and instead took a side trail. His mistake was understandable because the side trail was a well-worn path that showed heavier and more frequent use than the Nez Perce trail. The Salish Indians had established the side trail as a route to fishing sites on a nearby river. It was a costly mistake, which resulted in adding a full day to the corps' passage through the mountains. The good news that day was that the hunters dispatched earlier to find the missing horse and colt rejoined the group with the missing horse; the colt was not found.

Teaching Point:

Assessing the Situation. The captains were unaware at this point that Toby had missed an important turn and added another day to their crossing of the mountains. Using the METT-TC factors, update the captains' estimate of the situation at day four in the mountains.

Day 5
Stand 4
(Colt Killed Camp)
and
Stand 5
(Whitehouse Pond and Snow Bank Camp)

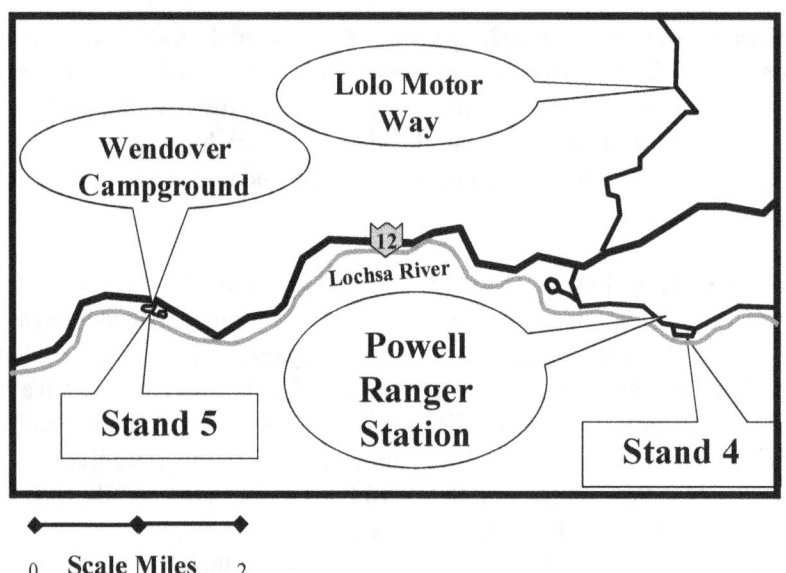

Map 5-4

Stand 4
Colt Killed Camp
(14 September 1805)

Directions: Continue west on US 12 to mile marker 162 and turn left into the Powell Ranger Station. (Note: this stand may be done in the parking lot of the ranger station or, with the permission of the rangers, at the helicopter pad. The helicopter pad is the location of the 14 September campsite.)

Orientation (See Visual 5-2, Appendix D): We're currently located in the Lochsa River Valley. The captains referred to the river as the Flathead River or Kooskooskee River. Toby led the group from the vicinity of the previous stand (The Road Not Taken) down the ridge and then along a small tributary creek to this location.

Situation: Late in the day, Toby recognized he had lost the Nez Perce trail. The road should have remained on ridge tops and not descended into a river valley. The Corps of Discovery camped that evening on the banks of the Kooskooskee River (today's Lochsa) just opposite a small pine island and made plans to find the correct road the next day. The long march and heavy labor of moving the pack animals along the mountain trails had exhausted the men. To make matters worse, the hunters had no success in bringing in any meat. Ironically, today's game-rich Bitterroot Mountains were not rich in game in 1805. It wasn't until the later settlement of the plains drove deer and elk into the mountains that the Bitterroot Mountains became the game paradise it is today. The daily labor of moving through the mountains costs a person 4,000 to 5,000 calories a day (three MREs provide approximately 4,000 calories). Each man needed about 8 to 10 pounds of meat per day to meet his daily requirement. Lewis attempted to ease their hunger with a meal of portable soup, but the men wanted meat. Therefore, the captains agreed to kill one of the colts for food.

Vignette 1: "... none of the hunters killed any thing except 2 or 3 pheasants; on which, without a miracle it was impossible to feed 30 hungry men and upwards, besides some Indians. So Capt. Lewis gave out some portable soup, which he had along, to be used in cases of necessity. Some of the men did not relish this soup, and agreed to kill a colt; which they immediately did, and set about roasting it; and which appeared to me to be good eating..." (Sergeant Gass, 14 September 1805, quoted in Gary Moulton, ed., *The Journals of the Lewis & Clark Expedition*, vol. 10, 142.)

Vignette 2: "Encamped opposit a Small Island at the mouth of a branch on the right side of the river which is at this place 80 yards wide, Swift and Stony, here we wer compelled to kill a Colt for our men & Selves to eat for the want of meat & we named the South fork Colt killed Creek, and this river we Call *Flathead* River. The Mountains which we passed to day much worst than yesterday the last excessively bad & Thickly Strowed with falling timber… our men and horses much fatigued…" (Captain Clark, 14 September 1805, quoted in Gary Moulton, ed., *The Journals of the Lewis & Clark Expedition*, vol. 5, 205.)

Teaching Point:

Logistics. Lewis' extensive logistics planning and preparations played a major role in the success of the expedition. Examples include the whiskey supply lasting till July 1805 and the tobacco lasting till March 1806. What was the status of the corps' feeding plan at the end of day four in the mountains?

Stand 5
Whitehouse Pond and Snow Bank Camp
(15 September 1805)

Directions: Continue west on US 12 and watch for mile marker 159. Then turn left into the Wendover Campground. Park near the interpretive sign and take the path to a small clearing next to the river.

Orientation (See Visual 5-2, Appendix D): The Colt Killed Camp is approximately 4 miles upriver. The corps route came down the north side of the Lochsa and paralleled US 12 to the present location of Wendover Campground. The woods to the northwest are the base of Wendover Ridge.

Situation: Toby recognized he had lost the trail and was looking for a way to rejoin the Indian road. He led the group down Kooskooskee River about 4 miles to a long ridge that provided a route back up to the mountains. The ridge reached down to the river and, at its base, was 3,200 feet above sea level. It then climbed for 6 miles back to the Indian road along a major east-to-west spine of the mountains at about 5,800 feet. The Corps of Discovery spent the majority of the day climbing the mountainside to reach the main Indian road to the west. The climb was incredibly difficult because of the steep ascent and the abundance of deadfall timber blocking the route. At one point in the climb, the horse carrying Clark's field desk rolled down a 40-yard slope. The horse survived, but the desk was smashed. Approximately halfway up the ridge, the captains halted the group at a spring to rest and let the stragglers catch up. They had hoped to establish a night camp at the top of the ridge but could not find water, so they continued west a short distance. Clark halted the group at an old snow bank to make camp. They melted some of the snow to make the evening meal of portable soup. The corps had made only 12 miles that day, and the captains were somewhat discouraged. They had expected a six-day passage, and now, at day five in the mountains, they could see nothing but mountains in every direction.

Vignette 1: "We set out early, the morning Cloudy, and proceeded on Down the right Side of [Kooskooskee] River over Steep points rockey and buschey as usial, for 4 miles to an old Indian fishing place, here the road leaves the river to the left and assends a *mountain* winding in every direction to get up the Steep assents & to pass the emence quantity of falling timber which had falling from dift causes i.e., fire & wind and has

175

deprived the Greater part of the Southerly Sides of this mountain of its gren timber, 4 miles up the mountain I found a Spring and halted for the rear to come up and to let our horses rest and feed, about 2 hours the rear of the party came up much fatigued & horses more So, Several horses Sliped and rolled down Steep hills which hurt them verry much The one which Carried my desk and Small trunk Turned over and roled down a mountain for 40 yards & lodged against a tree, broke the Desk the horse escaped and appeared but little hurt. Some others very much hurt…

From this mountain I could observe high ruged mountains in every direction as far as I could See. with the greatest exertion we Could only make 12 miles up this mountain and encamped on the top of the mountain near a Bank of Old Snow about 3 feet deep lying on the Northern Side of the <hills> mountain and in Small banks on the top and leavel parts of the mountain…" (Captain Clark, 15 September 1805, quoted in Gary Moulton, ed., *The Journals of the Lewis & Clark Expedition*, vol. 5, 206-207.)

Vignette 2: "Having breakfasted on colt, we moved on down the river 3 miles, and again took the mountains. In going up, one of the horses fell, and required 8 or 10 men to assist him in getting up again. We continued our march to 2 o'clock when we halted at a spring and dined on portable soup and a handful of parched corn. We then proceeded on our journey over the mountains to a high point, where, it being dark, we were obliged to encamp. There was here no water; but a bank of snow answered as a substitute; and we supped upon soup." (Sergeant Gass, 15 September 1805, quoted in Gary Moulton, ed., *The Journals of the Lewis & Clark Expedition*, vol. 10, 142-143.)

Teaching Point:

Updating the Estimate. Again using today's METT-TC factors, update the captains' estimate for crossing the mountains. Factors to consider include: fatigue; Toby the guide has lost the trail twice, one minor detour of three miles and one major detour that cost a full day; lack of game and forage in the mountains; one colt killed for emergency rations; and Clark's statement: "From this mountain I could observe high rugged mountains in every direction as far as I could see."

Day 5
- Stand 6 (Lonesome Cove Camp)
- Stand 7 (Sinque Hole Camp)
- Stand 8 (Sherman Peak)
- Stand 9 (Horse Steak Meadow)
- Stand 10 (Weippe Prairie)

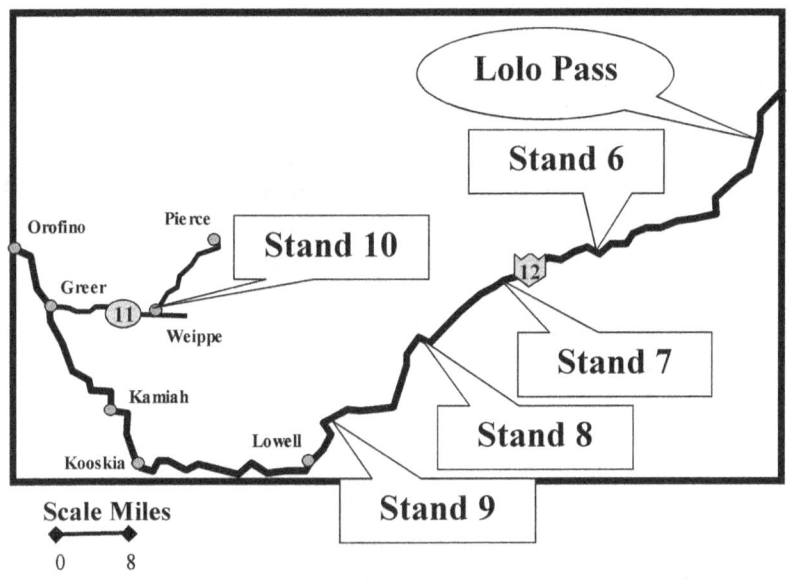

Map 5-5

**Stand 6
Lonesome Cove Camp
(16 September)**

Directions: Continue west on US 12 and park at the Colgate Licks Interpretive Signs.

Orientation (See Visual 5-3, Appendix D): The trail the Corps of Discovery followed was about 5 miles to the north and parallel to the modern highway.

Situation: The Corps of Discovery continued to struggle to the west on 16 September, the sixth day in the mountains. Their plight worsened when it snowed all day, adding 4 inches on top of several existing inches of snow; and Clark, the one who rarely complained, feared his feet would freeze. The route was incredibly difficult and greatly taxed the strength of the men and horses. To make it easier on the weary men, Clark forged ahead with one man to break the trail, establish a camp and get a fire going. The corps stumbled into Clark's camp that evening, having made only 13 miles. The captains ordered a second colt killed for food to help revive the spirits of the men.

Vignette 1: "some of the men without Socks raped rags on their feet, and loaded up our horses and Set out without any thing to eat, and proceeded on… all being tired & hungry, obledged us to kill another colt…" (Private Whitehouse, 16 September 1805, quoted in Gary Moulton, ed., *The Journals of the Lewis & Clark Expedition*, vol. 11, 318-319.)

Vignette 2: "… proceeded over the most terrible mountains I ever beheld…" (Sergeant Gass, 16 September 1805, quoted in Gary Moulton, ed., *The Journals of the Lewis & Clark Expedition*, vol. 10, 143.)

Vignette 3: "began to Snow about 3 hours before Day and Continud all day the Snow in The morning 4 Inches deep on The old Snow, and by night we found it from 6 to 8 Inches deep... I have been wet and as cold in every part as I ever was in my life, indeed I was at one time fearfull my feet would freeze in the thin Mockersons which I wore... men all wet cold and hungary. Killed a Second Colt which we all Suped hartily on and thought it fine meat… to describe the road of this day would be a repitition of yesterday excpt the Snow which made it much wors…" (Captain Clark, 16 September 1805, quoted in Gary Moulton, ed., *The Journals of the Lewis & Clark Expedition*, vol. 5, 209.)

Teaching Point:

Motivation. *Motivation* gives subordinates the will to do everything they can to accomplish a mission. How did the captains and NCOs motivate the Corps of Discovery to continue moving west?

Stand 7
Sinque Hole Camp
(17-18 September)

Directions: Continue west on US 12 to the vicinity of mile marker 136. Park at the Eagle Mountain Pack Bridge turnout.

Orientation (See Visual 5-3, Appendix D): The Indian trail the corps followed is parallel to the modern highway. The Sinque [Sink] Hole Camp is approximately 5.5 miles to the north.

Situation: The challenge of crossing the mountains was not only difficult for the members of the Corps of Discovery but also extremely hard on the horses. The horses were in very poor condition because of heavy physical labor and the lack of food. On the night of 17 September, the NCOs should have directed the men to hobble the horses to prevent them from wandering away to find food. However, they failed to direct the hobbling, and as a result, all the animals scattered to find forage. The men spent the next morning gathering the horses. One of the horses was found several miles to the rear. It was the mare of the colt killed the previous day; she was searching for her missing colt. All of this caused a significant delay, and by the time the horses were packed for movement, the corps was not ready to depart until 1:00 p.m.

Again the trail was "excessively bad," and they were only able to make 10 miles that day. One of their significant challenges was the deep snow. The captains could see the mountain valleys below them had no snow, but they kept to the Indian trail along the top of the ridges. They were determined to proceed along the trail, knowing it was the established route to the Nez Perce homeland. They also knew from experience that the river valley would be clogged with even more deadfall than the current route was. That evening they camped near a sinkhole, and the captains ordered the last colt killed for the evening meal.

The captains discussed their situation and determined that the corps was near its breaking point. The food supply was almost gone; men and horses alike were near starvation. They considered two options, retreat to Travelers' Rest for the winter or continue to the west. In their analysis they decided retreat was not a viable option. They did not have the strength or supplies to backtrack six days to the Bitterroot Valley; in fact they would rather die than give up. Their only hope for survival was to continue to the west out of the "terrible mountains." The captains decided to split the corps in a "do-or-die" attempt to overcome the terrain. A small advance party of the strongest men and horses would forge ahead rapidly to find food, and the main body would struggle along as best as it could. The advance party would then come back and rescue the main body as soon as it found food. They also decided that Clark, the stronger of the two captains, would lead the advance party.

The next morning, 18 September 1805, Clark moved ahead with six men. He believed the advance party could move at double or triple the corps' current rate of march because it was unencumbered with pack animals. He also reasoned his smaller group, traveling light and fast, had a better chance of finding game and could leave excess food along the trail for the following main body. He was determined to get out of the mountains, find food, and rescue Lewis' party.

Vignette 1: "Camped at a small Branch on the mountain near a round deep Sinque hole full of water..." (Private Whitehouse, 17 September 1805, quoted in Gary Moulton, ed., *The Journals of the Lewis & Clark Expedition*, vol. 11, 319.)

Vignette 2: "The want of provisions together with the difficuely of passing those emence mountains dampened the Spirits of the party which induced us to resort to Some plan of reviving ther sperits. I deturmined to take a party of the hunters and proceed on in advance to some leavel Country, where there was game to kill ...& send it back..." (Captain Clark, 18 September 1805, quoted in Gary Moulton, ed., *The Journals of the Lewis & Clark Expedition*, vol. 5, 213.)

Vignette 3: "Captain Clark set out this morning to go ahead with six hunters. there being no game in these mountains we concluded it would be better for one of us to take the hunters and hurry on to the leavel country a head and there hunt and provide some provisions <for> while the other remained with and brought on the party the latter of these was my part..." (Captain Lewis, 18 September 1805, quoted in Gary Moulton, ed., *The Journals of the Lewis & Clark Expedition*, vol. 5, 211.)

Teaching Point:

Honor and Duty. FM 22-100 states that *honor* holds all other Army values together. In what ways does the decision to send Clark ahead demonstrate that the captains, NCOs, and men of the Corps of Discovery understood our present-day Army value of honor?

**Stand 8
Sherman Peak
(18 September 1805)**

Directions: Continue west on US 12 to the vicinity of mile marker 121. Park the group at the river access for Fish Creek and walk down to the river for a view of the creek.

Orientation (See Visual 5-4, Appendix D): The Indian trail is north of and parallel to the highway. Sherman Peak is 6 miles to the north, and the Hungry Creek Camp is 4.5 miles northwest along the creek.

Situation: The Corps of Discovery dined the morning of 18 September on what remained of the colt killed the night before. At daylight Clark moved out with his small advance party. After traveling about 20 miles, a glimmer of hope encouraged Clark when he saw, in the far distance, an "immense plain and level country," the end of the mountains. He had climbed to the top of a nearby ridge for a view to the west. Today the ridge is called Sherman Peak or Spirit Revival Ridge. Clark made another 12 miles that day, totaling 32 miles over rugged and difficult terrain. Finding no game that day, Clark named a nearby creek Hungry Creek to commemorate the group's hunger.

Lewis had also resumed writing in his journals on 18 September; he had made only two entries during the previous three weeks. He had intended to depart with the corps soon after sunrise that morning, but, again, difficulties with the horses delayed the corps' departure. It appears Lewis had given specific instructions for the care of the horses the night before, but Private Willard had somehow failed to carry out his portion of the instructions and lost one of the mares. Lewis didn't want to lose the morning searching for the horse, so he moved the group out at 8:30 a.m. without Willard who he left behind to search for the missing horse. Late that afternoon Private Willard rejoined the group without the horse. Lewis' group, encumbered by its late start and the slow-moving pack animals, made only 18 miles that day, 14 less than Clark's advance party. Lewis' journal entry for 18 September showed his understanding of their critical situation. The men and horses were nearing starvation, but their dependence on the packhorses precluded the possibility of killing another horse for food.

Vignette 1: "a fair morning cold I proceeded on in advance with Six hunters... from the top of a high part of the mountain at 20 miles I had a view of an emence Plain and leavel Countrey to the S W & West at a great distance. made 32 miles and Encamped on a bold running Creek passing to the left which I call *Hungry Creek* as at that place we had nothing to eate..." (Captain Clark, 18 September 1805, quoted in Gary Moulton, ed., *The Journals of the Lewis & Clark Expedition*, vol. 5, 213-214.)

Vignette 2: "I directed the horses to be gotten up early being determined to force my march as much as the abilities of horses would permit. the negligence of one of the party Willard who had a spare horse <in> not attending to him and bringing him up last evening was the cause of our detention this morning until ½ after 8 A M when we set out..." (Captain Lewis, 18 September 1805, quoted in Gary Moulton, ed., *The Journals of the Lewis & Clark Expedition*, vol. 5, 211.)

Vignette 3: "we marched 18 miles this day and encamped on the side of a steep mountain... We dined & suped on a skant proportion of portable soup... a little bears oil and about 20 lbs. of candles form our stock of provision, the only recourses being our guns & packhorses. the first is but a poor dependence in our present situation where there is nothing upon earth exept ourselves and a few small pheasants, small gray Squirrels, a blue bird of the vulture kind..." (Captain Lewis, 18 September 1805, quoted in Gary Moulton, ed., *The Journals of the Lewis & Clark Expedition*, vol. 5, 211-213.)

Teaching Point:

Will. Captain Lewis had previously demonstrated the inner drive of *will* from the top of Lemhi Pass when he discovered that the hope of a waterborne northwest passage did not exist. How does the corps' situation in the Bitterroot Mountains demonstrate the will of the captains and their men?

Stand 9
Horse Steak Meadow
(19 September 1805)

Directions: Continue west on US 12 to the vicinity of mile marker 105 and turn into the APGAR Recreation Campground. Follow the campground road to the right and park where the group has a view of the mountains to the northwest.

Orientation (See Visual 5-4, Appendix D): The historical trail is parallel to the highway. Horse Steak Meadow is 11 miles to the north, and the Cedar Creek Camp is 10 miles to the northwest.

Situation: The Corps of Discovery continued to move in two groups on 19 September 1805. Clark departed the Hungry Creek camp at daylight and continued his rapid pace to get out of the mountains. His hunters happened on a lost Indian horse early in the morning, and the unfortunate animal quickly became the hungry men's breakfast. They ate what they needed and then hung the rest in a tree for Lewis and the main body of the corps. Today the site is remembered as Horse Steak Meadow. Clark's route took them over two mountain ridges, and because of the tremendous amount of deadfall, they were only able to make 22 miles. He remarked in his journal that having to go around the profusion of fallen timber actually doubled the 22 miles they traveled. He summed up his description of the route with the simple but telling words, "road bad."

Lewis' group also managed to break camp and move out at daylight. Perhaps his disciplining of Private Willard the morning before had affected how the men cared for their horses. Following along Clark's path, Lewis also climbed to the top of Sherman Peak and saw the distant prairies, which he estimated where about 60 miles away. Despite his belief that the prairies were a three- or four-day march away, he allowed old Toby to boost morale by claiming the prairies were within one hard day's march. Toby's estimate was actually closer than Lewis', as the prairies were, as the crow flies, only 30 miles from Sherman Peak. However, Toby's estimate did not take into account that the mountain trail was "excessively dangerous" or the poor condition of the men and horses. Strong, well-provisioned men and horses might have been able to make it in one day, but the corps was suffering from malnutrition and in the early stages of starvation. Because of their malnutrition, the men were also very susceptible to infections, and many of them were sick. It is a testament to Lewis' and the sergeants' leadership that they managed to make 18 miles that day.

Vignette 1: "Set out early. Proceeded on up the [Hungry] Creek, passing through a Small glade at 6 miles at which place we found a horse. I derected him killed and hung up for the party after takeing a brackfast off for our Selves which we thought fine after Brackfast proceed on up the Creek two miles & left it to our right passed over a mountain... and through much falling timber... road bad..." (Captain Clark, 19 September 1805, quoted in Gary Moulton, ed., *The Journals of the Lewis & Clark Expedition*, vol. 5, 216.)

Vignette 2: "One of our horses fell down the precipice about 100 feet, and was not killed, nor much hurt: the reason was, that there is no bottom below, and the precipice, the only bank, which the creek has; therefore the horse pitched into the water, without meeting with any intervening object, which could materially injure him... Having heard nothing from our hunters, we again supped upon some of our portable soup. The men are becoming lean and debilitated, on account of the scarcity and poor quality of the provisions on which we subsist: our horses' feet are also becoming very sore. We have, however, some hopes of getting soon out of this horrible mountainous desert, as we have discovered the appearance of a valley or level part of the country about 40 miles ahead. When this discovery was made there was as much joy and rejoicing among the corps, as happens among passengers at sea, who have experienced a dangerous and protracted voyage, when they first discover land on the long looked for coast..." (Sergeant. Gass, 19 September 1805, quoted in Gary Moulton, ed., *The Journals of the Lewis & Clark Expedition*, vol. 10, 144-145.)

Vignette 3: "the road was excessively dangerous along this creek being a narrow rockey path generally on the side of steep precipice... we encamped on the Stard. side of it in a little raviene, having traveled 18 miles over a very bad road. we took a small quantity of portable soup, and retired to rest much fatiegued. several of the men are unwell of the disentary. brakings out, or irruptions of the Skin, have also been common with us for some time..." (Captain Lewis, 19 September 1805, quoted in Gary Moulton, ed., *The Journals of the Lewis & Clark Expedition*, vol. 5, 215.)

Teaching Point:

Selfless Service and Teamwork. Why is *selfless service* an essential element of *teamwork*? In what ways does the corps' crossing of the Bitterroot Mountains demonstrate selfless service and teamwork?

Day 5
Stand 10
(Weippe Prairie)

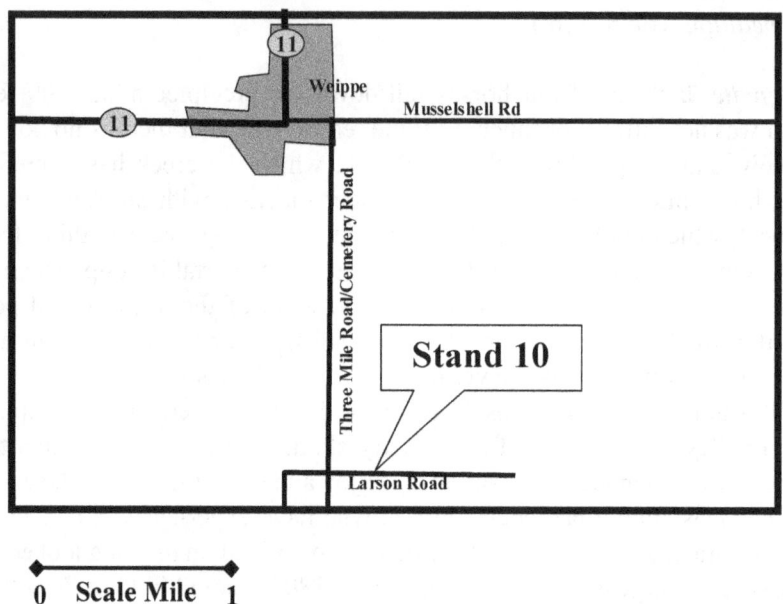

Map 5-6

Stand 10
Weippe Prairie
(20 – 23 September 1805)

Directions: Continue to follow US 12 to the west and pass through Kooskia and Kamiah, Idaho. At the town of Greer, take Route 11 to the east out of the river valley onto the upper prairie to Weippe. When Route 11 turns to the left in the center of Weippe, go straight instead for .2 miles and then turn right on Cemetery Road. At 1.7 miles, turn left on Larson Road and watch for the Lewis and Clark interpretive sign. Park and orient the group toward the prairie beyond the signs.

Orientation (See Visual 5-5, Appendix D): These prairies are part of the traditional homeland of the Nez Perce Indians. The Corps of Discovery entered the prairies from the Bitterroot Mountains to the east.

Situation: On 20 September, Clark's group marched out of the mountains onto the prairie and saw an Indian village in the distance. About a mile from camp, they came upon three Indian boys. The encounter surprised and frightened the boys, as Clark and his men were dirty, unshaven, and near starvation. Indian legend later described them as human-like creatures with hair on their faces and eyes like fish. The Nez Perce had a long-standing prophecy that strange men would come from the east and change things forever. In accordance with the prophecy, they provided a cordial welcome to the white men. Clark called them the Cho-pun-ish or pierced noses; they referred to themselves as the NeMeePoo, the people. He found the first camp about 3 miles southeast of present-day Weippe on Jim Ford Creek. It was occupied mainly by women, children, and elderly, because the warriors were away raiding Shoshone camps to the southwest. The elders of the first camp led them to a second village about 1 mile southwest of Weippe, where the women provided buffalo meat, dried salmon, berries, and camas to the starved men. Unfortunately, Clark and many of the men overate and made themselves sick.

Back in the mountains, Lewis' group again had problems collecting the horses that had scattered to find food. Lewis didn't seem to be overly concerned about the delay and devoted a full page in his journal to the description of a species of bird he had never seen before. He finally got the group packed and on the road at about 10 a.m. They soon found the horsemeat left by Clark, but Lewis wanted to make up the time they had lost that morning while collecting the horses. Therefore, he packed up the horsemeat and kept the group moving until 1 o'clock. He then allowed the men to rest and dine on the horsemeat. Unfortunately, Private Lepage allowed Lewis' packhorse to stray and Lewis again delayed the group's departure to search for the horse. At 3 p.m. he decided to leave two good men behind to continue the search while he continued west with the remainder of the group. The men made about 15 miles before they stopped to camp. That night they dined well on the remainder of the horsemeat.

The next day, 21 September, Captain Clark's first priority was to send help back to his friend Lewis and the remainder of the Corps of Discovery. He loaded a packhorse with roots and three large Salmon and sent it with Private Reubin Field back into the mountains to find Lewis. Clark spent the remainder of the day gathering intelligence from the Nez Perce about the route to the Pacific. The camp elders made up a map for Clark that showed the route to the Pacific. They also informed him of a greater chief that lived near the river to the west. Clark then traveled to the camp of Chief Twisted Hair on the Clearwater River just to the south of present-day Orofino, Idaho. He arrived there about 11 p.m., and it appears that Clark and Chief Twisted Hair struck up an almost immediate friendship. Clark also met another individual who, unbeknownst to the corps, became very influential in the survival of the corps. Clark simply referred to her as a squaw. Nez Perce tradition calls her Watkuweis, or "Gone from home and come back." She had spent time earlier as a captive of white men, yet seemed to have an overall positive impression of the strange people from the east. Later, when the Nez Perce elders discussed whether they should continue to befriend the white men or kill them, hers was the influential voice that convinced the elders to do them no harm.

That same day, Lewis delayed his group's departure to allow time for the two men sent back for the missing horse to catch up. He waited until 11 a.m. and then moved out, even though the missing men and horse had not arrived. Despite their leisurely morning of rest, the group was only able to make 11 miles that day. The road was extremely bad, and the march quickly tired the worn-out men and horses. Lewis was able to provide his men with a "hearty meal" that evening. They dined on a wolf, a few grouse, some crayfish, and the last of the horsemeat. Despite the good meal that night, Lewis expressed some concern about the next day in his journal entry. Perhaps he felt the men had only one more day left in them before they collapsed from exhaustion and sickness. He seemed determined to get them out of the mountains the next day. He was worried about procuring another day's supply of food and closed his journal entry with a deep concern about his and the men's health.

Lewis wanted to get an early start the next morning, their 12th day in the mountains. He had directed the horses hobbled the night before, but once again, one man failed to comply. It was 11 a.m. before they could get on the road. However, this did allow the two men left hunting the other horse time to finally catch up with the group. They had found the missing horse and retrieved the baggage it had carried. Unfortunately, they later not only lost that horse again, but also the one they had taken back with them. They consequently marched into camp carrying the recovered baggage on their backs. Good news came a few miles farther to the west that morning when Lewis' party met Reubin Field with the packhorse loaded with food. Later that day they marched out onto the prairie. Lewis had "triumphed over the mountains."

Clark had spent that same day, 22 September, briefly exploring the Clearwater River looking for trees suitable for canoes. He and Chief Twisted Hair had then returned to the Weippe Prairie, hoping to join Lewis and the remainder of the corps. On the return trip, Clark, riding a borrowed horse, was thrown three times, which gave him a bad limp for several days. The two captains met that evening at the Nez Perce village near present-day Weippe, Idaho. Clark probably wanted to share what he had learned about the route to the Pacific and to develop future plans with Lewis, but he realized Lewis first needed to eat and rest. Remembering his experience with eating too much his first day out of the mountains, Clark warned Lewis about the danger of overeating. However, Lewis failed to heed the warning and suffered the consequences.

Vignette 1: "I find myself verry unwell all the evening from eateing the fish & roots too freely..." (Captain Clark, 20 September 1805, quoted in Gary Moulton, ed., *The Journals of the Lewis & Clark Expedition*, vol. 5, 223.)

Vignette 2: "we had proceeded about 2 miles when we found the greater part of a horse which Capt Clark had met with and killed for us. he informed me by note that he should proceed as fast as possible to the leavel country which lay to the S.W. of us, which we discovered from the hights of the mountains on the 19th there he intended to hunt untill our arrival. at one oclock we halted and made a hearty meal on our horse beef much to the comfort of our hungry stomachs. here I larnt that one of the Packhorses with his load was missing and immediately dispatched Baptiest Lapage who had charge of him, to surch for him. he returned at 3 OC without the horse. The load of the horse was of considerable value consisting of merchandize and all my stock of winter cloathing. I therefore dispatched two of my best woodsmen in search of him..." (Captain Lewis, 20 September 1805, quoted in Gary Moulton, ed., *The Journals of the Lewis & Clark Expedition*, vol. 5, 218.)

Vignette 3: "we killed a few Pheasants, and I killed a prairie woolf which together with the ballance of our horse beef and some crawfish which we obtained in the creek enabled us to make one more hearty meal, not knowing where the next was to be found... I find myself growing weak for the want of food and most of the men complain of a similar deficiency, and have fallen off very much..." (Captain Lewis, 21 September 1805, quoted in Gary Moulton, ed., *The Journals of the Lewis & Clark Expedition*, vol. 5, 226.)

Vignette 4: "Notwithstanding my positive directions to hubble the horses last evening one of the men neglected to comply. he plead ignorance of the order. this neglect however detained us untill ½ after eleven OCk at which time we renewed our march, our course being about west..." (Captain Lewis, 22 September 1805, quoted in Gary Moulton, ed., *The Journals of the Lewis & Clark Expedition*, vol. 5, 228.)

Vignette 5: "the pleasure I now felt in having tryumphed over the rocky Mountains and decending once more to a level and fertile country where there was every rational hope of finding comfortable subsistence for myself and party can be more readily conceived than expressed, nor was the flattering prospect of the final success of the expedition less pleasing..." (Captain Lewis, 22 September 1805, quoted in Gary Moulton, ed., *The Journals of the Lewis & Clark Expedition*, vol. 5, 229.)

Vignette 6: "I found Capt Lewis & the party Encamped, much fatigued, & hungry, much rejoiced to find something to eate of which They appeared to partake plentifully. I cautioned them of the Consequences of eating too much..." (Captain Clark, 22 September 1805, quoted in Gary Moulton, ed., *The Journals of the Lewis & Clark Expedition*, vol. 5, 230.)

Vignette 7: "Capt. Lewis & 2 men verry Sick this evening..." (Captain Clark, 23 September 1805, quoted in Gary Moulton, ed., *The Journals of the Lewis & Clark Expedition*, vol. 5, 232.)

Teaching Point:

Host Nation Support. Lewis placed much value on *host nation support* in his logistics planning. One of the best examples is the importance the captains placed on finding the Shoshone Indians before attempting to cross the Rocky Mountains. Did Lewis' logistics planning take into account the critical support the Nez Perce provided to the Corps of Discovery?

Day 5
Stand 11
(Clearwater River)

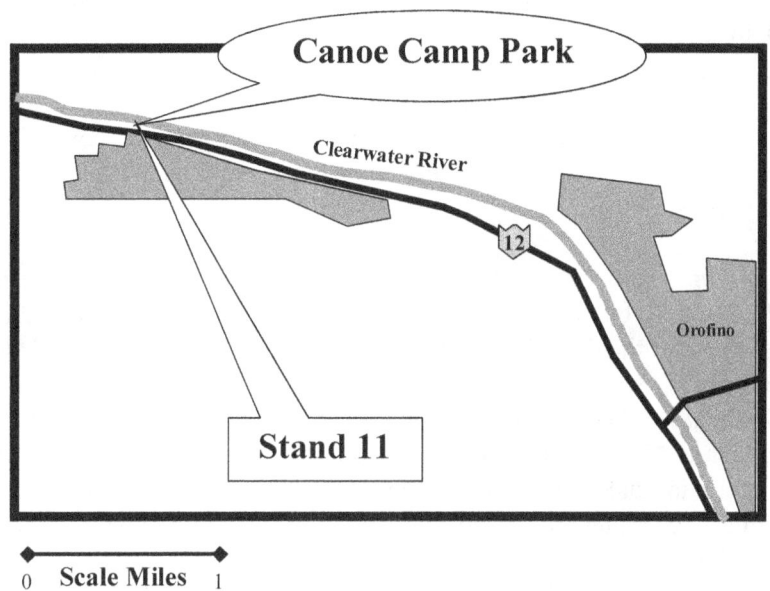

Map 5-7

Stand 11
Clearwater River
(23 - 25 September 1805)

Directions: Return to Greer and proceed north on US 12. Pass through Orofino, Idaho, and enter Canoe Camp Park. Walk to the reproduction of the dugout canoe.

Orientation (See Visual 5-6, Appendix D): The captains called today's Clearwater River the Kooskooskee River. The Corps of Discovery came down from the mountain prairie to the river, then paralleled the river to this vicinity.

Situation: The Corps of Discovery spent the remainder of 23 September 1805 giving gifts, trading, and making speeches with the Nez Perce Indians. Then on the 24th they moved down to the Clearwater River. During the move, Lewis and several men were very sick, and the others had to hold them on their horses. All of this was probably very entertaining to the Nez Perce. Most of what we know about this phase of the journey comes from the journal entries of Captain Clark, Sergeants Gass and Ordway, and Private Whitehouse. Unfortunately, Lewis either stopped writing for several weeks or his journals for this time period were lost. Clark was worried about the onset of winter and wanted to be on the move again. He also needed Lewis to assist in the planning and preparation of the move. He therefore administered to Lewis a frequent regimen of the powerful Rush's "Thunderclappers" to purge his body and hopefully make him well. However, Lewis was too sick again on the 25th to do anything but lie around. Meanwhile, Clark and Twisted Hair hunted for trees, which they found several miles downstream, to make into canoes.

On 26 September, Clark moved the corps to the area where he had found the large trees, which, in time, they called Canoe Camp. They remained at the camp for 10 days, working the large ponderosa pine logs into canoes. It is believed that, along with Lewis, up to half of the corps was sick. The canoe work was difficult for those well enough to participate. Lack of food was once again a challenge. The area around the camp was steep and dry and lacked an abundance of game. The party survived by bartering with the Nez Perce for salmon, camas roots, and camas bread. The journal entries also mentioned the eating of "a fat dog," a coyote, and horse soup. Interestingly, no mention is made of Sacagawea during this time. It is unknown whether she was numbered among the sick or the well.

By 1 October, most of the men had recovered sufficiently to resume work. However, Lewis was apparently not well enough to walk around until 4 October.

The corps made final preparations to depart the Canoe Camp and the Nez Perce on 6 October 1805. The men dug a large cache for extra supplies and made arrangements for the Nez Perce to care for their horses. Clark shaved the foremane of all the horses and branded them "U.S. Capt. M. Lewis" to identify them later. The next day, 7 October 1805, the soldiers packed their canoes and prepared to depart on their final westward trek down the Clearwater, Snake, and Columbia Rivers to the Pacific Ocean. It had taken 40 horses to get the corps and its supplies over the mountains. All was now packed into five canoes, which must have sat dangerously low in the water. Twisted Hair, who had agreed to accompany them for a time, wisely decided to walk on the shore. The corps departed Canoe Camp at 3 p.m.; now, for the first time in 18 months, they moved with the flow of the river. One month later, on 7 November 1805, Clark finally saw the broad estuary of the Columbia River flowing into the Pacific Ocean. The corps had fulfilled President Jefferson's dream of crossing the continent.

Vignette 1: "We assembled the principal Men as well as the Chiefs and by Signs informed them where we came from where bound our wish to inculcate peace and good understanding between all the red people &c. which appeared to Satisfy them much..." (Captain Clark, 23 September 1805, quoted in Gary Moulton, ed., *The Journals of the Lewis & Clark Expedition*, vol. 5, 231.)

Vignette 2: "the party in general are So weak and feeble that we git along Slow with the canoes..." (Private Whitehouse, 30 September 1805, quoted in Gary Moulton, ed., *The Journals of the Lewis & Clark Expedition*, vol. 11, 336.)

Vignette 3: "We are all in high spirits expecting we shall be able to descend the River tomorrow. This place we named Canoe Camp..." (Private Whitehouse, 6 October 1805, quoted in Gary Moulton, ed., *The Journals of the Lewis & Clark Expedition*, vol. 11, 339.)

Vignette 4: "Great joy in camp we are in *View* of the *Ocian*, this great Pacific Octean which we have been So long anxious to See..." (Captain Clark, 7 November 1805, quoted in Gary Moulton, ed., *The Journals of the Lewis & Clark Expedition*, vol. 6, 33.)

Teaching Points:

Loyalty and Duty. Lewis' preparation for the expedition included a two-week course on medical treatment from the most talented medical minds in the country. Lewis, in turn, passed on his knowledge to Clark. During the course of the expedition, the captains delivered a baby and treated various illnesses and injuries. Journal entries also note the captains massaging and pulling thorns from the men's feet. The value of the early 19th-century medical treatments was dubious at best and often did more harm than good. However, what can we learn about the Army values of *loyalty* and *duty* from the captains' determination to provide the best medical care contemporary science had to offer and the Corps of Discovery's ability to survive in the wilderness?

The US Army's Contribution to the Success of the Expedition. Evaluate President Jefferson's original decision to turn to the Army for the mission of exploring the West. What factors allowed the Army to complete the mission successfully?

IV. Integration Phase for the Lewis and Clark Staff Ride

As defined in *The Staff Ride* by Dr. William G. Robertson, a staff ride consists of three phases. The first phase is "The Preliminary Study Phase." This phase is conducted before the visit to the battlefield and prepares the student for the visit. It may take various forms, including classroom instruction, individual study, or a combination of the two. The second phase is "The Field Study Phase." This phase is conducted on the battlefield and better allows students to understand historical events through analysis of the actual terrain. The third and final phase of a staff ride is "The Integration Phase." No staff ride is complete without an integration phase, and it is critical for the students to understand what happened, why it happened, and, most important, what can be to be learned from the study of the battle. The staff ride leader can conduct the integration phase on the battlefield immediately after completing the field study phase. However, it is recommended that, when possible, students have some time for personal reflection and thought. Thus the integration phase may best be conducted the day after the field study phase ends.

The staff ride leader can organize the integration phase based on the unit, time available, and training objectives. The leader can conduct the integration phase like an after-action review or may simply lead a discussion with the students on what they learned. The following are potential integration phase topics that the staff ride leader could use.

Army Values. Army values remind us and tell the rest of the world—the civilian government we serve, the nation we protect, even our enemies—who we are and what we stand for. The trust soldiers and DA civilians have for each other and the trust the American people have in us depends on how well we live up to Army values. They are the fundamental building blocks that enable us to discern right from wrong in any situation. Army values are consistent; they support one another. You can't follow one value and ignore another. (Quoted from FM 22 –100, *Army Leadership*, 2-2).

The Lewis and Clark Expedition exemplified the values that have guided the American soldier to the present day. Thomas Jefferson himself described Meriwether Lewis:

Of courage undaunted, possessing a firmness & perseverance of purpose which nothing but impossibilities could divert from its direction, careful as a father of those committed to his charge, yet steady in the maintenance of order & discipline... honest, disinterested, liberal, of sound understanding and a fidelity to truth so scrupulous that whatever he should report would be as certain as if seen by ourselves. (Quoted in Stephen E. Ambrose's *Undaunted Courage*, iii.)

"Without the courage, determination, skill, and teamwork, not only of Lewis and Clark, but of each individual soldier, the Corps of Discovery would have fallen far short of its objective and may well have encountered disaster. The Spirit of the Corps lives on in the soldiers and values of today's Army."*

Loyalty. Bear true faith and allegiance to the US Constitution, the Army, your unit, and other soldiers. Since before the founding of the republic, the Army has respected its subordination to its civilian political leaders. This subordination is fundamental to preserving the liberty of all Americans. You began your Army career by swearing allegiance to the Constitution, the basis of our government and laws. Beyond your allegiance to the Constitution, you have an obligation to be faithful to the Army—the institution and its people—and to your unit or organization. (Quoted from FM 22 –100, *Army Leadership*, 2-2).

Few examples illustrate loyalty to country and institution as well as the examples of Lewis and Clark on their epic journey into the unknown. Discuss what the modern officer or soldier can learn about loyalty from a study of the Lewis and Clark Expedition.

Duty. Fulfill your obligations. Duty begins with everything required of you by law, regulation, and orders; but it includes much more than that. Professionals do their work not just to the minimum standard, but to the very best of their ability. Soldiers and DA civilians commit to excellence in all aspects of their professional responsibility so that when the job is done they can look back and say, "I couldn't have given any more."

Army leaders take the initiative, figuring out what needs to be done before being told what to do. What's more, they take full responsibility for their actions and those of their subordinates. Army leaders never shade the truth to make the unit look good—or even to make their subordinates feel good. Instead, they follow their higher duty to the Army and the nation. (Quoted from FM 22 –100, *Army Leadership*, 2-4.)

Captains Lewis and Clark understood and fulfilled their duty to the Army and to the soldiers they commanded. Discuss what you can learn from their example.

Respect. Treat people as they should be treated. Respect for the individual forms the basis for the rule of law, the very essence of what makes

---

* This paragraph is from the U.S. Army Center of Military History's brochure (CMH Pub 70-75-1) written by David W. Hogan, Jr. and Charles E. White.

America. In the Army, respect means recognizing and appreciating the inherent dignity and worth of all people. This value reminds you that your people are your greatest resource. Army leaders honor everyone's individual worth by treating all people with dignity and respect.

As America becomes more culturally diverse, Army leaders must be aware that they will deal with people from a wider range of ethnic, racial, and religious backgrounds. Effective leaders are tolerant of beliefs different from their own as long as those beliefs don't conflict with Army values, are not illegal, and are not unethical. As an Army leader, you need to avoid misunderstandings arising from cultural differences. Actively seeking to learn about people and cultures different from your own can help you do this. Being sensitive to other cultures can also aid you in counseling your people more effectively. You show respect when you seek to understand your people's background, see things from their perspective, and appreciate what's important to them.

As an Army leader, you must also foster a climate in which everyone is treated with dignity and respect regardless of race, gender, creed, or religious belief. Fostering this climate begins with your example: how you live Army values shows your people how they should live them. However, values training is another major contributor. Effective training helps create a common understanding of Army values and the standards you expect. When you conduct it as part of your regular routine—such as during developmental counseling sessions—you reinforce the message that respect for others is part of the character of every soldier and DA civilian. Combined with your example, such training creates an organizational climate that promotes consideration for others, fairness in all dealings, and equal opportunity. In essence, Army leaders treat others as they wish to be treated.

As part of this consideration, leaders create an environment in which subordinates are challenged, where they can reach their full potential and be all they can be. Providing tough training doesn't demean subordinates; in fact, building their capabilities and showing faith in their potential is the essence of respect. Effective leaders take the time to learn what their subordinates want to accomplish. They advise their people on how they can grow, personally and professionally. Not all of your subordinates will succeed equally, but they all deserve respect.

Respect is also an essential component for the development of disciplined, cohesive, and effective warfighting teams. In the deadly confusion of combat, soldiers often overcome incredible odds to accomplish the mission and protect the lives of their comrades. This spirit of selfless service and duty is built on a soldier's personal trust and regard for fellow soldiers. A leader's willingness to tolerate discrimination or harassment on any basis, or a failure to cultivate a climate of respect, eats away at this trust and erodes unit cohesion. But respect goes beyond issues of discrimination and harassment; it includes the broader issue of civility, the way people treat each other and those they come in contact with. It involves being sensitive to diversity and one's own behaviors that others may find insensitive, offensive, or abusive. (Quoted from FM 22 –100, *Army Leadership*, 2-5.)

The members of the Corps of Discovery exemplified the Army value of respect by treating everyone with dignity and respect. Discuss how this contributed to the success of the operation.

Selfless Service. Put the welfare of the nation, the Army, and subordinates before your own. You have often heard the military referred to as "the service." As a member of the Army, you serve the United States. Selfless service means doing what's right for the nation, the Army, your organization, and your people—and putting these responsibilities above your own interests. The needs of the Army and the nation come first. This doesn't mean that you neglect your family or yourself; in fact, such neglect weakens a leader and can cause the Army more harm than good. Selfless service doesn't mean that you can't have a strong ego, high self-esteem, or even healthy ambition. Rather, selfless service means that you don't make decisions or take actions that help your image or your career but hurt others or sabotage the mission. The selfish superior claims credit for work his subordinates do; the selfless leader gives credit to those who earned it. The Army can't function except as a team, and for a team to work, the individual has to give up self-interest for the good of the whole. (Quoted from FM 22 –100, *Army Leadership*, 2-6.)

The captains always placed their country's interests first and their own second. Discuss how today's Army leaders can benefit from their example.

Honor. Live up to all the Army values. Honor provides the "moral compass" for character and personal conduct in the Army. Though many people struggle to define the term, most recognize instinctively those with a keen sense of right and wrong, those who live such that their words and deeds are above reproach. The expression "honorable person," therefore, refers to both the character traits an individual actually possesses and the fact that the community recognizes and respects them.

Honor holds Army values together while at the same time being a value itself. Together, Army values describe the foundation essential to develop leaders of character. Honor means demonstrating an understanding of what's right and taking pride in the community's acknowledgment of that reputation. Military ceremonies recognizing individual and unit achievement demonstrate and reinforce the importance the Army places on honor.

For you as an Army leader, demonstrating an understanding of what's right and taking pride in that reputation means this: Live up to all the Army values. Implicitly, that's what you promised when you took your oath of office or enlistment. You made this promise publicly, and the standards—Army values—are also public. To be an honorable person, you must be true to your oath and live Army values in all you do. Living honorably strengthens Army values, not only for yourself but for others as well: all members of an organization contribute to the organization's climate. By what they do, people living out Army values contribute to a climate that encourages all members of the Army to do the same.

How you conduct yourself and meet your obligations defines who you are as a person; how the Army meets the nation's commitments defines the Army as an institution. For you as an Army leader, honor means putting Army values above self-interest, above career and comfort. For all soldiers, it means putting Army values above self-preservation as well. This honor is essential for creating a bond of trust among members of the Army and between the Army and the nation it serves. Army leaders have the strength of will to live according to Army values, even though the temptations to do otherwise are strong, especially in the face of personal danger. (Quoted from FM 22 –100, *Army Leadership*, 2-7.)

The captains lived in an age when life without honor was worse than death. They acted based on values, which they had clearly made their own: loyalty to their fellow soldiers; the duty to stand by them, regardless of the circumstances; and the personal courage to act, even in the face of great danger. Discuss the role that honor plays in today's Army.

Integrity. Do what's right—legally and morally. People of integrity consistently act according to principles—not just what might work at the moment. Leaders of integrity make their principles known and consistently act in accordance with them. The Army requires leaders of integrity who possess high moral standards and are honest in word and deed. Being honest means being truthful and upright all the time, despite pressures to do otherwise. Having integrity means being both morally complete and true to yourself. As an Army leader, you're honest to yourself by committing to and consistently living Army values; you're honest to others by not presenting yourself or your actions as anything other than what they are. Army leaders say what they mean and do what they say. If you can't accomplish a mission, inform your chain of command. If you inadvertently pass on bad information, correct it as soon as you find out it's wrong. People of integrity do the right thing not because it's convenient or because they have no choice. They choose the right thing because their character permits no less. Conducting yourself with integrity has three parts: separating what's right from what's wrong, always acting according to what you know to be right, even at personal cost, and saying openly that you're acting on your understanding of right versus wrong.

Leaders can't hide what they do: that's why you must carefully decide how you act. As an Army leader, you're always on display. If you want to instill Army values in others, you must internalize and demonstrate them yourself. Your personal values may and probably do extend beyond the Army values, to include such things as political, cultural, or religious beliefs. However, if you're to be an Army leader and a person of integrity, these values must reinforce, not contradict, Army values. (Quoted from FM 22–100, *Army Leadership*, 2-8.)

The captains understood the value of integrity. They made their principles known and consistently acted in accordance with them. Discuss what we can learn from their example.

Personal Courage. Face fear, danger, or adversity (physical or moral). Personal courage isn't the absence of fear; rather, it's the ability to put fear aside and do what's necessary. It takes two forms, physical and moral. Good leaders demonstrate both.

Physical courage means overcoming fears of bodily harm and doing your duty. It's the bravery that allows a soldier to take risks in combat in spite of the fear of wounds or death.

In contrast, moral courage is the willingness to stand firm on your values, principles, and convictions—even when threatened. It enables leaders to stand up for what they believe is right, regardless of the consequences. Leaders who take responsibility for their decisions and actions, even when things go wrong, display moral courage. Courageous leaders are willing to look critically inside themselves, consider new ideas, and change what needs changing.

Moral courage is sometimes overlooked, both in discussions of personal courage and in the everyday rush of business. Situations requiring physical courage are rare; situations requiring moral courage can occur frequently. Moral courage is essential to living the Army values of integrity and honor every day.

Moral courage often expresses itself as candor. Candor means being frank, honest, and sincere with others while keeping your words free from bias, prejudice, or malice. Candor means calling things as you see them, even when it's uncomfortable or you think it might be better for you to just keep quiet. It means not allowing your feelings to affect what you say about a person or situation. (Quoted from FM 22 –100, *Army Leadership*, 2-9.)

At times physical and moral courage blended together during the corps' journey into the unknown. The captains understood that doing the right thing might not only be unpopular, but dangerous as well. Discuss how the captains demonstrated personal courage and what we can learn from their example.

V. Support for a Lewis and Clark Staff Ride

1. Information and Assistance.

    a. The Staff Ride Division of the Combat Studies Institute at Fort Leavenworth can provide advice and assistance on every aspect of the expedition. Resources include files of historical data, detailed knowledge of the expedition, and familiarity with the route.

        Address:
        US Army Command and General Staff College
        Combat Studies Institute
        ATTN: ATZL-SWI
        Fort Leavenworth, Kansas 66027-6900
        Telephone:
        DSN 552-2122/2080 Commercial (913) 684-2122/2080
        www-cgsc.army.mil/csi/index.htm

    b. Lewis and Clark Interpretive Center. The center includes a permanent exhibit hall, a theater, retail store, and a traveling exhibit hall. The exhibits detail the 1804-1806 journey of the Lewis and Clark Expedition with focus on their interactions with the Plains Indians. There is a fee to enter the center, and prior coordination, especially for large groups, is recommended.

        Address:
        Lewis and Clark Interpretive Center
        4201 Giant Springs Road
        Great Falls, MT
        Phone: 406- 727-8733
        www.fs.fed.us/r1/lewisclark/recreation/lcic/lcic.shtml

    c. Boat Tours, Gates of the Mountains. Facilities include a gift shop, restrooms and picnic facilities. Tour personnel can assist with brochures and information about this portion of the expedition. Prior coordination, especially for large groups, is recommended.

        Address:
        Gates of the Mountains
        P.O. Box 478
        Helena, MT 59624
        Phone: 406-458-5241
        www.gatesofthemountains.com

d. Sacajawea [Sacagawea] Interpretive Cultural and Education Center. Facilities include a small museum, gift shop, restrooms, picnic facilities, and a walking tour. Park personnel can assist with brochures and information about this portion of the expedition. Prior coordination, especially for large groups, is recommended.

>Address:
>Sacajawea Center
>200 Main St.
>Salmon, Idaho 83467
>Phone: 208-756-1188
>www.sacajaweacenter.org

e. Travelers' Rest State Park. Facilities include a small museum, restrooms, and a walking tour. Park personnel can assist with brochures and information about this portion of the expedition. Prior coordination, especially for large groups, is recommended.

>Address:
>Travelers' Rest State Park
>6550 Mormon Creek Road
>P.O. Box 995
>Lolo, MT 59847
>Phone: 406-273-4253
>www.travelersrest.org

f. Lolo Trail and Lolo Pass Visitor Center includes a small museum, restrooms and a walking tour. Park personnel can assist with brochures and information about the Lolo Trail. Prior coordination, especially for large groups, is recommended.

>Address:
>Lolo Trail and Lolo Pass Visitor Center
>Highway 12
>Lolo, MT 59847
>Phone: 208-942-3113

2. Logistics.

   a. Meals. Restaurants, grocery stores, and fast-food establishments are available along the route in most of the towns in Montana and Idaho. However, driving times between towns can be significant, and stops should be planned in advance.

   b. Lodging. Most of the larger towns include hotel and motel accommodations. The staff ride itinerary (Section III of this handbook) includes recommended start and stop locations for each day of the trip.

   c. Medical. Most of the larger towns include medical facilities.

3. Other considerations.

   a. Do not trespass on private property without prior approval from the owner.

   b. Make provisions for liquids and food, since much of the expedition route is in rural areas.

   c. Ensure that your group has proper clothing for inclement weather. Violent thunderstorms can occur in any season. The recommended time window for a visit to the area is June to September.

   d. Plan your driving routes and timetables carefully (the Combat Studies Institute can provide assistance in planning).

Appendix A

Members of the Expedition[1]

Officers

Captain Meriwether Lewis (1774-1809)
Virginia
First Infantry

Lewis joined the Army in 1794 and served in the Ohio Valley and the Old Northwest Territory, where he became friends with William Clark. In 1801, Lewis was appointed as President Thomas Jefferson's private secretary, while retaining his military rank. Two years later, Jefferson chose Lewis as commander of the expedition. Following the return of the expedition in 1806, Lewis became governor of the Louisiana Territory, but he encountered financial difficulties that caused him severe emotional problems. On the Natchez Trace in Tennessee, Lewis took his own life in September 1809.

Second Lieutenant William Clark (1770-1838)
Virginia/Kentucky

The younger brother of General George Rogers Clark, William had served in the Army for four years, participating in the campaigns of General Anthony Wayne in the Northwest Territory before resigning his commission in 1796 to attend to the family business. Because of the Army seniority system, Clark received a second lieutenant's commission instead of a captaincy promised to him by Lewis when he rejoined the military as Lewis' second in command. But he and Lewis concealed this from the members of the expedition, who always referred to him as Captain Clark. After the expedition, Clark had a distinguished political career, including the governorship of the Missouri Territory.

Noncommissioned Officers

Sergeant Charles Floyd (1782-1804)
Kentucky

One of the "Nine Young Men from Kentucky," Floyd was made a sergeant before the expedition began. Lewis regarded him as "a young man of much merit." Floyd is remembered principally as the only Corps of Discovery fatality on the journey. He died on 20 August 1804, near present-day Sioux City, Iowa, probably from what modern medical experts believe was a ruptured appendix. Floyd kept a journal until a few days before his death.

Sergeant Patrick Gass (1771-1870)
Pennsylvania
First Infantry

Recruited at Fort Kaskaskia from Captain Russell Bissell's company of the First Infantry, Gass had joined the Army in 1799 after serving in a volunteer Ranger unit. His skill as a carpenter was of great value to the expedition. Gass was promoted to sergeant in August 1804, following the death of Floyd. In 1807, Gass was the first to publish his journal. He stayed in the Army and served in the War of 1812 but was discharged after losing an eye in an accident. Gass was the last known survivor of the expedition.

Sergeant John Ordway (1775-1817)
New Hampshire
First Infantry

The only member of the corps who was a sergeant in the Army before the expedition, Ordway was recruited at Fort Kaskaskia from Captain Russell Bissell's company of the First Infantry. He was well educated and became the senior sergeant of the expedition. He took care of the daily administration and, in the absence of the two captains, was in charge of the expedition. Ordway was the only member of the Corps of Discovery to keep his journal faithfully throughout the expedition. His accounts of Indian life are invaluable.

Sergeant Nathaniel Pryor (1772-1831)
Virginia/Kentucky

Pryor was a widower and cousin of Charles Floyd. Pryor was one of the "Nine Young Men from Kentucky." Lewis and Clark considered him to be "a man of character and ability" and, after the expedition, helped him secure an officer's commission in the Army. Pryor rose to the rank of captain and participated in the Battle of New Orleans in 1814. He later served as a government agent for the Osage Indians in 1830-31.

Corporal Richard Warfington (1777 - ?)
North Carolina
Second Infantry

Transferred from Captain John Campbell's company of the Second Infantry Regiment as a corporal, Warfington was both reliable and efficient. When his enlistment expired during the expedition, Lewis and Clark asked him not to take his official discharge but to retain his rank and authority and command the return party to St. Louis in 1805. The captains believed Warfington was the only trustworthy member of the return party, and they wanted to ensure the safety of their dispatches, journals, and specimens sent to President Jefferson. Warfington accepted command of the return party and completed his mission so successfully that he even managed to keep alive a prairie dog and four magpies Lewis had sent to Jefferson. Lewis later recommended that Warfington receive a bonus beyond his regular pay.

Privates

Private John Boley (Dates Unknown)
Pennsylvania
First Infantry

Recruited at Fort Kaskaskia from Captain Russell Bissell's company of the First Infantry Regiment, Boley had some disciplinary problems at Camp River Dubois and was designated for the return party. He later accompanied Zebulon Pike's expedition to the upper Mississippi in 1805 and continued with Pike to the southwest and the Rockies in 1806.

Private William Bratton (1778-1841)
Virginia/Kentucky

One of the "Nine Young Men from Kentucky," Bratton served the expedition as a hunter, blacksmith, and gunsmith. In the spring of 1806, he was incapacitated for several weeks by a mysterious back ailment, perhaps the longest period of serious illness experienced by any member of the Corps of Discovery. An Indiana sweat bath finally cured Bratton. After the expedition he served in the War of 1812.

Private John Collins (?-1823)
Maryland
First Infantry

Collins was recruited at Fort Kaskaskia from Captain Russell Bissell's company of the First Infantry Regiment. He was a good hunter but was frequently drunk and disobedient. He was court-martialed for stealing whiskey from the official supply while detailed to guard it. He received 100 lashes for his misconduct.

Private John Colter (1775-1813)
Virginia/Kentucky

One of the "Nine Young Men from Kentucky, " Colter was an excellent hunter and woodsman. On the return trip, he requested permission to leave the expedition at the Mandan villages so he could join a trapping party heading back up the Missouri River. He apparently became the first white man to see the region of present-day Yellowstone Park.

Private Pierre Cruzatte (Dates Unknown)

Half French and half Omaha Indian, Cruzatte was master boatman and fiddle player. Unlike the contract French boatmen, he and Francois Labiche were enlisted members of the expedition's permanent party. Blind in one eye and nearsighted in the other, Cruzatte accidentally shot Lewis while the two were hunting in August 1806. Lewis later paid tribute to Cruzatte's experience as a riverman and to his integrity. His fiddle playing often entertained the Corps of Discovery.

Private John Dame (1784 - ?)
New Hampshire
Regiment of Artillery

Recruited at Fort Kaskaskia from Captain Amos Stoddard's artillery company, Dame is mentioned only once in the journals. He was a member of the return party

Private Joseph Field (1772-1807)
Private Reubin Field (1771-1823?)
Virginia/Kentucky

The Field brothers were two of the "Nine Young Men from Kentucky." They were among the best shots and hunters in the Corps of Discovery and, with George Drouillard, accompanied the captains on special reconnaissance missions. Both were with Lewis in the fight with the Blackfeet on 17 July 1806.

Private Robert Frazer (? - 1837)
Virginia

There is no information on when Frazer joined the expedition or if he had previously been in the Army. He was not at first part of the permanent party, but he was transferred from the intended return party on 8 October 1804 to replace Moses Reed after the latter's expulsion. Frazer kept a journal and received special permission from the captains to publish it. But the publication never took place and the journal is apparently lost. Frazer's map of the expedition has survived.

Private George Gibson (? - 1809)
Pennsylvania/Kentucky

Another of the "Nine Young Men from Kentucky," Gibson was a good hunter and on occasion played the fiddle for the Corps of Discovery. He served as an interpreter, most likely through sign language.

Private Silas Goodrich (Dates Unknown)
Massachusetts

Just where Goodrich joined the expedition is not known, nor is there information regarding any prior military service he may have had. But he was one of the finest fishermen of the Corps of Discovery. After the expedition, Goodrich re-enlisted in the Army.

Private Hugh Hall (1772- ?)
Massachusetts
Second Infantry

Recruited at South West Point from Captain John Campbell's company of the Second Infantry Regiment, Hall was court-martialed with Collins for tapping into the official whiskey ration and getting drunk.

Private Thomas Howard (1779- ?)
Massachusetts
Second Infantry

Recruited at South West Point from Captain Campbell's company of the Second Infantry Regiment, Howard was the last member of the expedition court-martialed when he climbed over one of the walls of Fort Mandan after the gate had been closed. He was found guilty of "pernicious example" to the Indians, by showing them that the fort wall was easily scaled.

Private François Labiche (Dates Unknown)

Recruited at Fort Kaskaskia, Labiche was an enlisted member of the expedition, not a hired boatman. Like Cruzatte, he was an experienced boatman and Indian trader. He also spoke English, French, and several Indian languages. Lewis noted his services as an interpreter, recommending that he receive a bonus. Labiche accompanied Lewis to Washington after the expedition to interpret for the Indian chiefs.

Private Jean Baptiste Lepage (Dates Unknown)

Recruited at Fort Mandan, Lepage was a French-Canadian fur trader.

Private Hugh McNeal (Dates Unknown)
Pennsylvania

McNeal may have been in the Army prior to joining the expedition on 1 April 1804. A man with that name was on the Army rolls as late as 1811.

Private John Newman (1785-1838)
Pennsylvania
First Infantry

Recruited at Fort Massac from Captain Daniel Bissell's company of the First Infantry Regiment, Newman was expelled from the expedition following his court-martial for "having uttered repeated expressions of a highly criminal and mutinous nature." He remained with the expedition doing hard labor until sent back with the return party to St. Louis in April 1805.

Private John Potts (1776-1808?)
Germany
Second Infantry

Recruited at South West Point from Captain Robert Purdy's company of the Second Infantry Regiment, Potts was a miller by trade. Following the expedition, he joined Manuel Lisa's fur-trading venture to the upper Missouri and, with his friend John Colter, was ambushed by Blackfeet near the Three Forks of the Missouri. Potts was killed and Colter narrowly escaped.

Private Moses Reed (Dates Unknown)

Little is known about Reed's origin and background. In August 1804, he attempted to desert, was apprehended, tried, convicted, and expelled from the expedition. He remained with the Corps of Discovery doing hard labor until sent back with the return party to St. Louis in April 1805.

Private John Robertson (1780 -?)
New Hampshire
Regiment of Artillery

Recruited at Fort Kaskaskia from Captain Stoddard's artillery company, Robertson was initially a corporal when he joined the expedition. Robertson may have had some leadership problems, because on 4 January 1804, Clark admonished him for having "no authority" over his men. Robertson's failure to break up a fight at Camp River Dubois caused Clark to demote him to private. Robertson was most likely the first man to leave the expedition. On 12 June 1804, Joseph Whitehouse recorded in his journal that a private "belonging to Captain Stoddard's company of Artillery" was sent back to St. Louis with a trading party encountered coming downriver. Presumably Robertson returned to his artillery company, because there is no further record of him.

Private George Shannon (1785-1836)
Pennsylvania/Kentucky

The youngest Army member of the Lewis and Clark Expedition, Shannon joined Lewis at Maysville, Kentucky, and is listed as one of the "Nine Young Men from Kentucky." In the fall of 1804, he was lost for over two weeks and nearly starved to death. After the expedition, Shannon became a lawyer and later served as a senator from Missouri.

Private John Shields (1769-1809)
Virginia/Tennessee

The oldest member of the Corps of Discovery, and one of the few who were married, Shields is one of the "Nine Young Men from Kentucky." During the expedition, his skills as a blacksmith, gunsmith, and carpenter were invaluable. "Nothing was more peculiarly useful to us, in various situations," wrote Lewis, "than the skill of this man as an artist, in repairing our guns, accoutrements, &c." Lewis recommended that Congress give Shields a bonus for his services.

Private John Thompson (Dates Unknown)
This is virtually no information on John Thompson, other than Clark praising him as "a valuable member of our party." Thompson may have been a surveyor before joining the expedition.

Private Ebenezer Tuttle (1773-?)
Connecticut
Regiment of Artillery

Recruited at Fort Kaskaskia from Captain Stoddard's artillery company, Tuttle was a member of the return party in April 1805. The only mention of him in the journals is in the Detachment Order of 26 May 1804.

Private Peter Weiser (1781 - ?)
Pennsylvania
First Infantry

Recruited at Fort Kaskaskia from Captain Russell Bissell's company of the First Infantry Regiment, Weiser descended from the noted frontier diplomat Conrad Weiser. After the expedition he joined Manuel Lisa's fur-trading venture up the Missouri.

Private William Werner (Dates Unknown)
Little is known about William Werner. He had a fight with John Potts at Camp River Dubois and was convicted of being absent without leave at St. Charles, Missouri. Other than these incidents, the journals reveal little more about him.

Private Isaac White (1774 - ?)
Massachusetts
Regiment of Artillery

Recruited at Fort Kaskaskia from Captain Stoddard's artillery company, White was a member of the return party to St. Louis in April 1805. The only mention of him in the journals is in the Detachment Order of 26 May 1804.

Private Joseph Whitehouse (1775 - ?)
Virginia/Kentucky
First Infantry

Recruited at Fort Massac from Captain Daniel Bissell's company of the First Infantry Regiment, Whitehouse was initially expelled from the expedition for misconduct, but he was allowed to return after repenting. He kept a journal and often acted as a tailor for the other men. Whitehouse later served during the War of 1812 but deserted in 1817.

Private Alexander Willard (1778 - 1865)
New Hampshire
Regiment of Artillery

Recruited at Fort Kaskaskia from Captain Amos Stoddard's artillery company, Willard was convicted of sleeping while on guard duty, which was punishable by death. He was given 100 lashes instead and detailed to the return party in April 1805.² He was a blacksmith. Willard often assisted Shields in his work during the first year of the expedition. Willard later served during the War of 1812.

Private Richard Windsor (Dates Unknown)
First Infantry

Little is known about Richard Windsor, other than the fact that he was recruited at Fort Kaskaskia from Captain Russell Bissell's company of the First Infantry Regiment. Windsor was an experienced woodsman and productive hunter throughout the expedition.

Civilians

The Charbonneau Family

After Lewis and Clark, the most famous member of the expedition is Sacagawea. She was born around 1788, probably near Lemhi, Idaho, the daughter of a Shoshone chief. As a child she was kidnapped by the Hidatsa and sold into slavery to the Mandan. While with the Mandan, Sacagawea was sold or given to Toussaint Charbonneau, who made her his wife. On 11 February 1805, she gave birth to a son, Jean Baptiste. Lewis described Toussaint as a man "of no particular merit," while both captains acknowledged the indispensable service Sacagawea provided the Corps of Discovery. As Clark wrote, "a woman with a party of men is a token of peace."

Interpreter George Drouillard (? - 1810)
Canada

The son of a French-Canadian and a Shawnee mother, George Drouillard met Lewis at Fort Massac. Captain Daniel Bissell was probably employing Drouillard when Lewis recruited him for the expedition. Drouillard was known for his general skill as a scout, hunter, woodsman, and interpreter. Indeed, he was one of the best hunters of the expedition and often accompanied the captains on special reconnaissance missions. After the expedition, Drouillard became a partner in Manuel Lisa's fur-trading ventures on the upper Missouri and Yellowstone Rivers.

York (1770 - ?)
Virginia

York was Clark's companion from childhood, in the fashion of the slaveholding South. Clark legally inherited York in 1799. The journals indicated that he was large, strong, and perhaps overweight. He carried a rifle during the expedition and performed his full share of duties like the other members of the Corps of Discovery. York received his freedom in 1811 and then operated a wagon freight business in Tennessee and Kentucky.

Contract Boatmen[3]

Lewis and Clark hired 12 French boatmen, known as *engagés*, to help steer the keelboat and pirogues of the expedition. These men included:

E. Cann (1775 - 1836)
Mississippi

E. Cann was actually Alexander Carson, a man who had lived among the French so long that others thought of him as being French. He hired on with the expedition as a boatman and probably returned to St. Louis with the Return Party. One of his descendants was the famous "Kit" Carson.

Charles Caugee (Dates Unknown)

Captain Clark listed Charles Caugee in 4 July 1804 as one of the nine men hired. Other than that, nothing is known about him.

Joseph Collin (Dates Unknown)

Sergeant Gass mentions Collin in his journal as "a young man who formerly belonged to the North West Company." It appears he accompanied the Corps only as far as the Arikara Indian villages and was still living there when the Corps passed through again in 1806.

Jean Baptiste Deschamps (Dates Unknown)

It appears that Jean Baptiste Deschamps was recruited as a private in the US Army at Fort Kaskaskia to be the foreman of the French boatmen. He returned to St. Louis with the return party.

Charles Herbert (Dates Unknown)
Canada

St. Louis parish records show Hebert was married to Julie Hubert Dit La Croix in 1792. The records also list 11 baptized children. Captain Lewis listed him as an *engage* in May 1804. He was discharged at the Mandan village in the winter of 1804.

Jean Baptiste La Jeunesse (Unknown - 1806)

Jean Baptiste La Jeunesse was recruited as a private in the US Army to serve as a boatman. There is no record of his discharge. He may have remained at the Mandan village or returned to St. Louis.

La Liberté/Joseph Barter (Unknown - 1837)
Canada

While at Fort Kaskaskia, Lewis recruited La Liberte as a private in the US Army to serve as a boatman. He deserted soon afterward and was not mentioned again in the journals.

Etienne Malboeuf (1775[?] – Unknown)
Canada

Lewis recruited Etienne Malboeuf as a contract boatman at Fort Kaskaskia and paid him for his services on 4 October 1805. Jean Baptiste La Jeunesse was married to Malboeuf's sister Elisabeth.

Peter Pinaut (1776 – Unknown)
Shown as born "in the woods."

Pinaut was the son of a French trader and a Missouri Indian woman. He was listed as a member of the corps in May 1804. He probably returned to St. Louis with the return party.

Paul Primeau (Dates Unknown)
Canada

Lewis recruited Primeau as a contract boatman at Fort Kaskaskia and listed him as a member of the corps in May 1804. An 1807 record shows him owing George Drouillard $292.05, which he paid back in 1808. It is not known if he returned to St. Louis with the return party or remained on the upper Missouri.

François Rivet (1757 - 1852)
Canada

Hired at Fort Kaskaskia in 1804 as a contract boatman, Rivet, along with three other boatmen (Deschamps, Malboeuf, and Carson), remained at the Mandan village over the winter after they were discharged from the corps. Rivet then departed with the return party but later returned to the Mandan village and was living there when the corps passed through in 1806. He lived to be 95 and died in Oregon.

Peter Roi (Dates Unknown)

The family name of Roi was very common among the French in the St. Louis area. No specific details are known about Peter Roi.

Others

Rocque (Dates Unknown)
Unknown

The captains listed him as Rokey. However, Sergeant Ordway referred to him as Ross. The proper French name is believed to be Rocque. He served as a boatman along with the other *engages*. It appears that he remained along the upper Missouri and was still there when the corps returned in 1806, "We found a French man by the name of Rokey. Who was one of our engages as high as the Mandans. This man had spent all his wages and requested to return with us." (Captain Clark, 22 August 1806).

NOTES

[1] The US Army Center of Military History provided Appendix A for this the handbook. The Command Studies Institute added one footnote for Private Alexander Willard, biographical sketches for the 12 French contract boatmen, and one additional boatman, engage Rocque.

[2] Willard was subsequently reassigned to the Permanent Party.

[3] The Combat Studies Institute (CSI) added the biographical sketches for the 12 French contract boatmen, and one additional boatman, Engage Rocque. CSI obtained the information from Charles G. Clarke's book, *The Men of the Lewis and Clark Expedition*. Anton J. Pregaldin provided the information to Charles Clarke after extensive research in the Catholic parish registers of French pioneer families in the St. Louis area.

Appendix B

Detachment Orders

Detachment Orders
Camp River Dubois, February 20th 1804

[Lewis]

    The Commanding officer directs that during the absence of himself and Capt. Clark from camp, that the party shall consider them selves under the immediate command of Sergt. Ordway, who will be held accountable for the good police and order of the camp during that period, and will also see the subsequent parts of this order carried into effect.-

    The sawyers will continue their work until they have cut the necessary quantity of plank, the quantity wanting will be determined by Pryor; during the days they labor they shall receive each an extra gill of whiskey pr. day and be exempt from guard duty; when the work is accomplished, they will join the party and do duty in common with the other men.-

    The blacksmiths will also continue their work until they have completed the [articles?] contained in the memorandum with which I have furnished them, and during the time they are at work will receive each an extra gill of whiskey pr. day and be exempt from guard duty; when the work is completed they will return to camp and do duty in common with the detachment.-

    The four men who are engaged in making sugar will continue in that employment until further orders, and will receive each a half a gill of extra whiskey pr. day and be exempt from guard duty.-

    The practicing party will in further discharge only one round each per. day, which will be done under the direction of Sergt. Ordway, all at the same target and at the distance of fifty yards off hand. The prize of a gill of extra whiskey will be received by the person who makes the best show at each time of practice.-

    Floyd will take charge of our quarters and store and be exempt from guard duty until our return, the commanding officer hopes that this proof of his confidence will be justified by the rigid performance of the orders given him on that subject.-

    No man shall absent himself from camp without the knowledge and permission of Sergt. Ordway, other than those who have obtained permission from me to be absent on hunting excursions, and those will not extend their absence to a term by which they may avoid a tour of guard duty, on their return they will report themselves to Sergt. Ordway and receive his instructions.-

No whiskey shall in future be delivered from the contractor's store except for the legal ration, and as appropriated by this order, unless otherwise directed by Capt. Clark or myself-

Meriwether Lewis
Captain. 1st U.S. Regiment Infantry

Sergeant Ordway will have the men paraded this evening and read the enclosed orders to them.

M. Lewis

(Gary Moulton, ed., *The Journals of the Lewis & Clark Expedition*, vol. 2, 174-175.)

Detachment Orders
March 3rd 1804

[Lewis]

The commanding officer feels himself mortified and disappointed at the disorderly conduct of Reubin Fields, in refusing to mount guard when in the due routine of duty he was regularly warned; nor is he less surprised at the want of discretion in those who urged his opposition to the faithful discharge of his duty, particularly Shields, whose sense of propriety he had every reason to believe would have induced him rather to have promoted good order, than to have excited disorder and faction among the party, particularly in the absence of Captain Clark and himself: The commanding officer is also sorry to find any man, who has been engaged by himself and Captain Clark for the expedition on which they have entered, so destitute of understanding, as not to be able to draw the distinction between being placed under the command of another officer, whose will in such case would be their law, and that of obeying the orders of Captain Clark and himself communicated to them through Sergeant Ordway, who, as one of the party, has during their necessary absence been charged with the execution of their orders; acting from those orders expressly, and not from his own caprice, and who, is in all respects accountable to us for the faithful observance of the same.

A moments reflection must convince every man of our party, that were we to neglect the more important and necessary arrangements in relation to the voyage we are now entering in, for the purpose merely of remaining at camp in order to communicate our orders in person to the individuals of the party on mere points of police, they would have too much reason to complain; nay, even to fear the ultimate success of the enterprise in which we are all embarked. The abuse of some of the party with respect to the privilege heretofore granted them of going into the country, is not less displeasing; to such as have made hunting or other business a pretext to cover their design of visiting a neighboring whiskey shop, he cannot for the present extend this privilege; and does therefore most positively direct, that Colter, Boley, Weiser, and Robertson do not receive permission to leave camp under any pretext whatever for ten days, after this order is read on parade, unless otherwise directed hereafter by Captain Clark or himself. The commanding officers highly approve of the conduct of Sergeant Ordway. –

The carpenters, blacksmiths, and in short the whole party (except Floyd who has been specially directed to perform other duties) are to obey implicitly the orders of Sergeant Ordway, who has received our instructions on these subjects, and is held accountable to us for their due execution. –

Meriwether Lewis
Captain. 1st U.S. Regiment Infantry Commanding Detachment

Sergeant Ordway will read the within order to the men on the parade the morning after the receipt of the same. -

M. Lewis Captain.

(Gary Moulton, ed., *The Journals of the Lewis & Clark Expedition*, vol. 2, 178-179.)

Detachment Orders
Camp River Dubois, April 1st 1804

[Clark]

The Commanding officers did yesterday proceed to take the necessary enlistments and select the detachment destined for the expedition through the interior of the continent of North America; and [has] have accordingly selected persons herein after mentioned, as those which are to constitute their permanent detachment. (Viz).

William Bratton	+
John Colter	+
John Collins	+
Reubin Field	+
Joseph Field	
Charles Floyd	
Peter [Weiser]	
Ct Mll [court-martial?]	
Patrick Gass	+
George Gibson	
Silas Goodrich	+
Thomas P. Howard	
Hugh Hall	+
Hugh McNeal	
John Newman	+
John Ordway	+
Nathaniel Pryor	+
John Potts	+
Moses B Reed	
George Shannon	+
John Shields	+
John B Thompson	+
Richard Windsor	
William Werner	
Peter Weiser	(+)
Joseph Whitehouse	+ &
Alexander Willard	

The commanding officers do also retain in their service until further orders-: The following persons, Richard Warfington, Robert Frazer, John Robertson, & John Boley. [NB: Moses B. Read] who whilst they remain with the detachment shall be incorporated with the second, and third squads of the same, and are to be treated in all respects as those men who form the permanent detachment, except with regard to an advance of pay, and the distribution of arms and accoutrements intended for the expedition.

The following persons (Viz Charles Floyd, John Ordway, and Nathaniel Pryor are this day appointed sergeants. with equal power (unless when otherwise specially ordered). The authority, pay, and emoluments, attached to the said rank of sergeants in the military service of the United States, and to hold the said appointments, and be respected accordingly, during their good behavior or the Will and pleasure of the said commanding officers.

To insure order among the party, as well as to promote a regular police in camp, The commanding officers, have thought to divide the detachment into three squads, and to place a sergeant in command of each, who are held immediately responsible to the commanding officers, for the regular and orderly deportment of the individuals composing their respective squads.-

The following individuals after being duly balloted for, have fallen in the several squads as hereafter stated, and are accordingly placed under the direction of the sergeants whose name precedes those of his squad.

(Viz:) 1st Squad
Sergeant Nathaniel Pryor
Privates
George Gibson
Thomas P. Howard
George Shannon
John Shields
John Collins
Joseph Whitehouse
Peter Weiser
Hugh Hall

2nd Squad
Sergt. Charles Floyd
Privates
Hugh McNeal
Patrick Gass
Reubin Field
Joseph Field
John B. Thompson
[John Newman]
Richard Warfington
Robert Frazer

3rd Squad
Sergt. John Ordway
Privates
William Braton
John Colter
[Moses B. Reed]

225

Alexander Willard
William Werner
Silas Goodrich
John Potts
John Robertson
John Boley

The camp kettles, and other public utensils for cooking shall be produced this evening after the parade is dismissed; and an equal division shall take place of the same, among the noncommissioned officers commanding the squads. Those non-commissioned officers shall make an equal division of the proportion of those utensils between their own messes of their respective squads,- each squad shall be divided into two messes, at the head of one of which the commanding sergeant shall preside. The sergeants messes will consist of four privates only to be admitted under his discretion, the balance of each squad shall form the second mess of each Squad.

During the indisposition of Sergeant Pryor, George Shannon is appointed (protempor) to discharge his [and] the Said Pryor's duty in his squad.-

The party for the convenience of being more immediately under the eye of the several sergeants having charge of them, will make the necessary exchange of their bunks and rooms for that purpose as shall be verbally directed by us.-

Until otherwise directed, Sergeant John Ordway will continue to keep the roster and detail the men of the detachment for the several duties which it may be necessary, they should perform, as also to transcribe in a book furnished him for that purpose, those or such other orders as the commanding officers Shall think proper to publish from time, to time for the government of the Party.-

Signed
Meriwether Lewis
Wm. Clark

(Gary Moulton, ed., *The Journals of the Lewis & Clark Expedition*, vol. 2, 187-190.)

Detachment Orders
River a Dubois, April 7th 1804

[Ordway]

During the absence of the commanding officers at St. Louis, the party are to consider themselves under the immediate command of Sergeant John Ordway, who will be held accountable for the police; and good order of the camp, during that period. Every individual of the party will strictly attend to all necessary duties required for the benefit of the party; and to the regulations heretofore made which in now in force. Sergeant Floyd will stay in our quarters, attend to them, and the store; and to other duties required of him; he will also assist Sergeant Ordway as much as possible. -

Signed
Wm. Clark
Meriwether Lewis

(Gary Moulton, ed., *The Journals of the Lewis & Clark Expedition*, vol. 2, 193.)

Detachment Orders
April 21st 1804

[Ordway]

During the absence of the commanding officers at St. Louis the party are to be under the immediate command of Sergeant John Ordway agreeable to the orders of the 7th instant.

Signed
Wm. Clark Captain

(Gary Moulton, ed., *The Journals of the Lewis & Clark Expedition*, vol. 2, 206.)

Detachment Orders
River a Dubois, May the 4th 1804

[Ordway]

Orders, Corporal Warfington, Frazer, Boley, & the detachment late from Captain Stoddards Company will form a mess under the direction of the Corporal, who shall be held accountable for their conduct in Camp.-

Orders. The Sergeants are to mount as officers of the day during the time we delay at this place, and whilst on duty to command the detachment in the absence of the commanding officer- He is to see that the guard do their duty, and that the detachment attend to the regulations heretofore made and those which may be made from time to time. No man of the detachment shall leave camp without permission from the commanding officer present, except the French hands who have families may be allowed to stay with their families at this island.-

Sergt. Ordway for duty to day. Sergt. Floyd tomorrow & Sergt. Pryor the next day.-

Signed Wm. Clark
Captain Commanding

(Gary Moulton, ed., *The Journals of the Lewis & Clark Expedition*, vol. 2, 212.)

Orders
St. Charles Thursday the 17th May 1804

[Ordway]

A sergeant and four men of the party destined for the Missouri Expedition will convene at 11 oClock to day on the quarter deck of the boat, and form themselves into a court martial to hear and determine (in behalf of the Capt.) the evidences adduced against William Werner & Hugh Hall for being absent last night without leave; contrary to orders; -& John Collins 1st for being absent without leave- 2nd for behaving in an unbecoming manner at the Ball last night – 3rd for speaking in a language last night after his return tending to bring into disrespect the orders of the commanding officer

Signd. W. Clark Comdg.
Detail for Court martial

Segt. John Ordway Prs.

Members
R. Fields
R. Windsor
J. Whitehouse
Jo. Potts

The Court convened agreeable to orders on the 17th of May 1804

Sgt. John Ordway P. members Joseph Whitehouse, Rueben Field, Potts, Richard Windsor.

After being duly sworn the court proceeded to the trial of William Warner & Hugh Hall on the following Charges Viz: for being absent without leave last night contrary to orders, to this charge the prisoners plead guilty. The court of opinion that the prisoners Warner & Hall are both guilty of being absent from camp without leave it being a breach of the rules and articles of war and do sentence them each to receive twenty five lashes on their naked back, but the court recommend them from their former good conduct, to the mercy of the commanding officer.- at the same court was tried John Collins charged 1st for being absent without leave- 2d. for behaving in an unbecoming manner at the ball last night [and] 3dly for Speaking in a language after his return to camp tending to bring into disrespect the orders of the commanding officer- The prisoner pleads guilty to the first charge but not guilty to the two last charges.- after mature deliberation & agreeable to the evidence adduced. The court are of opinion that the prisoner is guilty of all the charges alleged against him it being a breach of the rules & Articles of War and do sentence him to receive fifty lashes on his naked back – The commanding officer approves of the proceedings & decision of the court martial and orders that the punishment of John Collins take place this evening at sun set in the presence of the party.- The punishment ordered to be inflicted on William Warner & Hugh Hall, is remitted under the assurance arriving from a confidence which the commanding officer has the sincerity of the recommendation from the court.- after the punishment, Warner Hall & Collins will return to their squads and duty-

The Court is dissolved.

Sign. Wm. Clark

(Gary Moulton, ed., *The Journals of the Lewis & Clark Expedition*, vol. 2, 235-237.)

Detachment Orders
May 26th 1804

[Lewis]

The Commanding Officers direct, that the three Squads under the command of Sergeants Floyd Ordway and Pryor heretofore forming two messes each, shall until further orders constitute three messes only, the same being altered and organized as follows---

1. Sergeant. Charles Floyd.

Privates:
2. Hugh McNeal
3. Patrick Gass
4. Reubin Field
5. John B Thompson
6. John Newman
7. Richard Windsor
+ Francois Rivet &
8. Joseph Field

9. Sergeant. John Ordway.

Privates.
10. William Bratton
11. John Colter
12. Moses B. Reed
13. Alexander Willard
14. William Warner
15. Silas Goodrich
16. John Potts &
17. Hugh Hall

18. Sergeant. Nathaniel Pryor.

Privates.
19. George Gibson
20. George Shannon
21. John Shields
22. John Collins
23. Joseph Whitehouse
24. Peter Weiser
25. Pierre Cruzatte &
26. Francois Labiche

 The commanding officers further direct that the remainder of the detachment shall form two messes; and that the same be constituted as follows. (viz)-

Patroon, Baptiste Deschamps

Engages
Etienne Malboeuf
Paul Primeau
Charles Hébert
[Jean] Baptiste La Jeunesse
Peter Pinaut
Peter Roi
Joseph Collin

1. Corporal. Richard Warfington.

Privates
2. Robert Frazer
3. John Boley
4. John Dame
5. Ebenezer Tuttle
6. Isaac White.

 The commanding officers further direct that the messes of the Sergts. Floyd, Ordway and Pryor shall until further orders form the crew of the Bateaux; the mess of the Patroon La Jeunesse will form the permanent crew of the red pirogue; Corpl. Warfington's mess forming that of the white pirogue. –

 Whenever by any casualty it becomes necessary to furnish additional men to assist in navigating the pirogues, the same shall be furnished by daily detail from the privates who form the crew of Bateaux, exempting only from such detail, Thomas P. Howard and the men who are assigned to the two bow and the two stern oars. – For the present one man will be furnished daily to assist the crew of the white pirogue; this man must be an expert boatman.—

 The posts and duties of the Sergts. shall be as follows-- when the bateaux is under way, one Sergt. shall be stationed at the helm, one in the center on the rear of the starboard locker, and one at the bow. The Sergt. at the helm, shall steer the boat, and see that the baggage on the quarterdeck is properly arranged and stowed away in the most advantageous manner; to see that no cooking utensils or loose lumber of any kind is left on the deck to obstruct passage between the berths-- he will also attend to the compass when necessary.--

The Sergt. at the center will command the guard, manage the sails, see that the men at the oars do their duty; that they come on board at a proper season in the morning, and that the boat gets under way in due time; he will keep a good lookout for the mouths of all rivers, creeks, islands and other remarkable places and shall immediately report the same to the commanding officers; he will attend to the issues of spirituous liquors; he shall regulate the halting of the bateaux through the day to give the men refreshment, and will also regulate the time of her departure taking care that not more time than is necessary shall be expended at each halt-- it shall be his duty also to post a sentinel on the bank, near the boat whenever we come too and halt in the course of the day, at the same time he will (accompanied by his two guards) reconnoiter the forest around the place of landing to the distance of at least one hundred paces. When we come too for the purpose of encamping at night, the Sergt. of the guard shall post two sentinels immediately on our landing; one of whom shall be posted near the boat, and the other at a convenient distance in rear of the encampment; at night the Sergt. must be always present with his guard, and his is positively forbidden to suffer any man his guard to absent himself on any pretext whatever; he will at each relief through the night, accompanied by the two men last off their posts, reconnoiter in every direction around the camp to the distance of at least one hundred and fifty paces, and also examine the situation of the boat and pirogues, and see that they ly safe and free from the bank.

It shall be the duty of the sergt. at the bow, to keep a good look our for all danger which may approach, either of the enemy, or obstructions which may present themselves to (the) passage of the boat; of the first he will notify the Sergt. at the center, who will communicate the information to the commanding officers, and of the second or obstructions to the boat he will notify the Sergt. at the helm; he will also report to the commanding officer through the Sergt. at the center all pirogues boats canoes or other craft which he may discover in the river, and all hunting camps or parties of Indians in view of which we may pass. He will at all times be provided with a setting pole and assist the bowman in poling and managing the bow of the boat. It will be his duty also to give and answer all signals, which may hereafter be established for the government of the pirogues and parties on shore.

The Sergts. will on each morning before our departure relieve each other in the following manner—The Sergt. at the helm will parade the new guard, relieve the Sergt. and the old guard, and occupy the middle station in the boat; the Sergt. who had been stationed the preceding day at the bow will place himself at the helm.-- The sergts. in addition to those duties are directed each to keep a separate journal from day to day of all passing occurrences, and such other observations on the country &c. as shall appear to them worthy of notice--

The Sergts. are relieved and exempt from all labor of making fires, pitching tents or cooking, and will direct and make the men of their several messes perform an equal portion of those duties.—

The guard shall hereafter consist of one sergeant and six privates & engages.—

Patroon Deschamps, Copl. Warfington, and George Drewyer [Drouillard], are exempt from guard duty; the two former will attend particularly to their pirogues at all times, and see that their lading is in good order, and that the same is kept perfectly free from rain or other moisture; the latter will perform certain duties on shore which will be assigned him form time to time: all other soldiers and engaged men of whatever description must perform their regular tour of guard duty.—

All details for guard or other duty will be made in the evening when we encamp, and the duty to be performed will be entered on, by the individual so warned, the next morning.-- provision for one day will be issued to the party on each evening after we have encamped; the same will be cooked on that evening by the several messes, and a proportion of it reserved for the next day as no cooking will be allowed in the day while on the march—

Sergt. John Ordway will continue to issue the provisions and make the details for guard or other duty.-- the day after tomorrow dried corn and grease will be issued to the party, the next day pork and flour, and the day following Indian meal and pork; and in conformity to that ration provisions will continue to be issued to the party until further orders.— should any of these messes prefer Indian meal to flour they may receive it accordingly— no pork is to be issued when we have fresh meat on hand. Labiche and Cruzatte will man the larboard bow oar alternately, and the one not engaged at the oar will attend as the bows-man, and when the attention of both these persons is necessary at the bow, their oar is to be manned by any idle hand on board.-

Meriwether Lewis Capt.
Wm. Clark Cpt.

(Gary Moulton, ed., *The Journals of the Lewis & Clark Expedition*, vol. 2, 254-258.)

Detachment Orders
Nadawa Island July 8th 1804.

[Lewis]

In order to insure a prudent and regular use of all provisions issued to the crew of the bateaux in future, as also to provide for the equal distribution of the same among the individuals of the several messes, The commanding officers do appoint the following persons to receive, cook, and take charges of the provisions which may from time to time be issued to their respective messes, (viz) John B. Thompson to Sergt. Floyd's mess, William Warner to Sergt. Orday's mess, and John Collins to Sergt. Pryor's Mess.- These superintendents of provision, are held immediately responsible to the commanding officers for a judicious consumption of the provision which they receive; they are to cook the same for their several messes in due time, and in such manner as is most wholesome and best calculated to afford the greatest proportion of nutriment; in their mode of cooking they are to exercise their own judgment; they shall also point out what part, and what proportion of the mess provisions are to be consumed at each stated meal (i.e.) morning, noon and night; nor is any man at any time to take or consume any part of the mess provisions without the privity, knowledge and consent of the superintendent. The superintendent is also held responsible for all cooking utensils of his mess. In consideration of the duties imposed by this order on Thompson, Warner, and Collins, they will in future be exempt from guard duty, tho' they will still be held on the roster for that duty, and their regular tour - shall be performed by some one of their respective messes; they are exempted also from pitching the tents of the mess, collecting firewood, and forks poles &c. for cooking and drying such fresh meat as may be furnished them; those duties are to be also performed by the other members of the mess.-

M. Lewis
Wm. Clark

(Gary Moulton, ed., *The Journals of the Lewis & Clark Expedition*, vol. 2, 359-360.)

Orders
August 26th 1804.

[Lewis]

The commanding officers have thought it proper to appoint Patrick Gass, a Sergeant in the Corps of Volunteers for North Western Discovery, he is therefore to be obeyed and respected accordingly.

Sergt. Gass is directed to take charge of the late Sergt. Floyd's mess, and immediately to enter on the discharge of such other duties, as by their previous orders been prescribed for the government of the sergeants of this corps.

The commanding officers have every reason to hope from the previous faithful services of Sergeant Gass, that this expression of their approbation will be still further confirmed, by his vigilant attention in future to his duties as a sergeant. The commanding officers are still further confirmed in the high opinion they had previously formed of the capacity, diligence and integrity of Sergt. Gass, from the wish expressed by a large majority of his comrades for his appointment as sergeant.

Meriwether Lewis
Captain 1st U.S. Regiment Infantry
Wm. Clark Captain &.

(Gary Moulton, ed., *The Journals of the Lewis & Clark Expedition*, vol. 3, 14-15.)

Orders
October the 8th 1804.

[Clark]

Robert Frazer being regularly enlisted and having become one of the Corps of Volunteers for North Western Discovery, he is therefore to be viewed & respected accordingly; and will be annexed to Sergeant Gass's mess.

Wm. Clark Captain &.
Meriwether Lewis
Captain 1st U.S. Regiment Infantry

River Marapa

(Gary Moulton, ed., *The Journals of the Lewis & Clark Expedition*, vol. 3, 152-153.)

Orders
13th of October 1804.

[Lewis and Clark]

A court Martial to consist of nine members will set to day at 12 o'clock for the trial of John Newman now under Confinement. Capt. Clark will attend to the forms & rules of a president without giving his opinion.

Detail for the Court Martial
Sergt. John Ordway
Sergeant Pat. Gass
Jo. Shield
H. Hall
Jo. Collins
Wm. Werner
Wm. Bratten
Jo. Shannon
(P Wiser)
Silas Goodrich

Meriwether Lewis Capt.
1st U.S. Regt. Infantry
Wm Clark Capt
Or [on?] E. N W D

In conformity to the above order the Court martial convened this day for the trial of John Newman, charged with "having uttered repeated expressions of a highly criminal and mutinous nature; the same having a tendency not only to destroy every principle of military discipline, but also to alienate the affections of the individuals composing this detachment to their officers, and disaffect them to the service for which they have been so sacredly and solemnly engaged."- The prisoner plead not guilty to the charge exhibited against him. The court after having duly considered the evidence adduced, as well as the defense of the said prisoner, are unanimously of opinion that the prisoner John Newman is guilty of every part of the charge exhibited against him, and do sentence him (under the articles of the [blank] section of the [blank] agreeably to the rules and articles of war, to receive seventy five lashes on his bear back, and to be henceforth discarded from the permanent party engaged for North Western discovery; two thirds of the court concurring in the sum and nature of the punishment awarded. The commanding officers approve and confirm the sentence of the court, and direct the punishment take place tomorrow between the hours of one and two P.M.- The commanding officers further direct that John Newman in future be attached to the mess and crew of the red pirogue as a laboring hand on board the same, and that he be deprived of his arms and accoutrements, and not be permitted the honor of mounting guard until further orders; the commanding officers further direct that in lue of the guard duty from which Newman has been exempted by virtue of this order, that he shall be exposed to such drudgeries as they may think proper to direct from time to time with a view to the general relief of the detachment.-

Meriwether Lewis Captain
1st U.S. Regiment Infantry
Wm. Clark Captain
Or [on?] E. N W D

(Gary Moulton, ed., *The Journals of the Lewis & Clark Expedition*, vol. 3, 170-171.)

Orders
Fort Clatsop January 1st 1806

The fort being now completed, the Commanding officers think proper to direct: that the guard shall be regularly relieved each morning at sunrise. The post of the new guard shall be in the room of the Sergeants respectively commanding the same. The sentinel shall be posted, both day and night, on the parade in front of the commanding officer's quarters; Tho' should he at any time think proper to remove himself to any other part of the fort, in order the better to inform himself of the designs or approach of any party of savages, he is not only at liberty, but is hereby required to do so. It shall be the duty of the sentinel also to announce the arrival of all parties of Indians to the Sergeant of the Guard, who shall immediately report the same to the commanding officers.

The Commanding Officers require and charge the garrison to treat the natives in a friendly manner; nor will they be permitted at any time, to abuse, assault or strike them; unless such abuse or assault or stroke be first given by the natives. Nevertheless it shall be right for any individual, in a peaceable manner, to refuse admittance to, or put out of his room, any native who may become troublesome to him; and should such native refuse to go when requested, or attempt to enter their rooms after being forbidden to do so; it shall be the duty of the Sergeant of the Guard on information of the same, to put such native out of the fort and see that he is not admitted during that day unless specially permitted; and the Sergeant of the Guard may for this purpose employ such coercive measures (not extending to the taking of life) as shall at his discretion be deemed necessary to effect the same.

When any native shall be detected in theft, the Sergt. of the guard shall immediately inform the commanding officers of the same, to the end that such measures may be pursued with respect to the culprit as they shall think most expedient.

At sunset on each day, the Sergt. attended by the interpreter Charbonneau and two of his guard, will collect and put out of the fort, all Indians except such as may specially be permitted to remain by the commanding officers, nor shall they be again admitted until the main gate be opened the ensuing morning.

At Sunset, or immediately after the Indians have been dismissed, both gates shall be shut, and secured, and the main gate locked and continue so until sunrise the next morning. The water-gate may be used freely by the garrison for the purpose of passing and re-passing at all times, tho' from sunset, until sunrise, it shall be the duty of the sentinel to open the gate for, and shut it after all persons passing and re-passing, suffering the same never to remain unfixed long[er] than is absolutely necessary.

It shall be the duty of the Sergt. of the Guard to keep the key of the meat house, and to cause the guard to keep regular fires therein when the same may be necessary, and also once at least in 24 hours to visit the canoes and see that they are safely secured; and shall further on each morning after he is relieved, make his report verbally to the commanding officers.—

Each of the old guard will every morning after being relieved furnish two loads of wood (each) for the commanding officers fire.

No man is to be particularly exempt from the duty of bringing meat from the woods, nor none except the cooks and interpreters from that of mounting guard.

Each mess being furnished with an ax, they are directed to deposit in the room of the commanding officers all other public tools of which they are possessed; nor (are) shall the same at any time hereafter be taken from the said deposit without knowledge and permission of the commanding officers; and any individual so borrowing the tools are strictly required to bring the same back the moment he has ceased to use them. And in no case shall they be permitted to keep them out all night.

Any individual selling or disposing of any tool or iron or steel instrument, arms, accoutrements or ammunition, shall be deemed guilty of a breach of this order, and shall be tried and punished accordingly.-

the tools loaned to John Shields are excepted from the restrictions of this order.

Meriwether Lewis
Capt. 1st U.S. Regt
Wm. Clark Capt

(Gary Moulton, ed., *The Journals of the Lewis & Clark Expedition*, vol. 6, 156-158.)

Appendix C

The Uniforms of the Lewis and Clark Expedition*

The Lewis and Clark expedition was a military operation. Of the 33 individuals who made the trip to the Pacific, there were two officers in command and 26 enlisted men. Previous scholarship has focused on the places visited and the discoveries made by the expedition; however, little has ever been written about the expedition's uniforms, arms, and accoutrements. This article and drawings show the uniforms, weapons, and accoutrements worn by the expedition at the time it left St. Louis. It does not address the items carried by civilians or show the modifications and replacements that occurred as time went on. Readers who have additional documents are encouraged to contact Dr. Charles H. Cureton at 757-788-3781 or e-mail at: curetonc@monroe.army.mil.

The United States Army at the time of the expedition was organized under the Military Peace Establishment of 16 March 1802. This organization allowed for two regiments of infantry, one regiment of artillery, a small corps of engineers, and the general staff. The Army establishment consisted of a total of 3,287 officers and men. All three line regiments provided soldiers to the expedition.[1]

The Officers

The commander of the expedition was Captain Meriwether Lewis of the 1st Infantry.[2] The uniform of the regiment was detailed in the standing orders of the 1st Infantry dated July 1802 and signed by Colonel John F. Hamtramck.[3] It was particularly detailed as to officer dress. The primary uniform for officers consisted of a dark blue woolen cutaway coat with red woolen collar (known in the period as a 'cape'), cuffs, and lapels. All buttonholes were trimmed in silver lace. The coat was lined in white woolen shaloon, and where the turnbacks for each skirt were secured, there were two red cloth diamonds edged in silver. Lieutenants were to wear a silver lace and bullion epaulet on the left shoulder, and captains wore a single silver epaulet on the right shoulder. The opposite shoulder had a dark blue strap edged in silver lace in place of a second epaulet. Field grade officers (majors, lieutenant colonels and colonels) wore two epaulets. Buttons for the officers of the 1st Regiment were silver with the regimental number, "1," surrounded by "UNITED STATES."[4] There were 10 buttons on each

---

* Text and uniform plates provided by Dr. Charles H. Cureton and Stephen J. Allie.

lapel, four on each cuff, four on the collar, four on each pocket, and three on each tail. A single small button secured the epaulet and another secured the opposite shoulder strap. Since sleeves fitted close to the arm, cuffs often closed with two or more small buttons placed vertically on the back slit. The coat closed in front with three hooks and eyes; the backward sweep of the front precluded the lapels buttoning over or the coat closing to the waist. Additional features from contemporary portraits show that by 1802, the skirts had the turnbacks sewn down in keeping with English military fashion. Portraits also show the turnbacks edged in red.

The coat was worn with a white woolen waistcoat and white woolen pantaloons in winter and a high-quality white linen waistcoat and white linen pantaloons in summer. Buttons for the waistcoats would have been regimental. Pantaloons came into fashion late in the previous century and were similar to breeches except the legs for pantaloons extended to the ankle instead of just below the knee. The regulation black cocked hat had a black silk cockade with small silver eagle that was held in place by silver lace and a regimental button. The cocked hat still showed vestiges of its tri-corn origins and had not yet become the bi-corn chapeau typical of the War of 1812 era. Around the crown of the hat would have been a silver cord and tassels. A white feather plume completed the headdress. Officer gloves were white buckskin, and when the officer was on duty he was to wear a red silk sash and a silver gorget. The boots prescribed for infantry officers were black and cut in the hussar style with either a scalloped or a pointed front peak and finished with a black tassel. Officers wore black leather or silk stocks in the same manner and for the same purpose as the modern cravat or tie is used.[5]

Officers had a less expensive undress coat for daily wear and for informal occasions. The undress coat was identical to the dress or uniform coat in all respects except that it omitted the silver lace trim from the buttonholes.[6] The waistcoat, pantaloons, boots, gorget, and sash remained as for the formal uniform. Officers of the 1st Infantry also had a red woolen roundabout (a tailless jacket similar to a sleeved waistcoat) for informal wear during winter months. It was worn with blue woolen pantaloons that were edged along the outseams in white. A simple fashionable black round hat (top hat) was also permitted for undress and fatigue. Some military round hats carried a cockade on the left side.

For use in inclement or cold weather, company grade officers were prescribed a dark blue surtout (overcoat). The surtout was made of a heavier weight wool than used for the uniform, and it extended well below the knee. It was double-breasted on the upper half and single-breasted to just below the waist. All buttons were regimental and the coat was lined in red and had a red collar. This overcoat had two capes that were 9 and 10 inches long.[7]

The second in command was Captain William Clark. This rank is problematic since Clark's commission was as a first lieutenant of artillery.[8] Lewis had wanted him returned to active duty as a captain; however, no vacancies in that grade existed so Clark had to accept the lower rank. Although Lewis designated William Clark a co-captain, it is unclear whether he went to the extent of wearing his epaulet on the right shoulder. Personal honor and integrity were the hallmarks of a gentleman and it is possible that Clark would not have presented himself as a captain unless he had official sanction from the War Department to do so. Regardless, other then in the placement of the epaulet, there was no difference in the dress of captains and lieutenants. In general, artillery officers wore the same uniform as infantry officers except the lace, buttons, and epaulets were gold instead of silver. The lace and epaulet(s) on the artillery coat were gold bullion.[9] All buttons were gilt and featured a cannon with USA&E (for the United States Artillery and Engineers) in script beneath.[10] Artillery coats were lined in red, thus the turnbacks were red with blue cloth diamonds edged in gold.[11] Except for having gilt artillery buttons, all other garments were as prescribed for infantry officers. Headdress was the same as infantry but with gold trim and devices in place of silver. There are no surviving general orders for artillery officers as were written for officers of the 1st Infantry. However, according to the illustrations in the Gass journal, Clark is shown consistently wearing a round hat, so that article was common to both artillery and infantry officers.[12] Gass's drawings also show Clark wearing the untrimmed undress coat, which would have been appropriate for the round hat. Clark's boots would have been black, made in the hussar style and with a black tassel.

Officers were armed with a spontoon and a sword. There was no regulation pattern for each; however, surviving spontoons follow the style shown in the illustrations. Swords for company grade officers could have either straight or curved blades, and both artillery and infantry officers carried their swords from a shoulder belt. Scabbards were black leather with either gilt or silver mountings according to the color of metal used for the hilt. Artillery officers had sword hilts and mountings in gilt corresponding to their buttons, while infantry officers had silver hilts and mountings. The color of the sword knot and belt plate matched the button color, silver for an officer of infantry and gold for artillery.

There are some issues regarding wear of the uniform. The uniform coat, undress coat, and roundabout were fitted garments and were cut differently from present-day styles. This is not to say that they were uncomfortable and ill suited; these garments were for an age that had different ideas as to the function of clothing than Americans do today. Sleeves were cut close to the arm and extended as far as the wrist. The cut of the coat at the area of the armscye was also unique and can be seen in the back views shown in the accompanying plates. Garments made between the mid 1760s and about 1819 had the armscye considerably inset, and this presented a somewhat narrow-shouldered look that is very distinctive. Not only was there a narrow-shouldered silhouette to the figure, the sleevehead was smoothly set into the armsyce such as to present a smooth line from coat to sleeve. There was certainly no ridge at the beginning of the sleeve as characteristic of present-day coats or most reproductions made using modern patterns. The position of the epaulet reflected the tailoring, that is, the epaulet strap buttoned on the collar and not on the shoulder and the strap did not extend beyond the armscye, it was the bullion that fell over the top of the sleeve. The epaulet laid close and conformed to the lines of the shoulder as shown. It did not stand up and project out over the sleeve as happened with epaulet design later in the century. Also, it is not generally appreciated that epaulets were very expensive items and could cost more then the coat, waistcoat, and pantaloons combined. This brings the question as to how much officers in the field wore their epaulets when on the march, on fatigue, or in camp. The cross strap, or bridle, that held the epaulet in place would by placement on either the right or left shoulder (or both if field grade) have indicated the officer's rank. It should also be pointed out that there was little difference in the epaulet itself for any rank except for general officers, who had stars on the strap; otherwise, it is the number and placement of the epaulet that indicated the wearer's rank. It is likely that Lewis and Clark would have saved their epaulets for special occasions. Last, when wearing the coat, the sash was worn over the waistcoat and under the coat; it was not worn outside of an open-faced coat. When wearing the roundabout, the sash was on the outside and tied over the sword belt.

    What happened to the two officers' uniforms over the next several years of arduous wear and tear is not known precisely. However, there are some considerations that should be mentioned. The frontier notwithstanding, Lewis and Clark were officers and gentlemen and would have attempted to maintain the dress standards of their class and rank for as long as was possible. America in this period was a very class-conscious society, and a person's dress and appearance were a fundamental part to their status and image. In all likelihood, Lewis and Clark had at least two uniforms, the undress and dress coats. Lewis should have had the roundabout as well, and both quite probably had their surtouts. They also had a number of shirts and socks for at least the early stages of the expedition. Given the importance placed on appearance, both officers would have contrived to set themselves apart from the enlisted men.

The Enlisted Men

The enlisted men of the expedition comprise two distinct groups. Half of the expedition members who made it to the Pacific coast and the men who returned the boats from the Mandan villages were enlisted in the Regular Army prior to the expedition.[13] Consequently, these men had regimental clothing issued by their original units and thus were dressed in the regulation uniform of the infantry and artillery. There is a surprising amount of information on the uniforms of this period, so it is possible to establish the appearance of these soldiers with some accuracy. A few general rules are necessary. Enlisted uniforms were similar in their general tailoring to officer clothing; however, their design was different and the materials used were of a lesser quality. Sergeants' uniforms and clothing were made of slightly better cloth but otherwise were identical in design to the rank and file dress.

The infantry uniform consisted of a dark blue cutaway coat, lined white with white turnbacks, and had red lapels, cuffs, and collars.[14] These coats were made according to a design approved in 1798, when Congress expanded the Army to meet the demands of a possible war with France. The massive expansion of the Army forced the Quartermaster Department to redesign the previous uniform with an eye toward reducing its cost. A more simplified uniform coat emerged that included a reduction in the number of coat buttons from 44 to 18. The lower number was accomplished by eliminating all collar, cuff, and pocket buttons and reducing to two the number of buttons on each tail. Furthermore, all lace trim as well as the rear pocket flaps were eliminated, and the turn-backs were non-functional. For all its color, this was a considerably simplified uniform and the changes reduced the cost of the coats from $2.50 to just over $.80.[15] As it happened, war with France never materialized and the Army was again reduced. This created a surplus of the 1798 pattern, and it was from these stocks of clothing that Lewis and Clark's infantry soldiers received their clothing issue. Infantry uniforms for enlisted men had pewter buttons instead of silver, but they were of the same design as officer buttons, that is, they had the regimental number in the center surrounded by "UNITED STATES." The number in the center might differ, however, as the uniforms produced for the expanded Army were for an establishment of 16 regiments. The Quartermaster Department had to use up the surplus stocks, so the soldiers of the two infantry regiments that survived the reduction were issued coats bearing regimental buttons numbered 1 through 16 without regard for the regiment to which they were actually assigned.[16] The supply of 1798 coats lasted until after the expedition had departed. At that time it was determined that new coats would be required for the 1804 issue and a new pattern was chosen. Consequently, when the expedition returned two years later, the Army had its enlisted men dressed in a different uniform.[17]

The remainder of the uniform followed officer dress but with several details unique to enlisted men. Waistcoats were made of a durable white wool, but the waistcoat had neither a collar nor pockets. The overalls were linen for summer with blue edging along the outseams and white wool with blue edging for winter. Though called overalls, the styles of this period were relatively close fitting and were called overalls because the base of the leg was open and extended to the ankle. Pantaloons differed in that they were shaped to the leg and tied at the base under the instep. Enlisted overalls were worn with short, black-painted linen gaiters that were closed with four small pewter buttons. The winter overalls were made of white wool and had the outside seam edged in blue. However, they were actually gaitered overalls, that is, the lower leg was cut so as to cover the shoe. These fitted over the top of the shoe and closed tightly around the calf with three small buttons.[18] Shoes were low quarter and were closed by buckles.

Enlisted headdress prescribed for infantry was distinctly different from what officers wore. The pattern resembled headdress adopted for the Legion of United States during the 1790s and was also similar in design to headdress adopted by the British army for certain units. The American version was a black felt round hat 5-7/8" tall and 7-3/16" wide, with a 3" brim edged with white worsted binding. Over the crown of the hat was a wire-reinforced 4"-wide strip of bearskin. On the left side was a white deer tail secured by a black leather cockade and pewter eagle.[19] For fatigue and when on the march, the bearskin, deer tail, and cockade were removed.

Undergarments consisted of white linen shirts for summer and woolen flannel shirts for winter. Shirts of the period were quite voluminous and extended to below the crotch. Since underwear was not issued to enlisted men, and were not generally worn anyway, the shirt performed this function and kept the outer garments from getting stained. The shirt was always worn with a black leather stock, which was generally made of a heavier leather then stocks worn by officers.

All noncommissioned rank was distinguished by epaulets. Normally, epaulets followed the button color but were made of worsted wool instead of the officer's bullion, white for infantry and yellow for artillery. To simplify acquisition and distribution of this article for the proposed expanded Army, however, the 1798 uniform had red epaulets for all noncommissioned officers regardless of their branch. Otherwise, the placement of epaulets mirrored that for company grade officers. Corporals wore a single epaulet on the left shoulder and sergeants wore theirs on the right. Sergeants also wore a scarlet worsted sash and carried a sword.[20]

The artillery uniform was identical to its infantry counterpart except for a few small details. The tail lining and turnbacks on the coat were red. Further, instead of the pewter infantry buttons, the uniform had brass buttons with similar artillery markings to those found on officer buttons.[21] In 1802, the artillery uniform was slightly modified. The buttonholes were trimmed with yellow worsted lace and the lapels were sewn permanently to the coat.[22] The artillery waistcoats differed from those of the infantry by having collars and brass buttons. Artillery overalls were the same as worn by infantry but with the outer seam edged in yellow. Another difference in their dress was that the men wore cocked hats of a pattern similar to the officer pattern, but the enlisted hat was bound in yellow lace and had a black leather cockade with gilt eagle and a white worsted plume.[23]

For fatigue, all enlisted men wore a linen roundabout. Basically a jacket, it closed with eight small pewter or brass buttons according to the branch. The pattern jacket remained in use with only minor changes for fashion until the 1850s, and it is the forerunner of the modern Battle Dress Utility worn by soldiers. Enlisted men attached to the Lewis and Clark expedition would also have had plain loose-fitting linen trousers and a Russian-sheeting (hemp cloth) fatigue frock. The latter was essentially a large overshirt.[24] The work uniform was completed with a cloth fatigue hat.[25] Based on the French army pattern, these hats resembled an old-fashioned night cap, that is, they were made of two triangular pieces of dark blue uniform cloth from the previous year's coat (the uniform being replaced annually) and were trimmed with red cloth salvaged from the same garment.

The basic uniform dress was to suffice for most weather conditions, hence the need to replace it annually, but the War Department did provide cold weather clothing. In winter, each company had a supply of watch coats at a ratio of one coat for every four to six enlisted men in the command. These coats were not issued to individual soldiers but were for use by the men as they stood watch, simply trading them off as the guard changed. These coats were made of a heavy drab melton wool. The term drab refers to a range of color between light gray and medium brown. Since watch coats were company property, none of the soldiers transferred from regular units had these garments. However, Lewis did receive 15 of these coats from the Quartermaster Department. The number of coats indicates that

247

they were probably intended for the 15 men specifically recruited for the expedition.[26] The other soldiers are believed to have had blanket coats of heavy white wool with blue trim. According to the standing orders for the 1st Infantry, sergeants were issued officer pattern surtouts but made of an inferior quality wool.[27]

Firearms and accoutrements carried by the infantry and artillery soldiers were as used by the rest of the Army. The musket and bayonet were of the model adopted in 1795. Since the 1795 musket was a flintlock, each soldier also had a brass brush and picker for keeping the pan clean when firing. The bayonet was carried in a black leather scabbard suspended from a shoulder belt. Ammunition was carried in a large black leather cartridge box of a pattern adopted by the Continental Army during the Revolutionary War. Soldiers also had their bedding blanket and personal items in a knapsack of the type produced initially for the Army in 1792. There is no evidence of either haversacks or canteens being provided to the expedition.

In addition to the soldiers from infantry and artillery units, there was a third group of 15 men recruited specifically for the expedition. As they were not affiliated with any regular unit, it was decided to provide them a distinctive dress. The notable feature of their uniform was a drab-colored coatee. All that is known about the coatees is from a list of materials delivered to Philadelphia tailor Francis Brown on 6 June 1803.[28] The pattern for the standard coat of the time would not fit on the allotted cloth. What could be cut was a double-breasted jacket of the sort referred to in the period as a roundabout or jacket. The term coatee described a coat having short skirts, and sometimes the skirts were so short as to make the garment almost indistinguishable from a roundabout or jacket. During the American Revolution, some quartermaster clerks used the terms *coatee* and *jacket* interchangeably. This pattern allowed for 18 coat buttons to close the front, two small buttons to close each cuff, and two small buttons to secure the shoulder straps.[29] The argument favoring a double-breasted jacket is supported by the absence of waistcoats for these soldiers. The regulation uniform coat required a waistcoat to cover the exposed area in front, and the absence of this garment suggests that it was not required.[30]

The recruit coatees were made from superfine milled drab cloth.[31] Superfine was a very high quality woolen cloth with a tight weave and heavily felted surface nap. The goods were so tight that exposed cut edges could be used without risk that the material would unravel. It was used for the very best civilian coats and officers' uniform coats. As such it was far superior to the woolen cloth used for enlisted men's coats by the Army. The decision for a closed front uniform coat was in keeping with changes occurring with enlisted men's dress in the British army, and it predates the closed-front coat adopted by the American Army in 1810.[32]

The remainder of the special detachment's uniform consisted of the surplus clothing intended for the expanded Army. Instead of the regular Army soldiers' white overalls, the 15 men received obsolete pattern blue woolen overalls edged along the outseam in white. Except for the watchcoats, their shoes, fatigue frocks, and both linen and flannel shirts were as issued to all soldiers.[33] No hats were provided to the recruits, and they are depicted in the "common hats" typical of the period.

In addition to the unique uniform, the new enlistees were armed with rifles. The weapon was the 1792/1794 contract rifle that was shortened and fitted with rifle sling swivels, which matched the slings drawn for them by Lewis.[34] As was customary for riflemen, they were also provided with a waist belt, a rifleman's pouch, powderhorn, knife and scabbard, and a tomahawk.[35] Lewis had 15 rifle pouches and powder horn sets produced by Robert C. Martin.[36] He also provided extra powder horns and cartridge boxes. Like the regulars, these men were provided backpacks and blankets, but again there is no evidence of haversacks or canteens being issued.[37]

The clothing, equipment, and arms carried by the expedition were sufficient to deal with any eventuality. Availability of fatigue clothing meant that the primary uniform garments would have been spared for a time. However, they are not likely to have lasted the length of the expedition. References in the expedition's journals suggest that later in the expedition, Lewis and Clark attempted to replace worn-out items of uniform with similar garments made of buckskin. Regardless of when and how the soldiers' clothing evolved, the military character of the expedition would have been evident from the arms, accoutrements, and equipment carried by its members.

Image Notes

Image 1. Captain of infantry in dress with sword and spontoon. The sash depicted is too dark; it would have been similar in color to the lapels. Sleeves were fitted close to the shape of the arm.

Image 2. Captain of infantry in dress, back view. Notice that the epaulet lays on top of the shoulder and complements the shoulder line.

Image 3. Captain of infantry in undress with sword. The undress coat simply omitted the lace but was otherwise identical in design to the dress coat. The sash should be red. Note that the fringe to the sash in this period was a continuation of the same thread used in the weave of the sash and did not have the separate bullion knots adopted in 1832.

Image 4. Infantry officer in roundabout, front view. Note the location of the sleevehead. The sash should be red.

Image 5. Infantry officer in roundabout, back view. The seams show the inset sleeve very clearly.

Image 6. Infantry officer in surtout. The sash should be red.

Image 7. Artillery officer in undress, off duty. The artillery uniform for officers was the same as for infantry officers but with gilt buttons and red lining. When off duty, officers were to dispense with the sash.

Image 8. Sergeant of infantry. The early years of the Army's existence were ones of great economy. Accoutrements manufactured during the Revolution continued to be issued, and the illustrations provided were without regard to the color of the button. The sword shown is from a pattern believed to have been issued to noncommissioned officers of the Regular Army at the turn of the century. Most extant swords have brass hilts but there are some examples in steel.

Image 9. Private of infantry. The knapsack was painted linen.

Image 10. Private of artillery. The artillery uniform was distinguished by the yellow lace, brass buttons, and cocked hat. Note the brass picker and brush. They were suspended from a button on the side nearest where the soldier would have held his musket or rifle when priming the pan in preparation for firing.

Image 11. Private of infantry in fatigue jacket. Note the close fit of the jacket and sleeves. The length of the sleeves extended to the hand. The fatigue hat was made of old uniform cloth and had the regimental number on the front.

Image 12. Private of infantry in fatigue frock. This shows the loose fit of the pullover frock and the close-fitting overalls.

Image 13. Private of artillery in watchcoat. The watchcoat is based on civilian overcoats of the period. Accoutrements were worn outside of the coat. Note the gaitered overalls.

Image 14. Sergeant of infantry in surtout, front view. The sergeant's version of the officer's surtout was similar in cut but made of lower-quality wool.

Image 15. Private in blanket coat. The three bars indicated the weight of the blanket wool.

Image 16. "Recruit" rifle uniform. It appears that both cartridge box and shot pouch with powder horn were provided to this group. The waistbelt for the knife and tomahawk is black leather and is based on extant civilian examples. They show the tomahawk suspended from a pouch made to hold the blade.

Image 17. "Recruit" back view. The coat is shown without tails. The absence of much cloth for lining or interfacing suggests a very simple garment.

NOTES

1. Heitman, Francis B., *Historical Register and Dictionary of the United States Army, Vol. 2*, Government Printing Office, Washington, DC, 1903, 569.
2. Heitman, Francis B., *Historical Register and Dictionary of the United States Army, Vol. 1*, Government Printing Office, Washington, DC, 1903, 631.
3. Hamtramck, Col. J. F., Standing Orders of the First Regiment of Infantry, 1802, Detroit, 26 July 1802, Orderly book collection (item 104), Library of Congress, Washington DC.
4. Albert, Alphaeus H., *Record of American Uniform and Historical Buttons with Supplement*, Boyerstown Publishing Company, Boyerstown, PA, 1973, 16-18.
5. The complete uniform is described in Hamtramck, Col. J. F., Standing Orders of the First Regiment of Infantry, 1802. The uniform is best illustrated by a portrait of Captain David Bissell, 1st Infantry, dated 1803, in the collection of the David Bissell Mansion, St. Louis Parks, St. Louis, MO.
6. Hamtramck, Col. J. F., Standing Orders of the First Regiment of Infantry, 1802, Detroit, 26 July 1802, Orderly book collection (item 104), Library of Congress, Washington DC.
7. Ibid.
8. Heitman, Francis B., *Historical Register and Dictionary of the United States Army, Vol. 1*, Government Printing Office, Washington, DC, 1903, 306.
9. United States Army, General Order, Headquarters, Loftus Heights, 2 January 1799, General Order Headquarters, Natchez, 26 February 1800, *Uniform of the Army of the United States, 1774-1889*, Quartermaster General, Washington, DC, 1890.
10. Albert, Alphaeus H., *Record of American Uniform and Historical Buttons with Supplement*, Boyerstown Publishing Company, Boyerstown, PA, 1973, 46-47.
11. United States Army, General Order, Headquarters, Loftus Heights, 2 January 1799, General Order Headquarters, Natchez, 26 February 1800, *Uniform of the Army of the United States, 1774-1889*, Quartermaster General, Washington, DC, 1890.
12. Gass, Patrick, *Journal of the Voyages and Travels of a corps of Discovery, Under the Command of Capt. Lewis and Capt. Clarke*, 3rd ed., Philadelphia, 1811, Reprinted by A. C. McClurg & Co., 1904.
13. Clarke, Charles G., *The Men of the Lewis and Clark Expedition*, The Arthur C. Clark Co., Spokane, WA, 2001.
14. United States Army, General Order, Headquarters, Loftus Heights, 2 January 1799, General Order, Headquarters, Natchez, 26 February 1800, *Uniform of the Army of the United States, 1774-1889*, Quartermaster General, Washington, DC, 1890.
15. Finke, Detmar H. & McBarron, H. Charles, The Infantry Enlisted Man's Coat, 1804-1810, Military Collector and Historian, Vol. XL No.4, Washington, DC, 1988, 162-164.
16. Albert, Alphaeus H., *Record of American Uniform and Historical Buttons with Supplement*, Boyerstown Publishing Company, Boyerstown, PA, 1973, 16-18.
17. Finke, Detmar H. & McBarron, H. Charles, The Infantry Enlisted Man's Coat, 1804-1810, Military Collector and Historian, Vol. XL, No.4, Washington DC, 1988, 162-164.
18. Finke, Detmar H. & Marko Zlatich, The Army Clothing Estimate for 1804, Military Collector and Historian, Vol. XLVI, No. 2, Washington DC, 1994, 55-58. XLIV, No.1, Washington DC, 1992, 32-33.
19. Zlatich, Marko, U.S. Infantry Hat, 1801-1811, Military Collector and Historian, Vol. XLIV, No.1, Washington DC, 1992, 32-33.

20. United States Army, General Order, Headquarters, Loftus Heights, 2 January 1799, General Order Headquarters, Natchez, 26 February 1800, *Uniform of the Army of the United States, 1774-1889*, Quartermaster General, Washington, DC, 1890.

21. Ibid.

22. Finke, Detmar H. & McBarron, H. Charles, The Infantry Enlisted Man's Coat, 1804-1810, Military Collector and Historian, Vol. XL No.4, Washington DC, 1988, 162-164.

23. United States Army, General Order, Headquarters, Loftus Heights, 2 January 1799, General Order Headquarters, Natchez, 26 February 1800, *Uniform of the Army of the United States, 1774-1889*, Quartermaster General, Washington, DC, 1890.

24. Finke, Detmar H., Army Linen Garments, 1801-1813, Military Collector and Historian, Vol. XLVI, No. 2, Washington DC, 1994, 50-51.

25. Hamtramck, Col. J. F., Standing Orders of the First Regiment of Infantry, 1802, Detroit, 26 July 1802, Orderly book collection (item 104), Library of Congress, Washington, DC.

26. Jackson, Donald, *Letters of the Lewis and Clark Expedition With Related Documents, 1783-1854*, University of Illinois Press, Urbana, 1962, 98, (note Jackson lists these as "Match Coats," which seems to be a miss-transcription of "Watch Coats.")

27. Hamtramck, Col. J. F., Standing Orders of the First Regiment of Infantry, 1802, Detroit, 26 July 1802, Orderly book collection (item 104), Library of Congress, Washington DC.

28. Jackson, Donald, *Letters of the Lewis and Clark Expedition With Related Documents, 1783-1854*, University of Illinois Press, Urbana, 1962, 92.

29. Shaw, Thomas G. and Abolt, Stephen, research used to reconstruct a reproduction "recruit coatee" for the Frontier Army Museum, Fort Leavenworth KS, 1998.

30. Ibid.

31. Jackson, Donald, *Letters of the Lewis and Clark Expedition With Related Documents, 1783-1854*, University of Illinois Press, Urbana, 1962, 92.

32. Shaw, Thomas G. and Abolt, Stephen, research used to reconstruct a reproduction "recruit coatee" for the Frontier Army Museum, Fort Leavenworth KS, 1998.

33. Jackson, Donald, *Letters of the Lewis and Clark Expedition With Related Documents, 1783-1854*, University of Illinois Press, Urbana, 1962, 98.

34. Ibid.

35. Ibid.

36. Ibid, 90.

37. Ibid, 98.

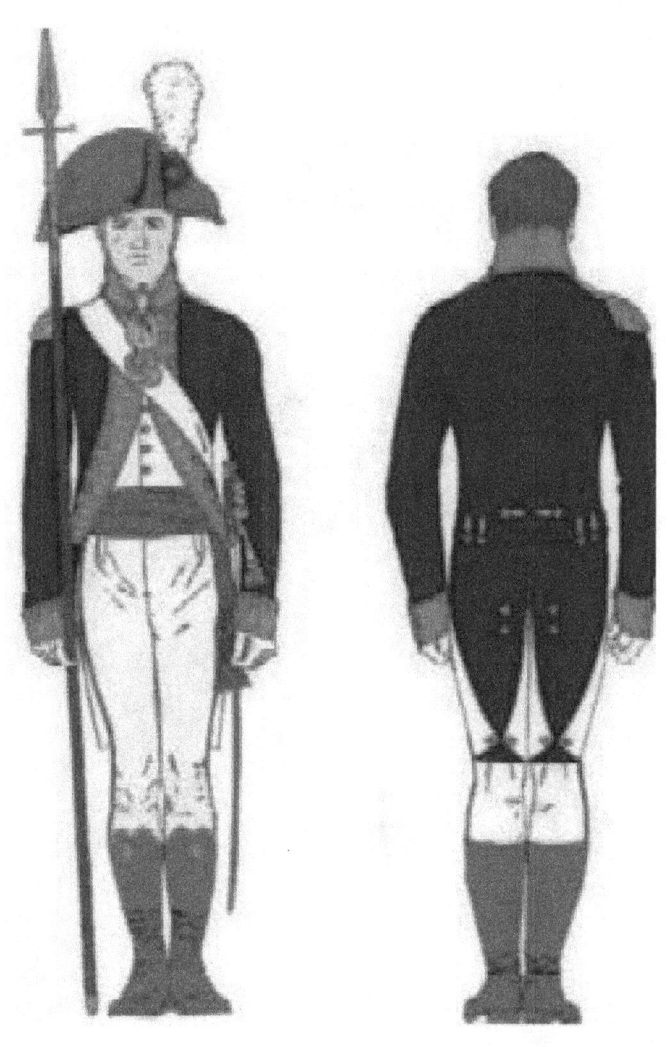

Image 1. Captain of infantry in dress with sword and spontoon.
Image 2. Captain of infantry in dress, back view.

Image 3. Captain of infantry in undress with sword.

Image 4. Infantry officer in roundabout, front view.
Image 5. Infantry officer in roundabout, back view.

Image 6. Infantry officer in surtout.
Image 7. Captain of artillery in undress, off duty.

Image 8. Sergeant of infantry, front view.
Image 9. Private of infantry, back view.

Image 10. Private of artillery.

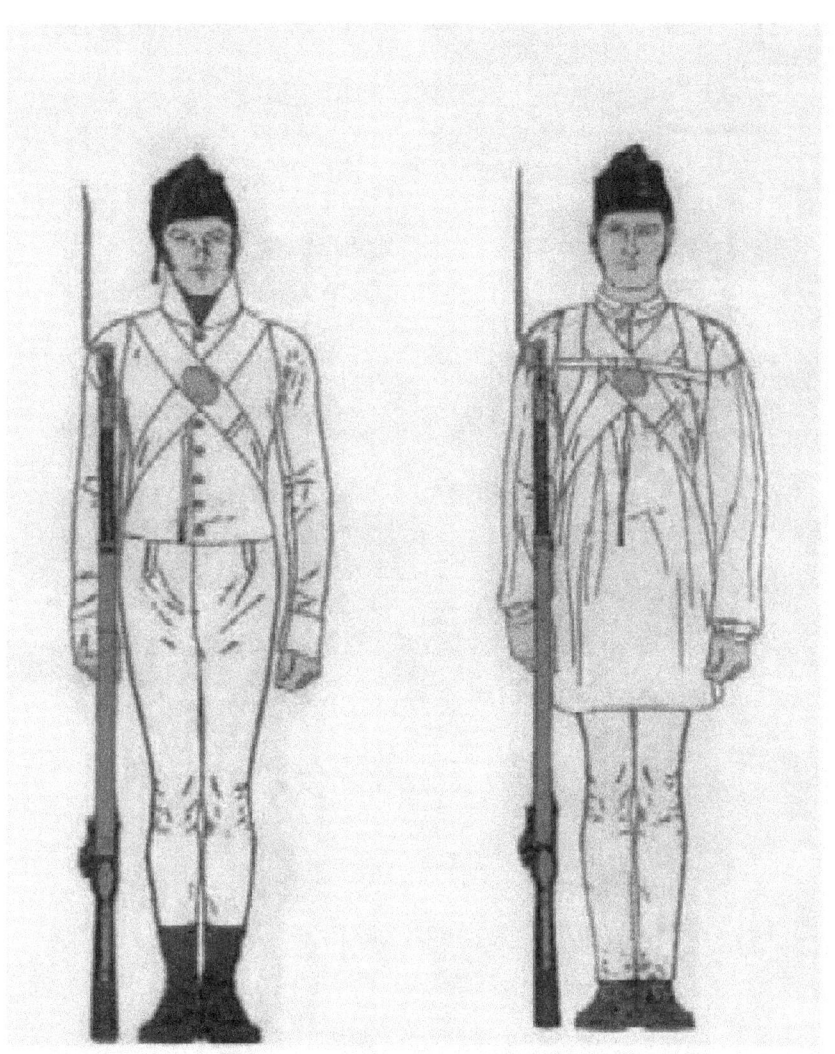

Image 11. Private of infantry in fatigue jacket.
Image 12. Private of infantry in fatigue frock.

Image 13. Private of artillery in watchcoat.
Image 14. Sergeant of infantry in surtout, front view.

Image 15. Private in blanket coat.

Image 16. "Recruit" rifle uniform, front view.
Image 17. "Recruit" uniform, back view.

Appendix D

Visuals

Day 1 Visuals

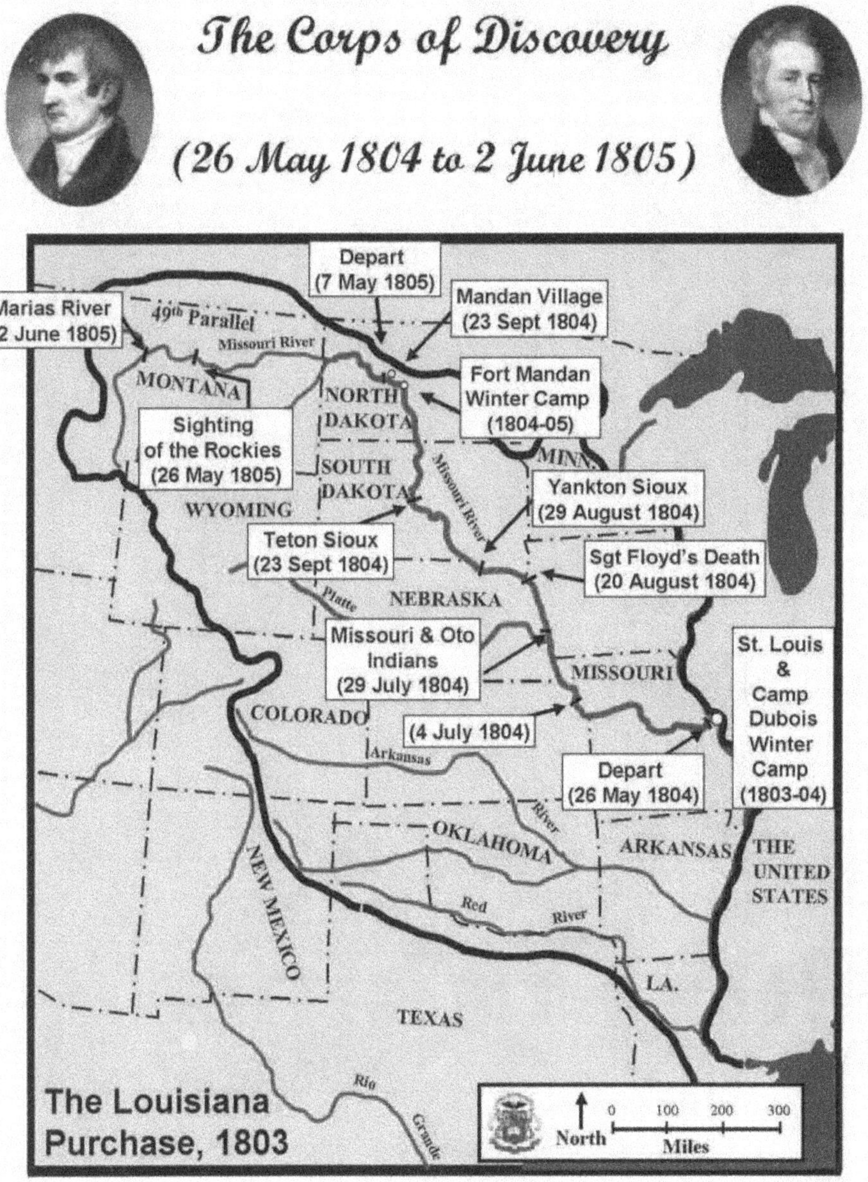

Visual 1-1

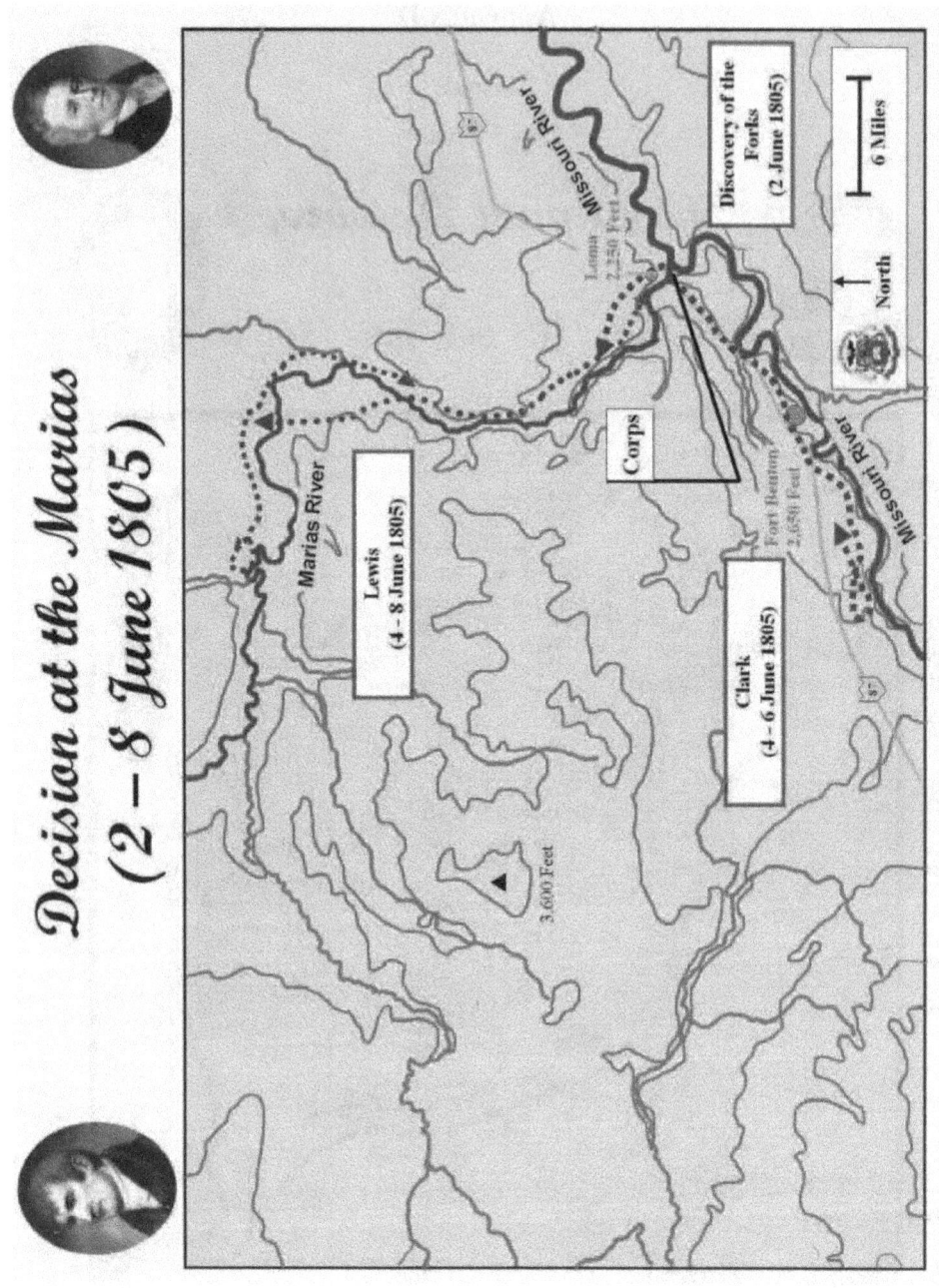

Visual 1-2

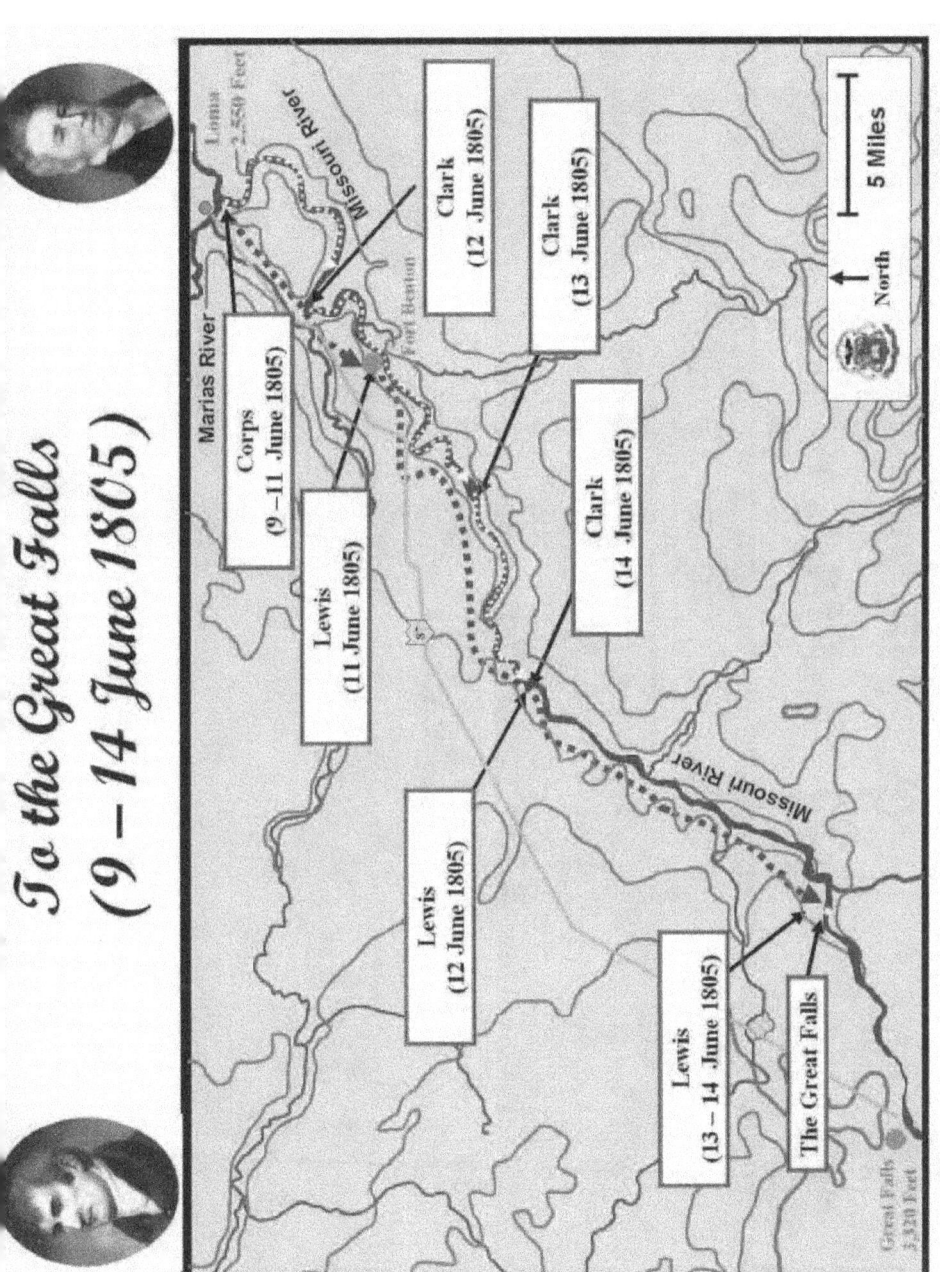

Visual 1-3

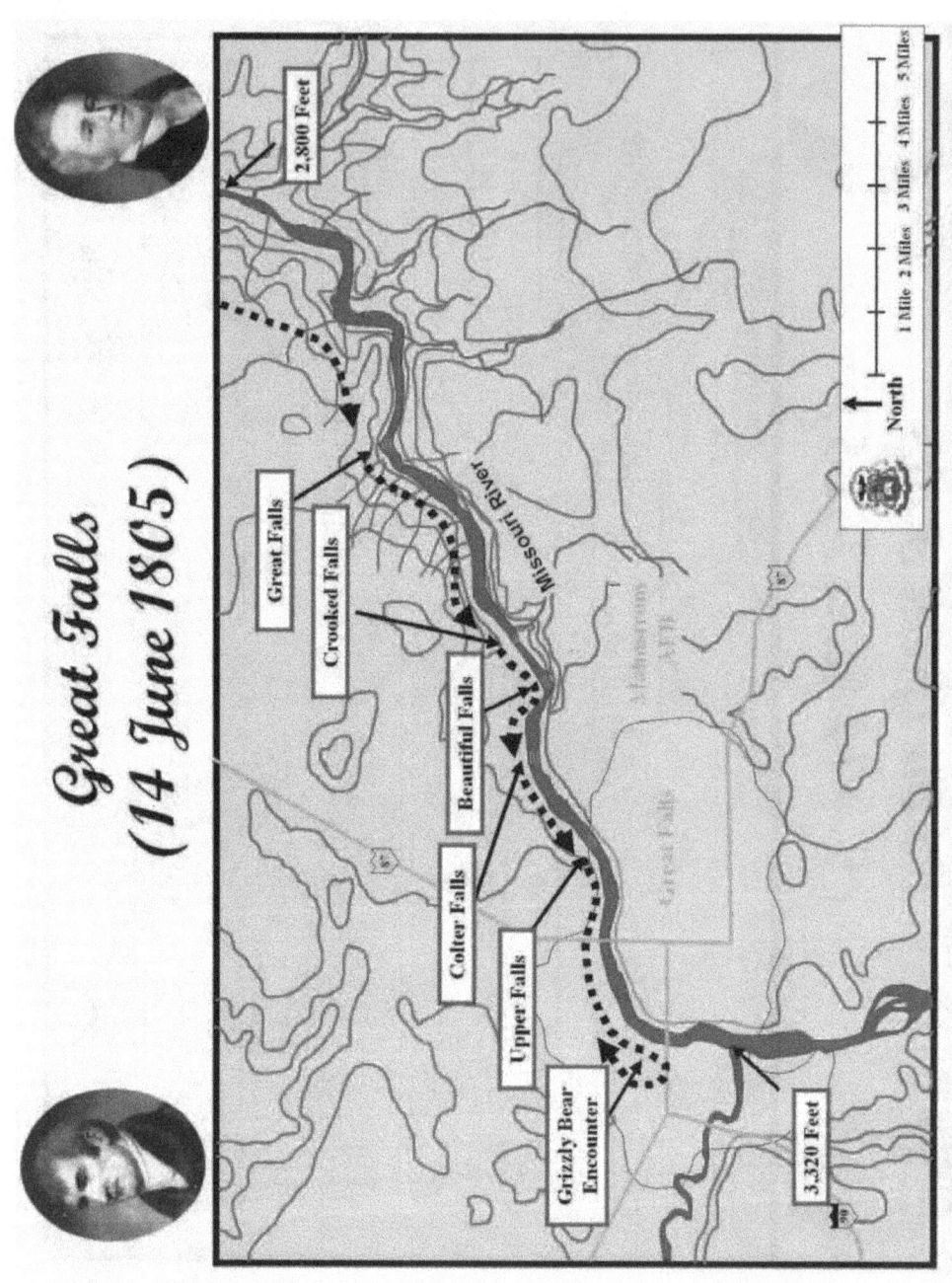

Visual 1-4

268

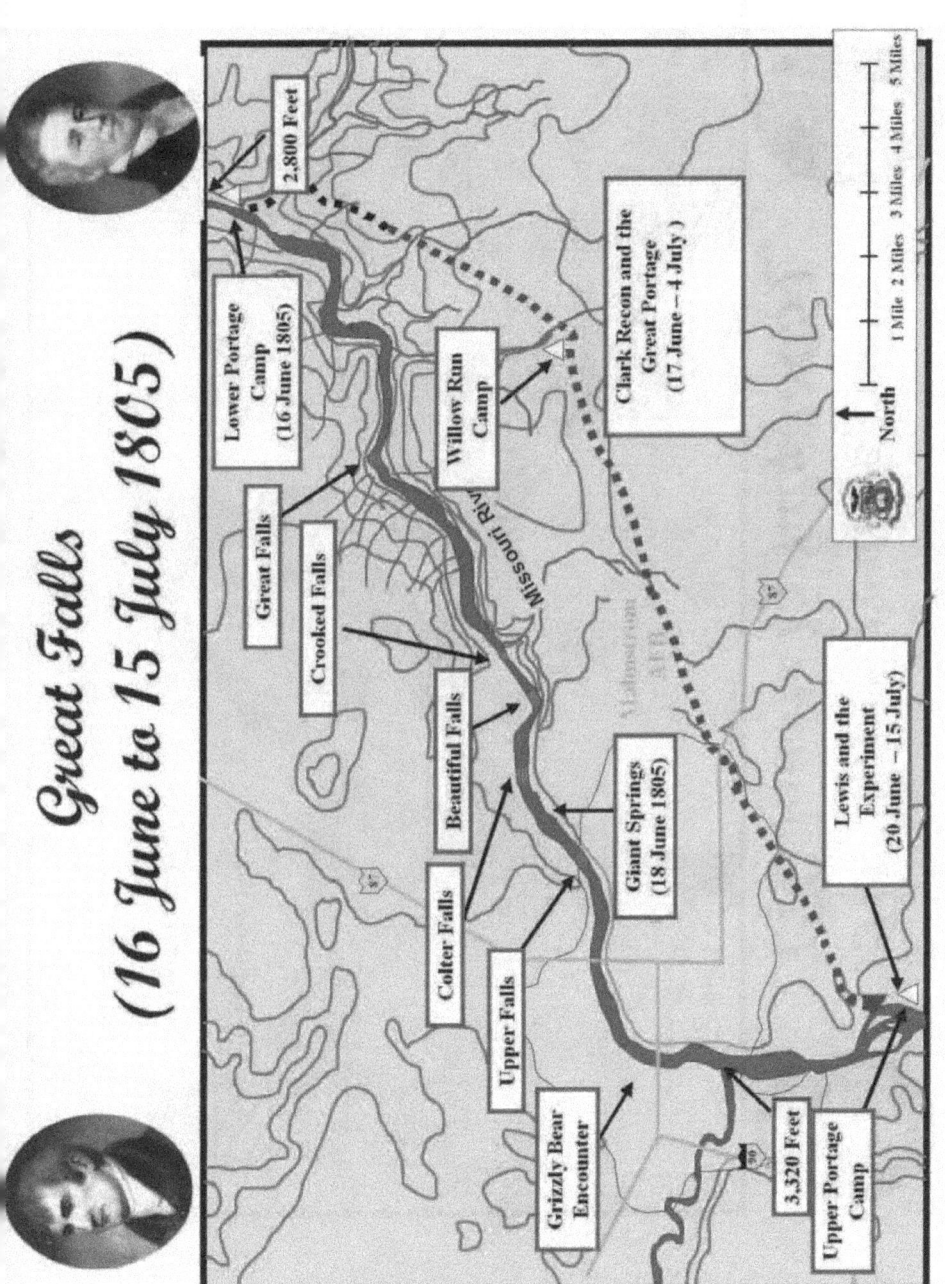

Visual 1-5

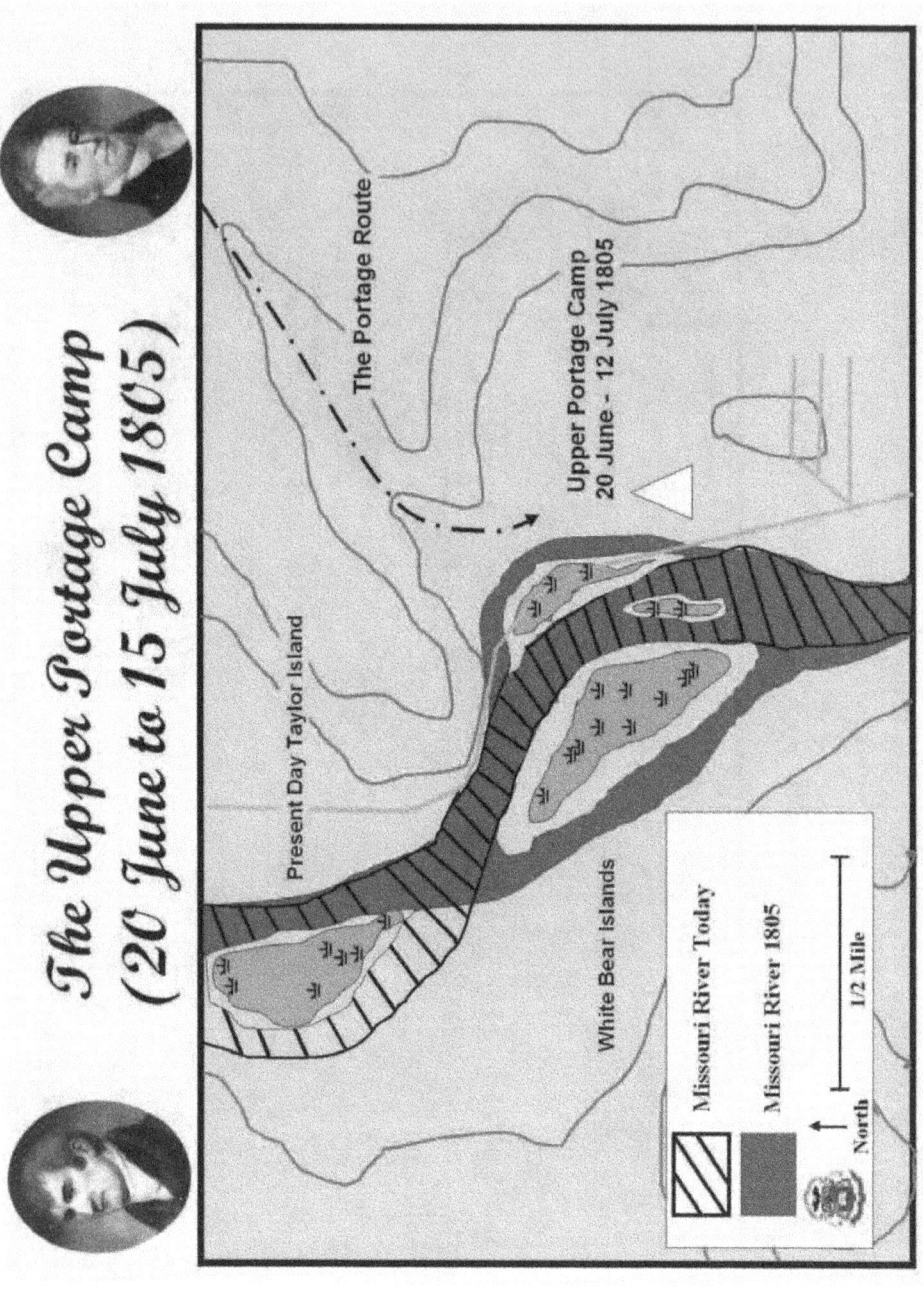

Visual 1-6

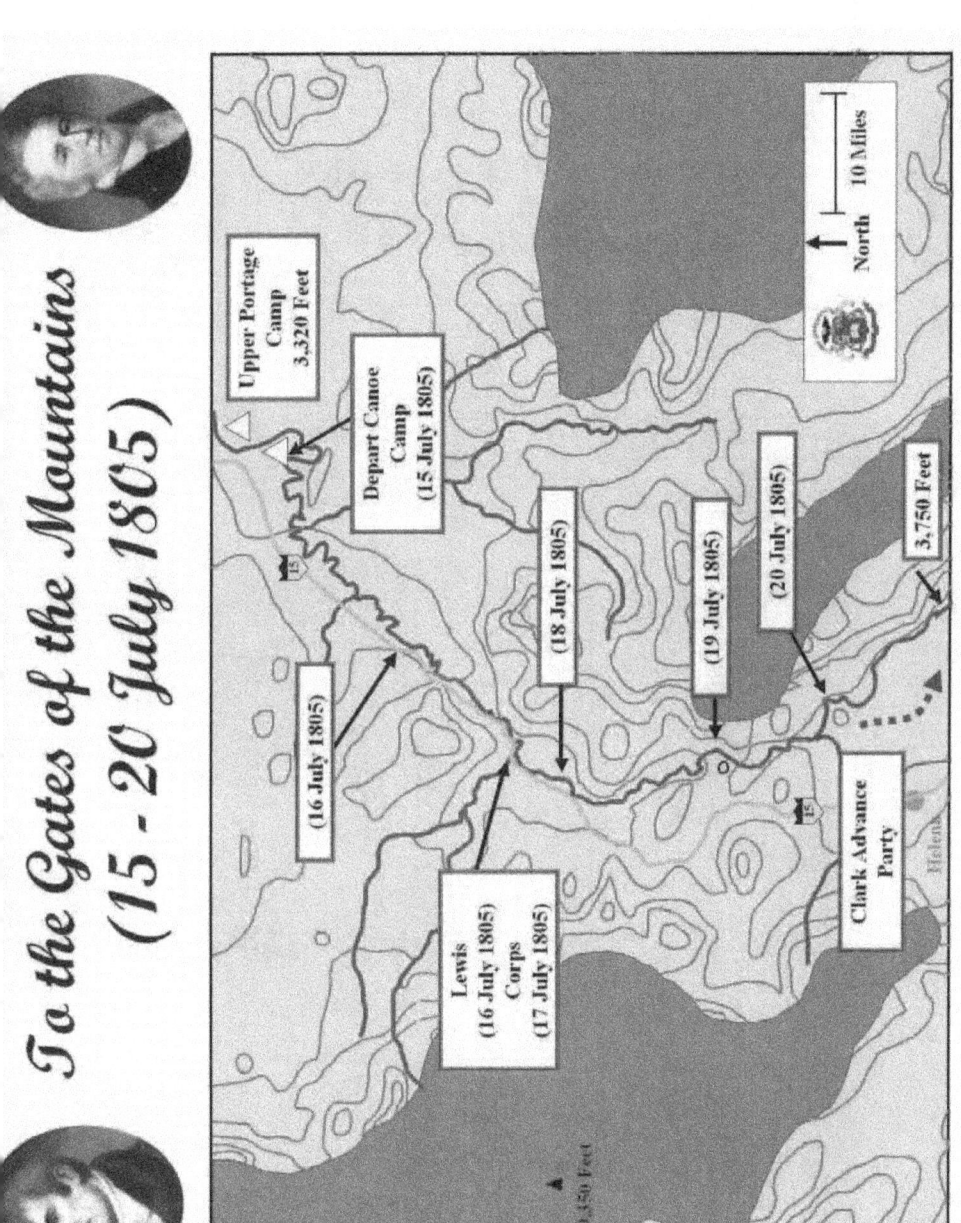

Visual 2-1

To the Three Forks
(20 - 25 July 1805)

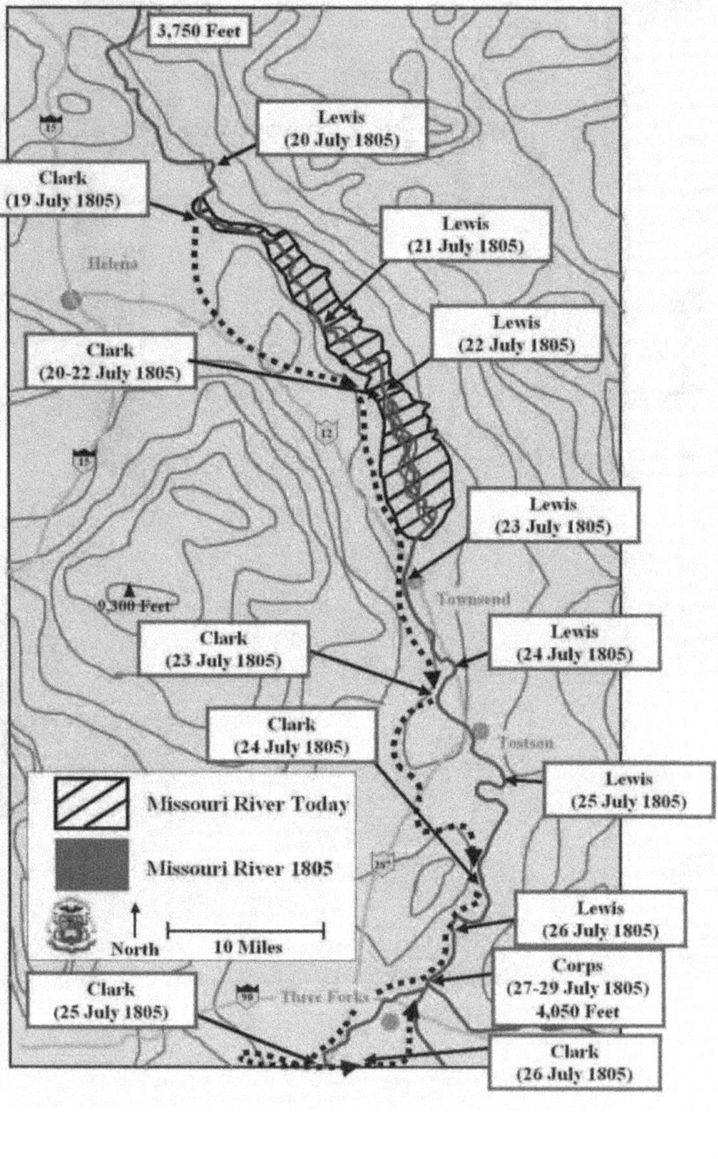

Visual 2-2

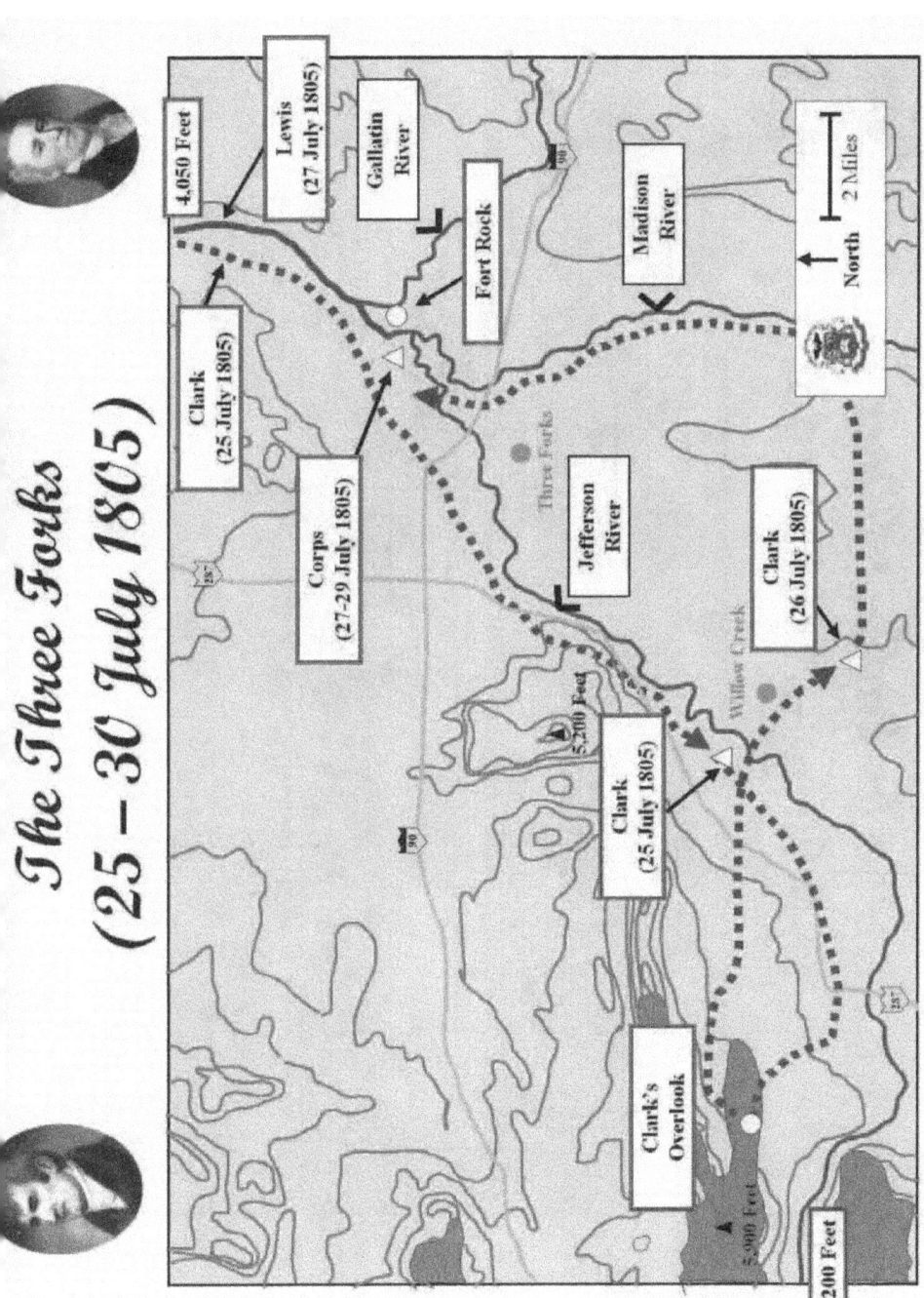

Visual 2-3

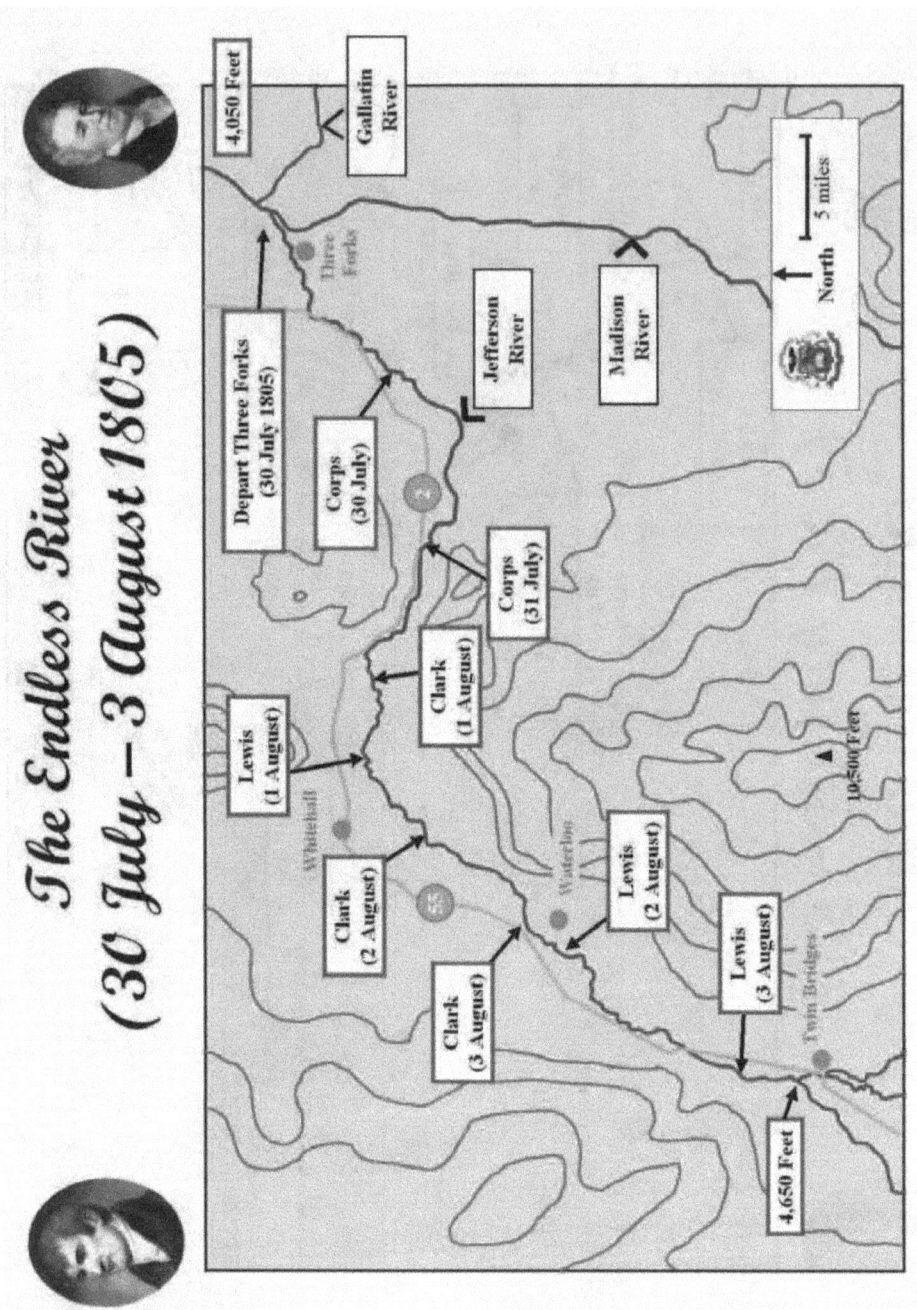

Visual 3-1

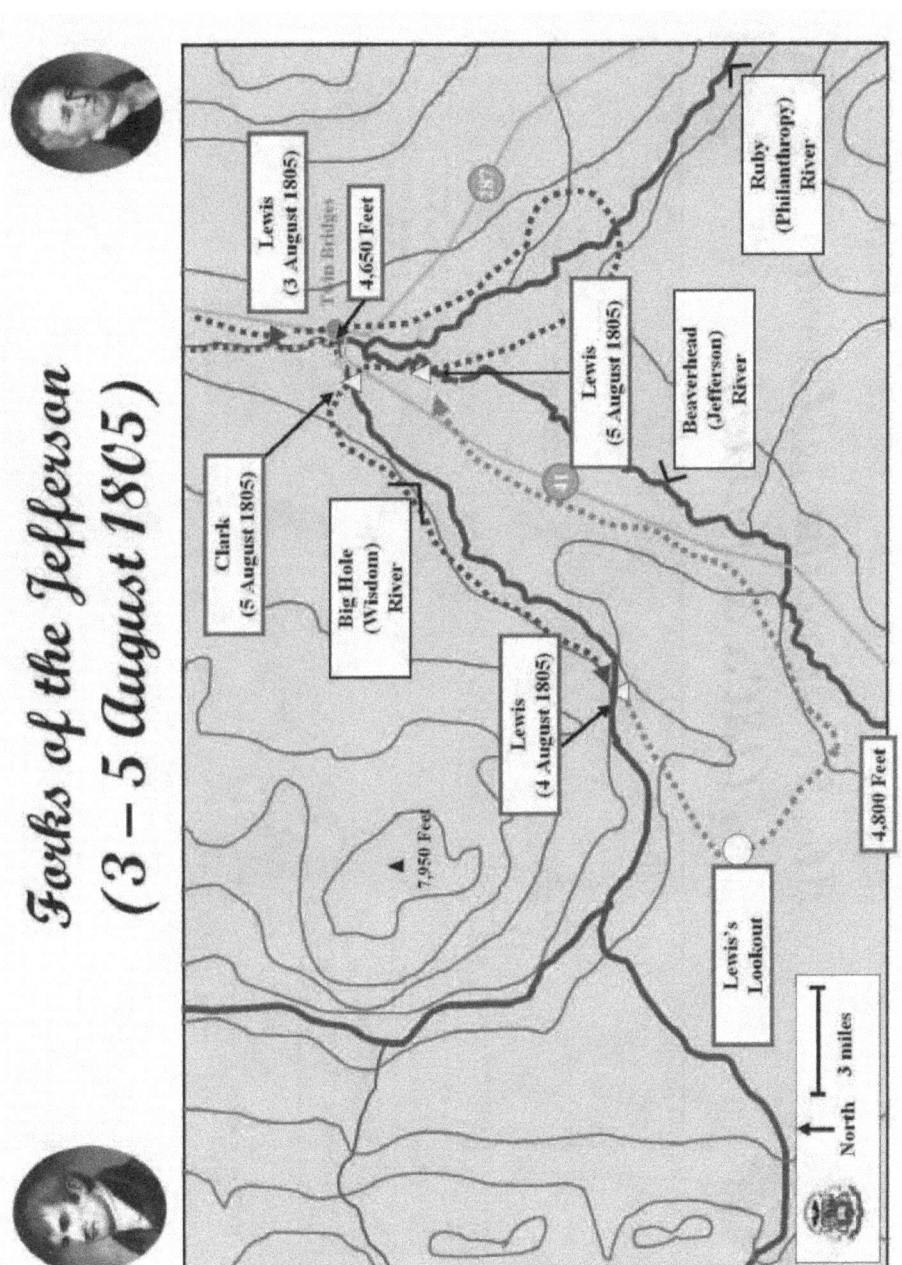

Visual 3-2

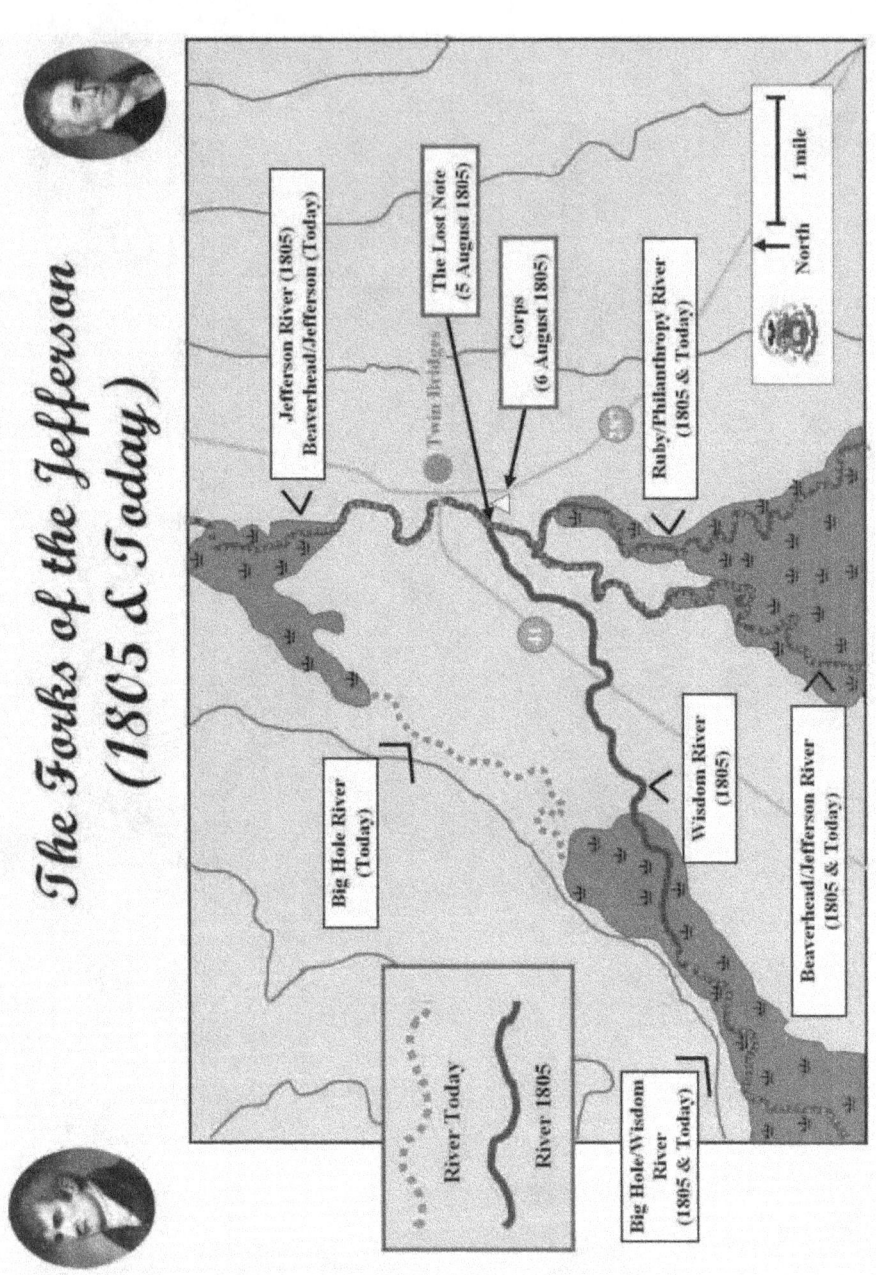

Visual 3-3

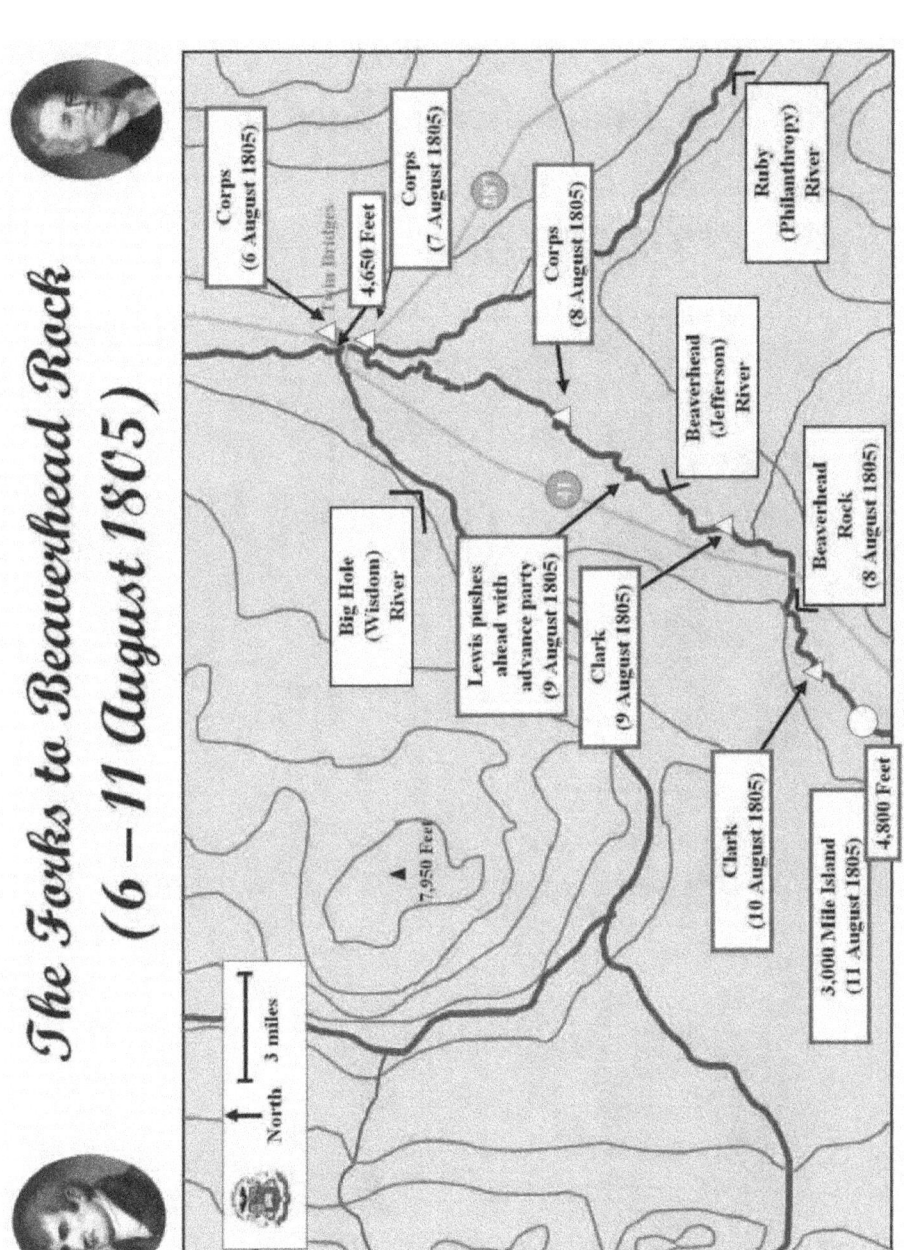

Visual 3-4

Beaverhead Rock to the Forks
(9 – 13 August 1805)

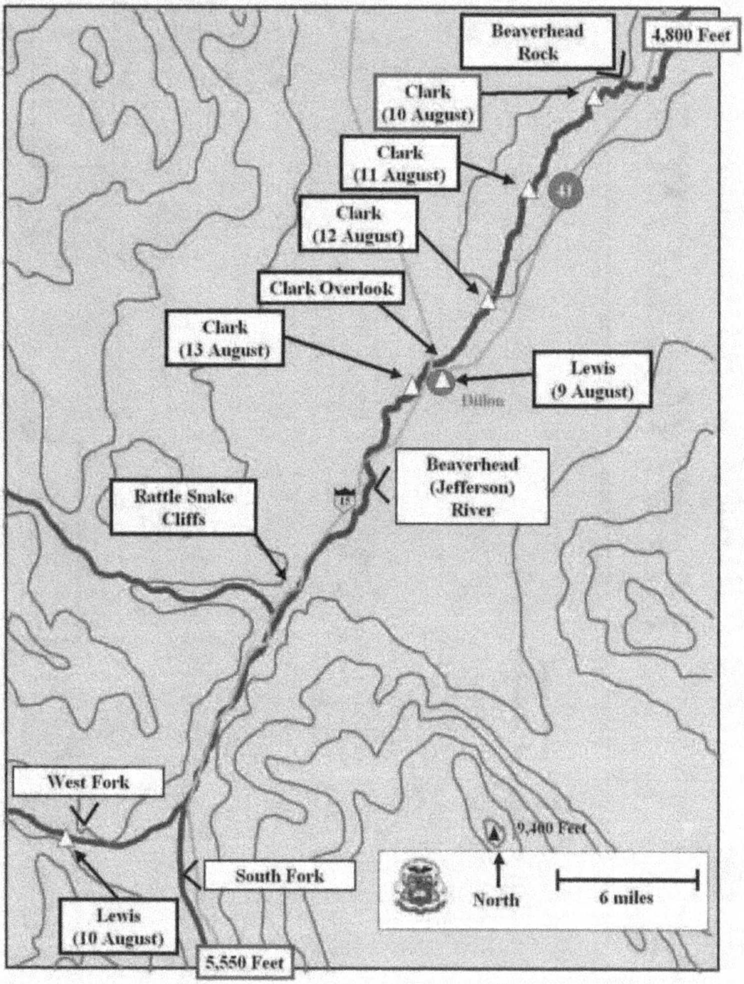

Visual 3-5

Camp Fortunate
17 – 24 August 1805

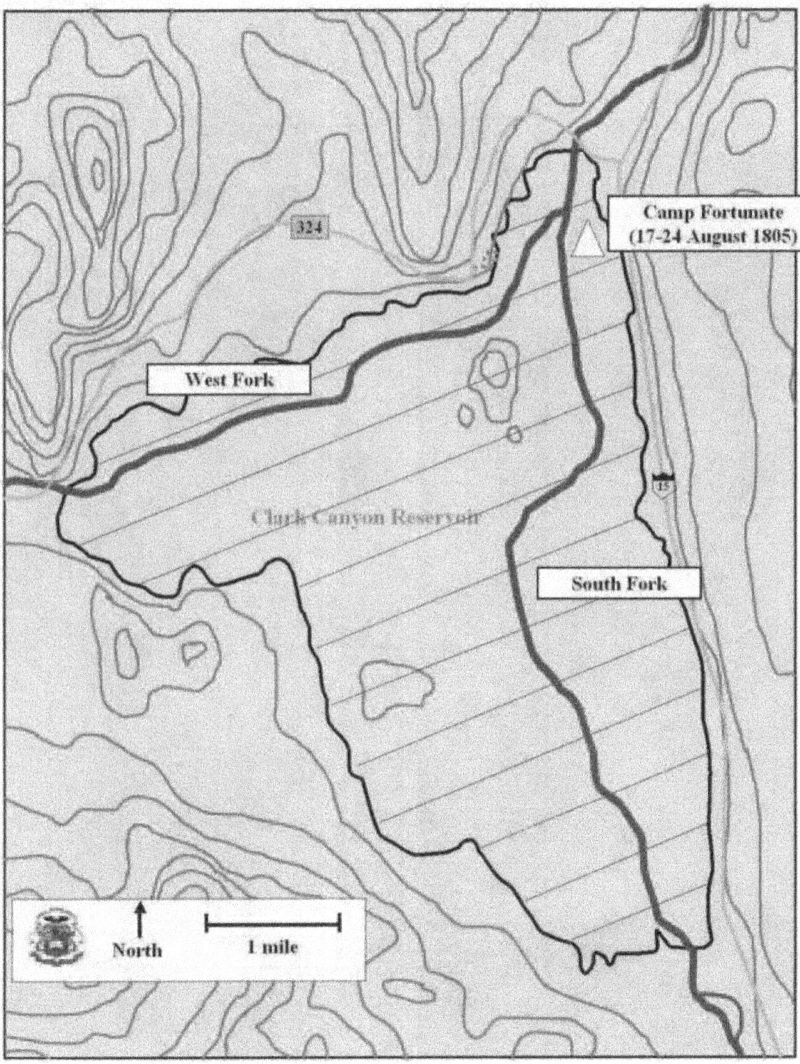

Visual 3-6

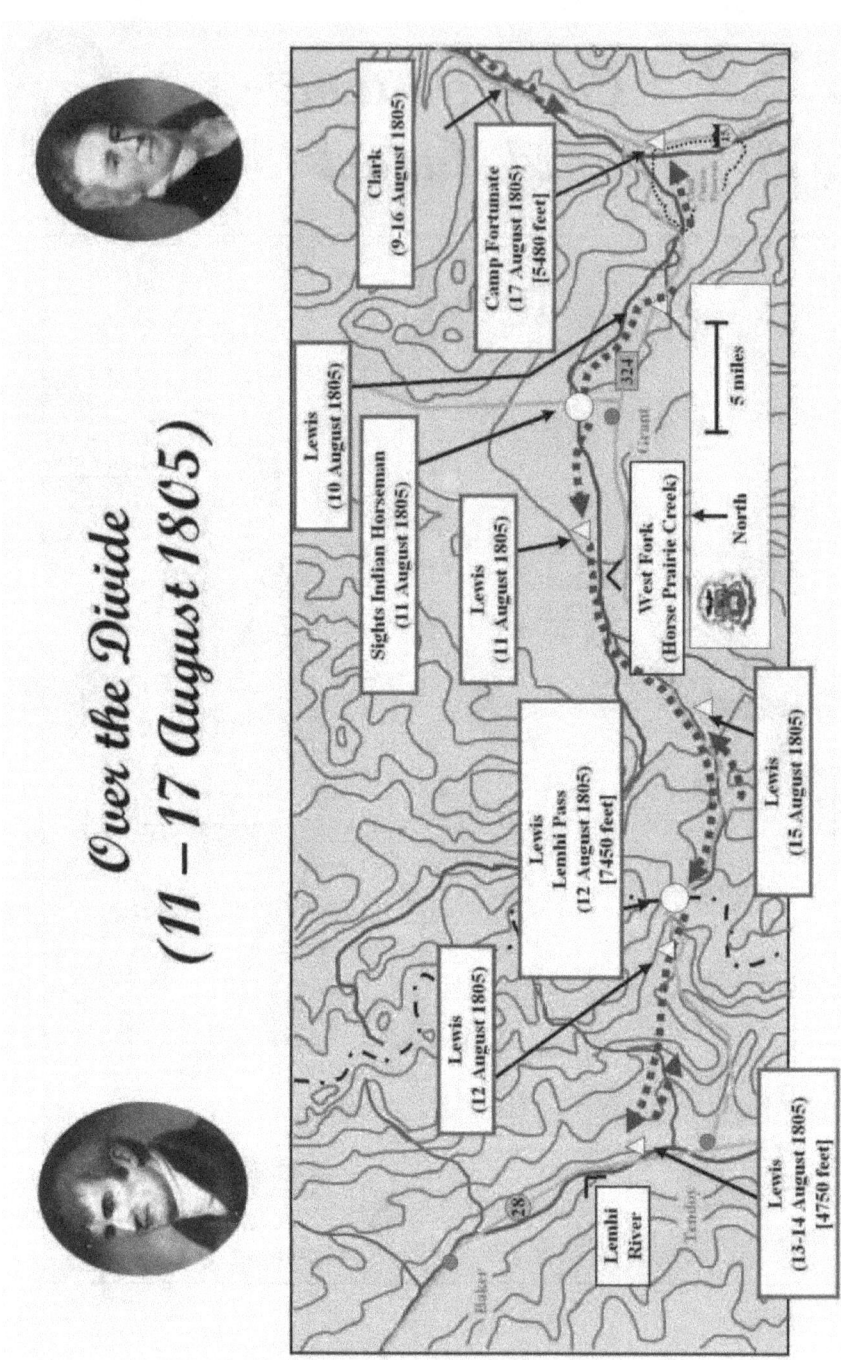

Visual 3-7

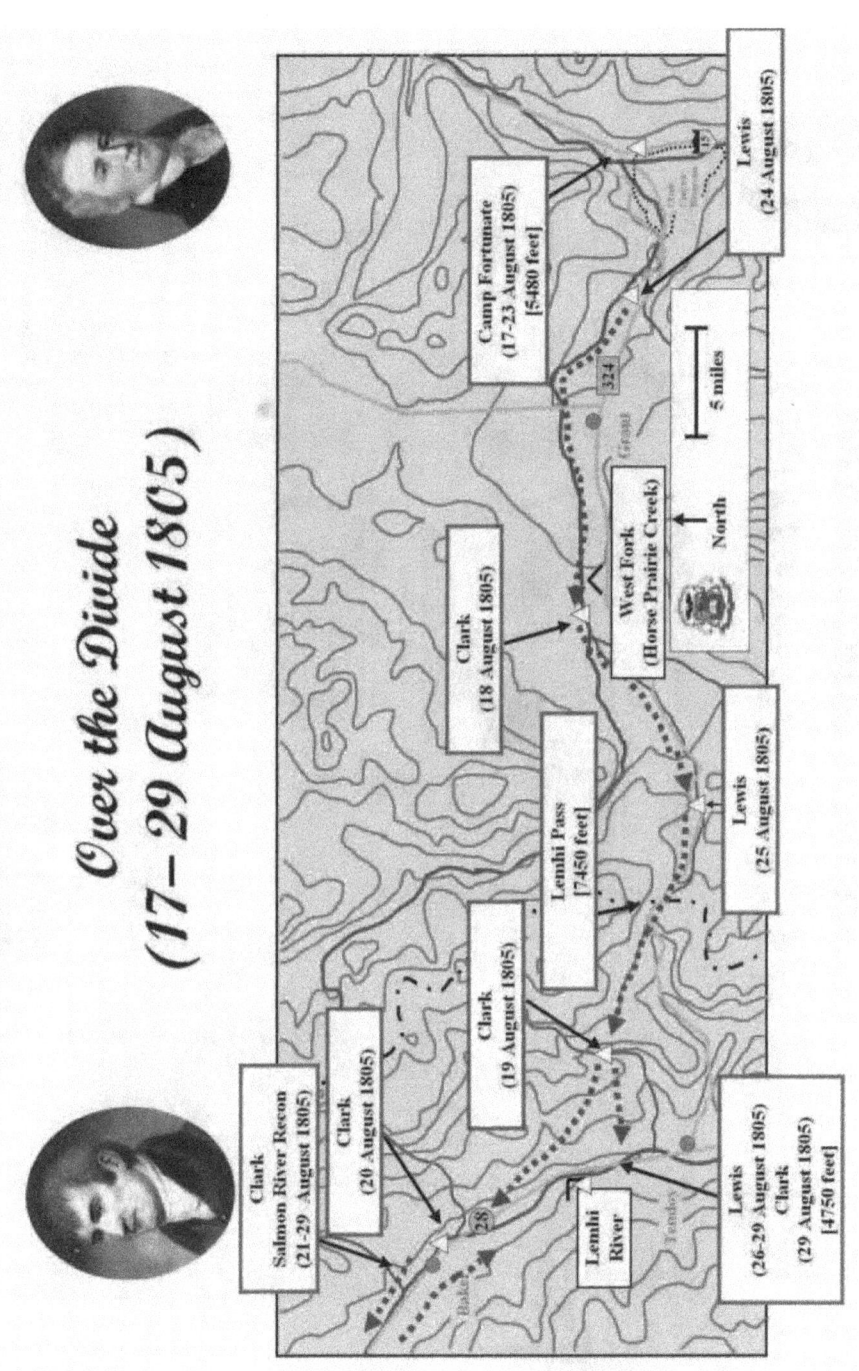

Visual 3-8

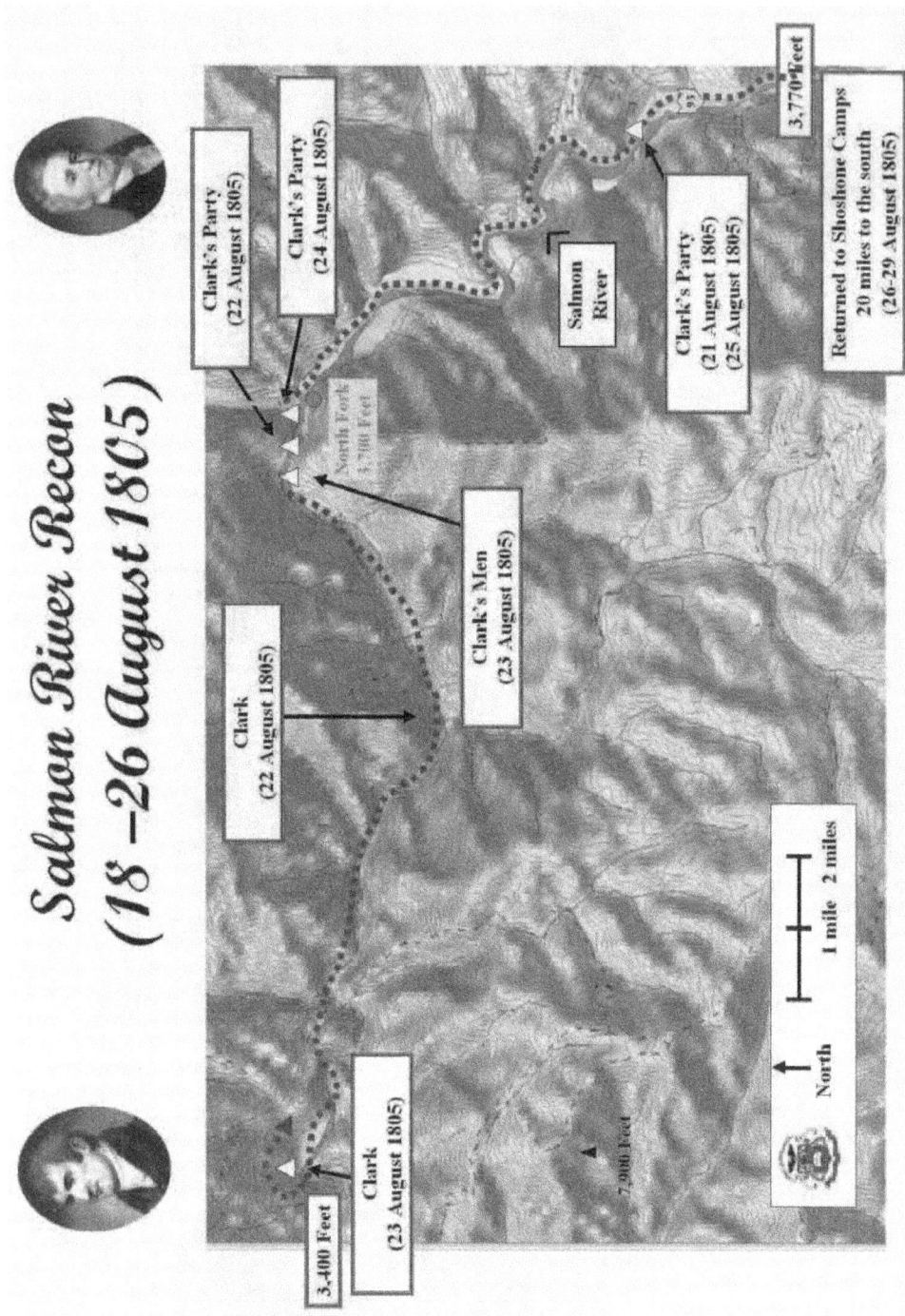

Visual 4-1

Lost Trail Pass and the Salish Indians
(30 August – 6 September 1805)

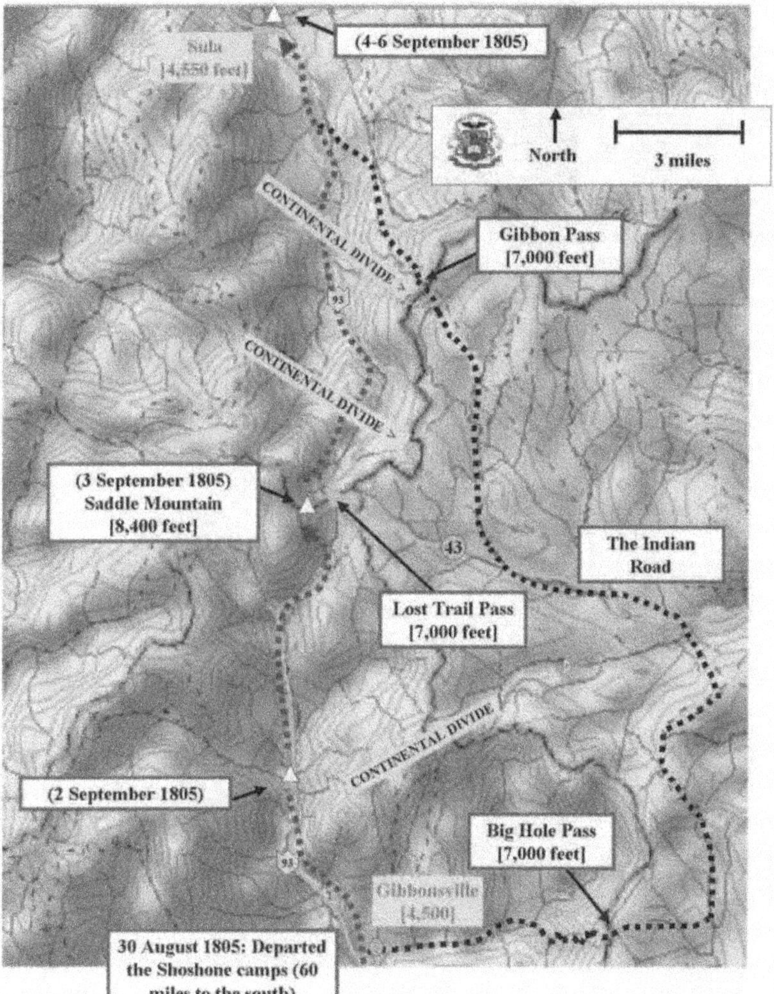

Visual 4-2

Bitterroot Valley
(6 – 10 September 1805)

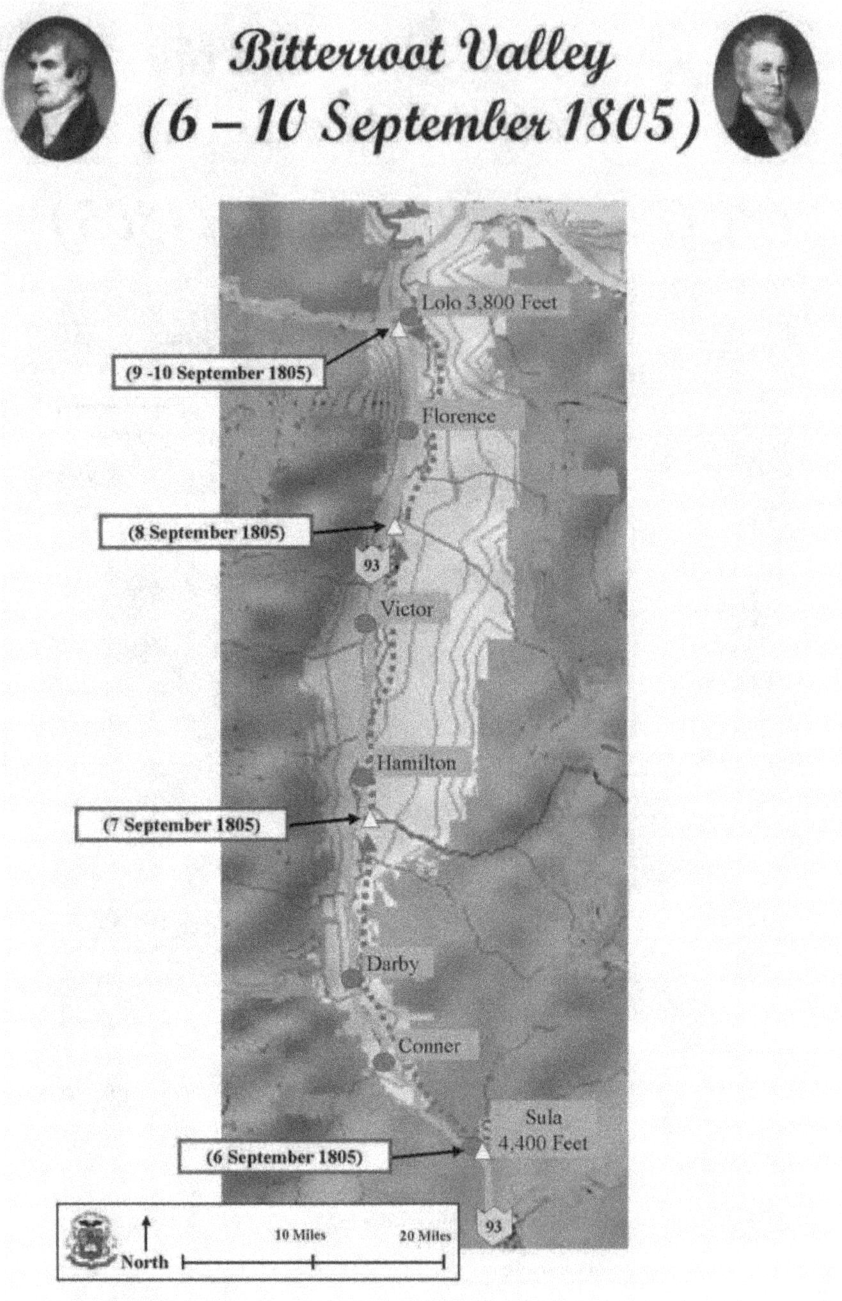

Lolo 3,800 Feet

(9 -10 September 1805)

Florence

(8 September 1805)

Victor

Hamilton

(7 September 1805)

Darby

Conner

Sula 4,400 Feet

(6 September 1805)

North | 10 Miles | 20 Miles

Visual 4-3

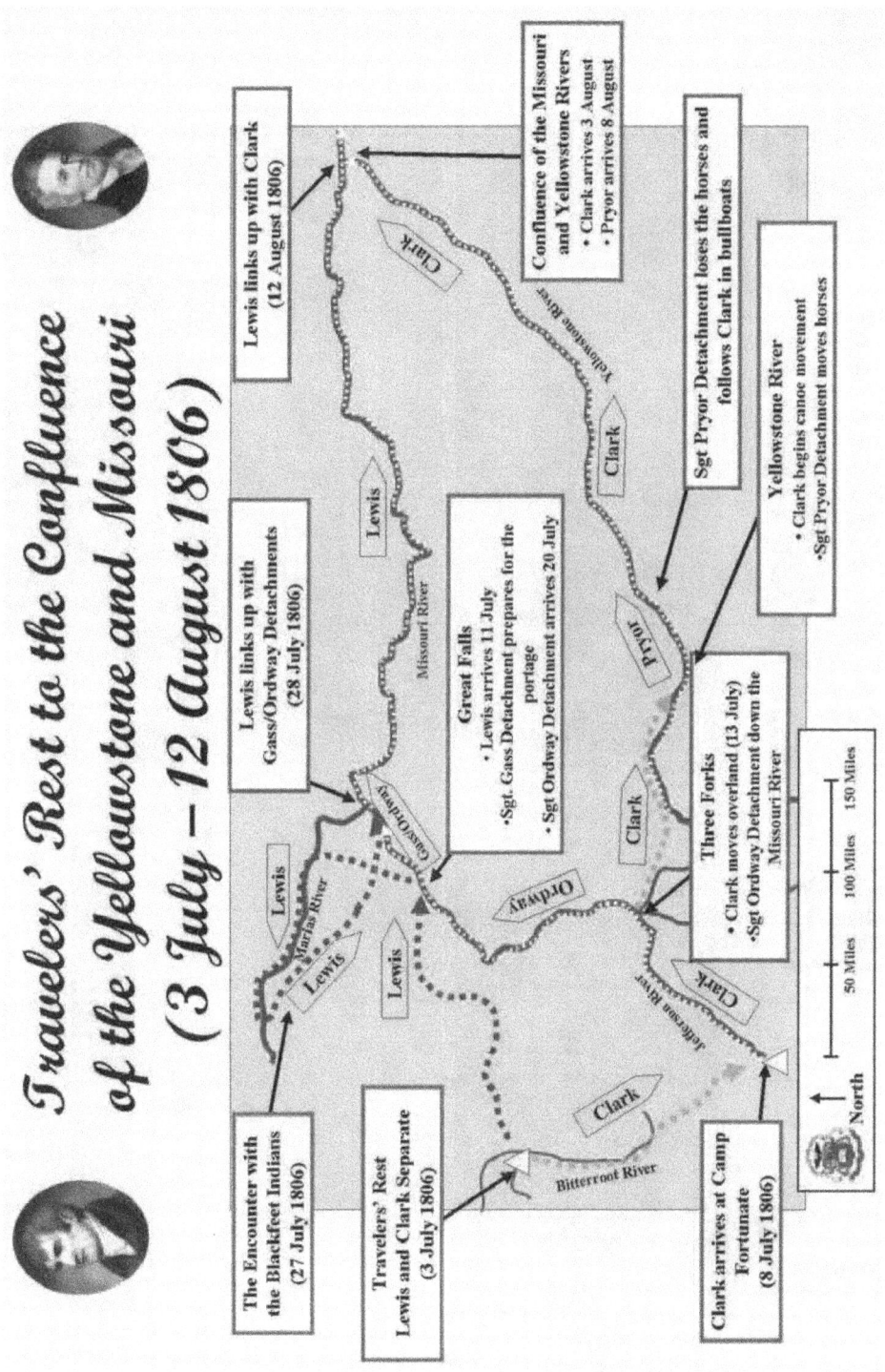

Visual 4-4

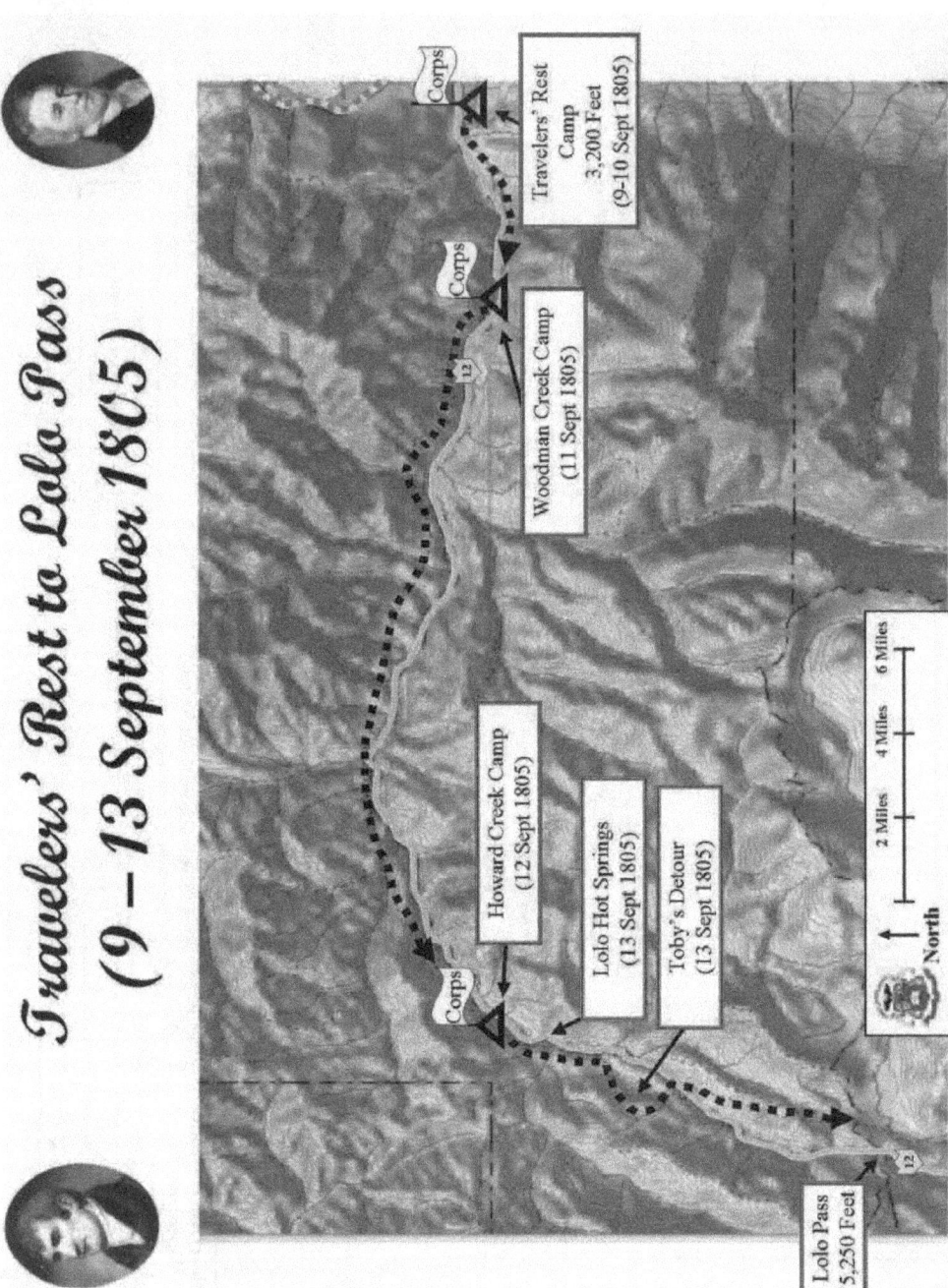

Visual 5-1

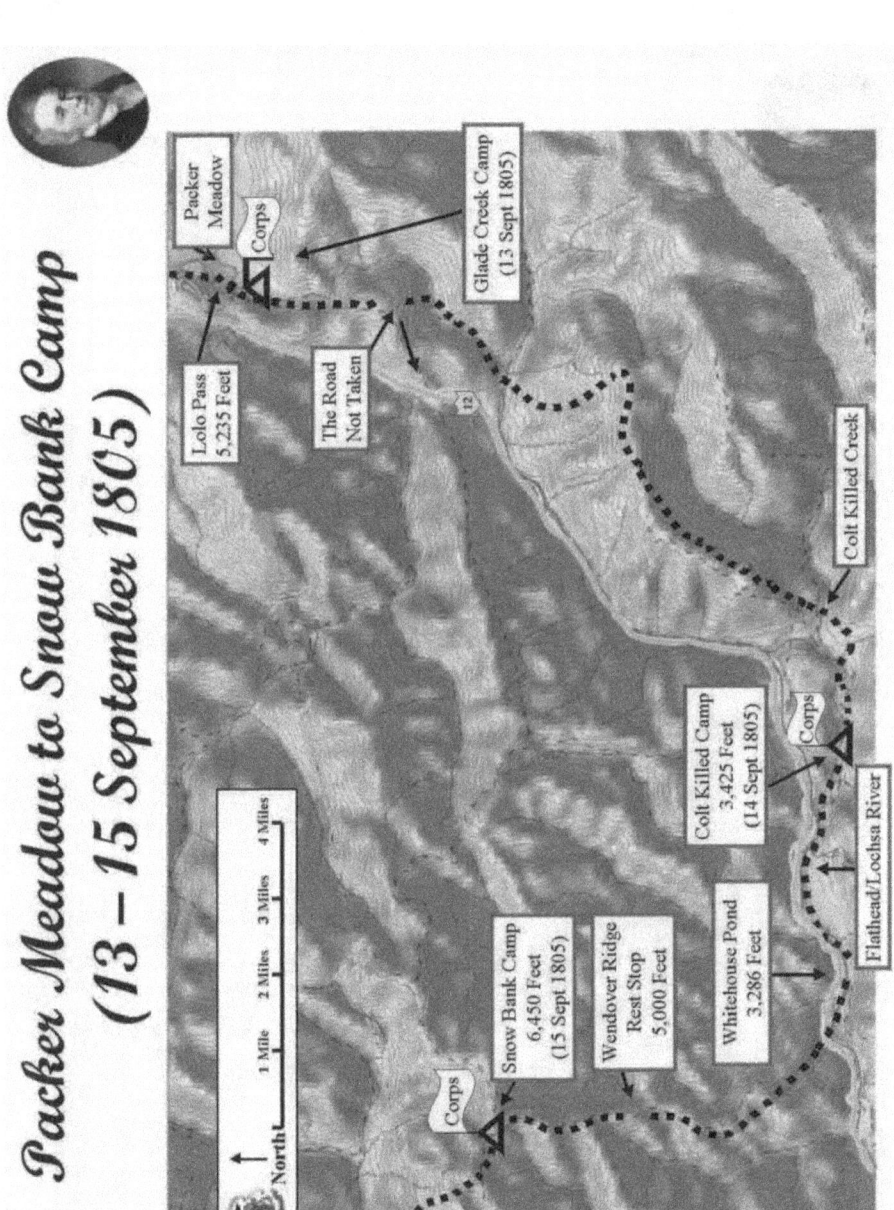

Visual 5-2

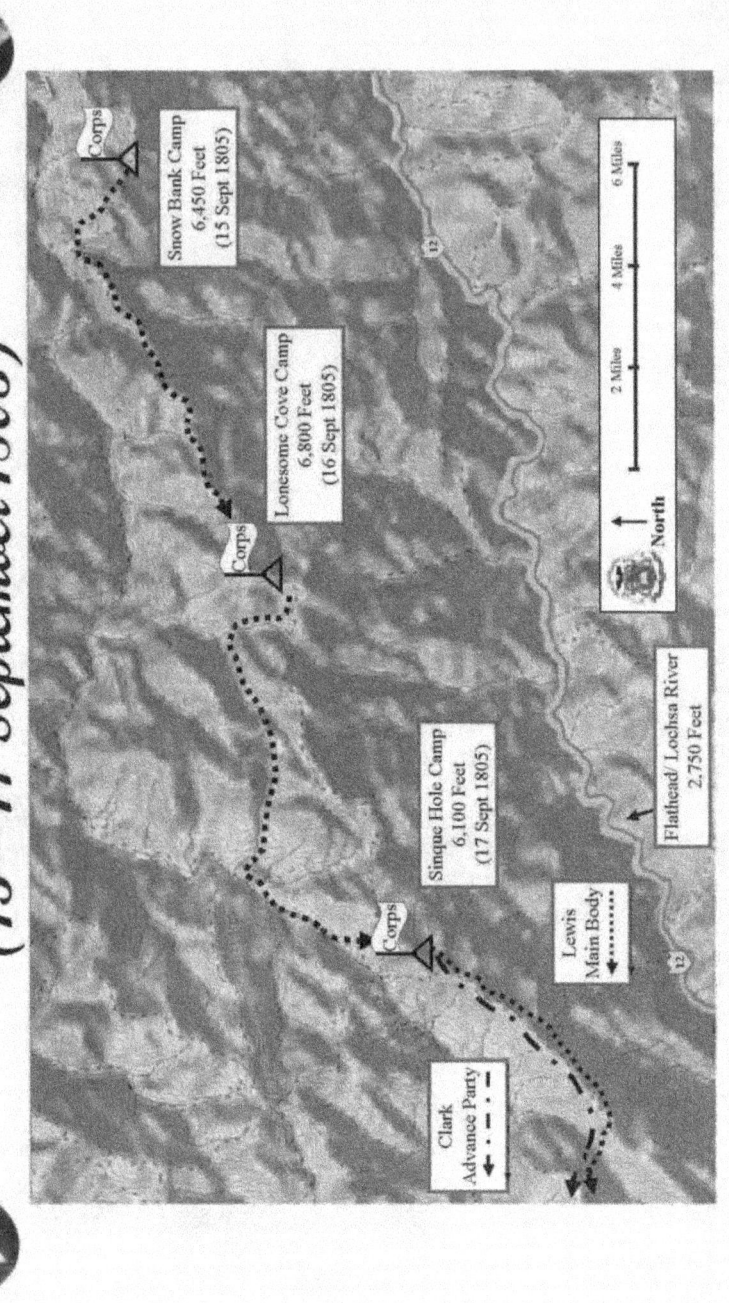

Visual 5-3

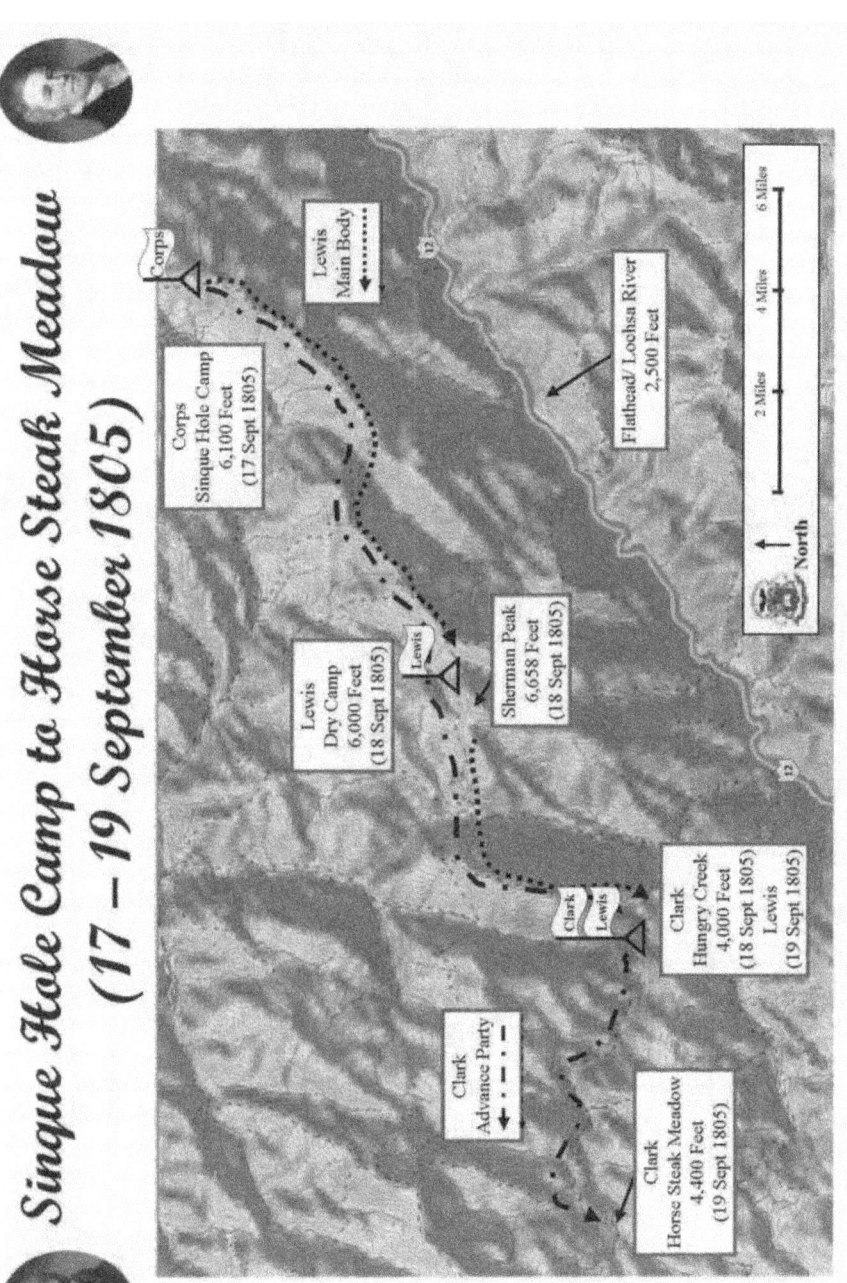

Visual 5-4

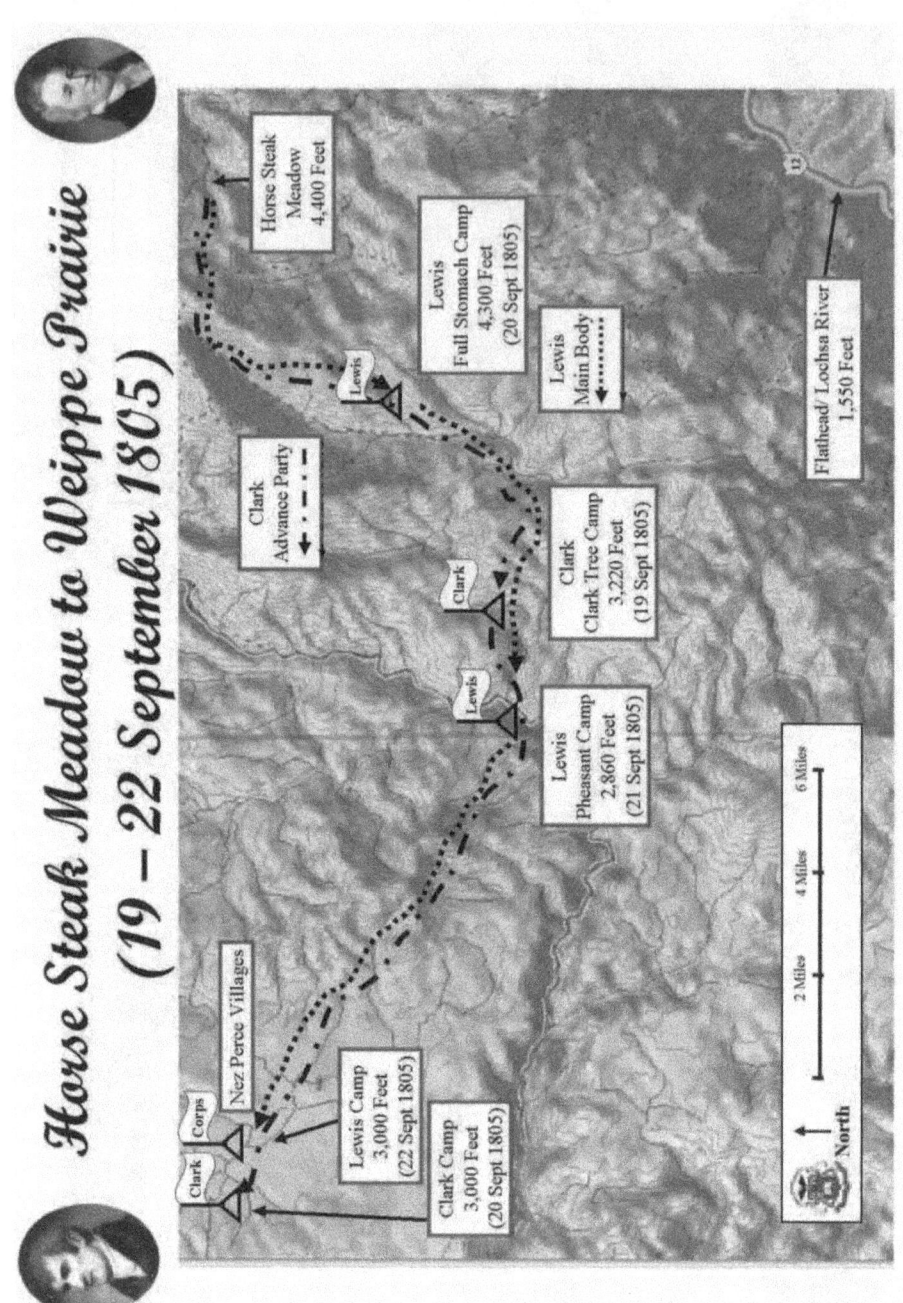

Visual 5-5

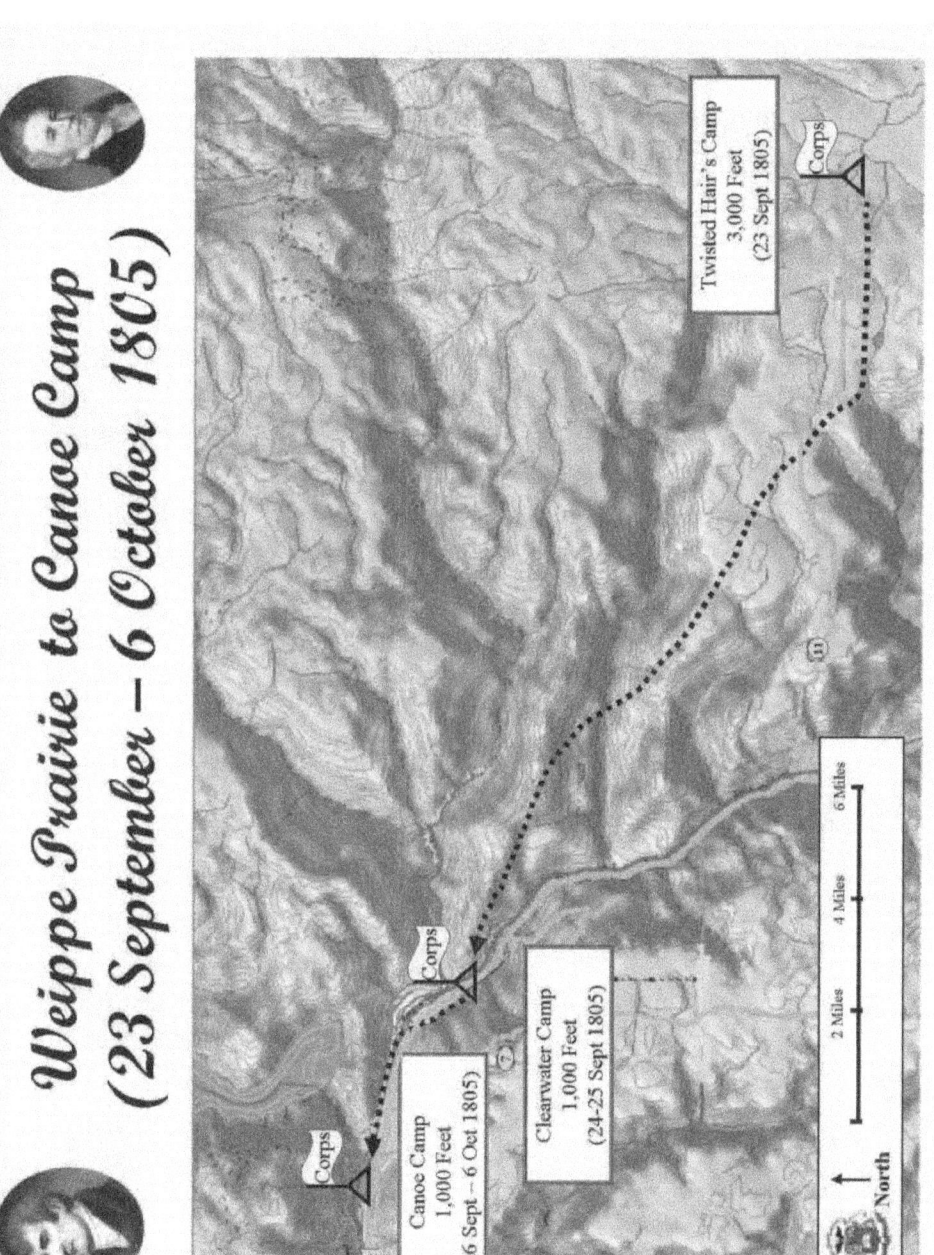

Visual 5-6

Bibliography

I. Conducting a Staff Ride

Robertson, William G. *The Staff Ride*. Washington, DC: U.S. Army Center of Military History, 1987.

II. The Journals of the Lewis and Clark Expedition

Journal entries are from *The Journals of the Lewis & Clark Expedition (August 30, 1803 – September 26, 1806)*, published as a project of the Center for Great Plains Studies by the University of Nebraska Press, 1986. Gary E. Moulton served as the editor for this outstanding and valuable project.

Moulton, Gary E., ed. *The Journals of the Lewis & Clark Expedition (August 30, 1803 – August 24, 1805), Vol. 2*. Lincoln and London: University of Nebraska Press, 1986.

_____. *The Journals of the Lewis & Clark Expedition (August 25, 1804 - April 6, 1805), Vol. 3*. Lincoln and London: University of Nebraska Press, 1987.

_____. *The Journals of the Lewis & Clark Expedition (April 7 – July 27, 1805), Vol. 4*. Lincoln and London: University of Nebraska Press, 1987.

_____. *The Journals of the Lewis & Clark Expedition (July 28 – November 1, 1805), Vol. 5*. Lincoln and London: University of Nebraska Press, 1988.

_____. *The Journals of the Lewis & Clark Expedition (November 2, 1805 – March 22, 1806), Vol. 6*. Lincoln and London: University of Nebraska Press, 1990.

_____. *The Journals of the Lewis & Clark Expedition (March 23 – June 9, 1806), Vol. 7*. Lincoln and London: University of Nebraska Press, 1991.

_____. *The Journals of the Lewis & Clark Expedition (June 10 – September 26, 1806), Vol. 8*. Lincoln and London: University of Nebraska Press, 1993.

_____. *The Journals of the Lewis & Clark Expedition, The Journals of John Ordway and Charles Floyd, Vol. 9*. Lincoln and London: University of Nebraska Press, 1995.

_____. *The Journals of the Lewis & Clark Expedition, The Journals of Patrick Gass, Vol. 10.* Lincoln and London: University of Nebraska Press, 1996.

_____. *The Journals of the Lewis & Clark Expedition, The Journals of Joseph Whitehouse, Vol. 11.* Lincoln and London: University of Nebraska Press, 1997.

III. Books

Ambrose, Stephen E. *Undaunted Courage: Meriwether Lewis, Thomas Jefferson, and the Opening of the American West.* New York: Simon & Schuster, 1996.

Appleman, Roy E. *Lewis & Clark.* Washington, DC: United States Department of the Interior, National Park Service, 1975.

Chuinard, Eldon. G. *Only One Man Died: The Medical Aspects of the Lewis & Clark Expedition.* Fairfield: Ye Galleon Press, 1998.

Clarke, Charles G. *The Men of the Lewis & Clark Expedition.* Lincoln and London: University of Nebraska Press, 2002.

DeKay, Ormonde. *The Adventures of Lewis and Clark.* New York: Random House. 1968.

Eastman, Gene and Mollie. *Bitterroot Crossing.* Moscow, ID: University of Idaho Library, 2002.

Edwards, Lawyn. "Clark, William." From the *Encyclopedia of American Military History, Volume 1.* Edited by Spencer C. Tucker. New York, Facts on File, Inc., 2003.

Fazio, James R. *Across the Snowy Ranges.* Moscow, ID: Woodland Press, 2001.

Goetzmann, William H. *Exploration and Empire: The Explorer and the Scientist in the Winning of the American West.* New York: Vintage Books. 1966.

Jackson, Donald, ed. *Letters of the Lewis and Clark Expedition, with Related documents: 1783-1854.* 2 Vols. 2nd ed. Urbana: University of Illinois Press, 1978.

Moore, Robert J. *Tailor Made, Trail Worn.* Farcountry Press, 2003

Plamondon II, Martin. *Lewis and Clark Trail Maps, A Cartographic Reconstruction, Volume II*. Pullman, Washington: Washington State Univeristy Press, 2001.

Schmidt, Thomas. *Guide to the Lewis and Clark Trail*. Washington, D.C.: National Geographic Society, 2002.

Winthrop, Riga, et al. *We Called this Creek Travellers' Rest*. Stevensville, MT: Stoneydale Press Publishing Company, 2003.

www.ingramcontent.com/pod-product-compliance
Lightning Source LLC
Chambersburg PA
CBHW071658160426
43195CB00012B/1508